MAKING MODERN AUSTRALIA

MAKING MODERN AUSTRALIA

The Whitlam Government's 21st Century Agenda

EDITED BY JENNY HOCKING

© Copyright 2017
© Copyright of this collection in its entirety is held by the editor, Jenny Hocking.
© Copyright of the individual chapters is held by the respective authors.
All rights reserved. Apart from any uses permitted by Australia's Copyright Act 1968, no part of this book may be reproduced by any process without prior written permission from the copyright owners. Inquiries should be directed to the publisher.

Monash University Publishing
Matheson Library and Information Services Building
40 Exhibition Walk
Monash University
Clayton, Victoria 3800, Australia
www.publishing.monash.edu

Monash University Publishing brings to the world publications which advance the best traditions of humane and enlightened thought.

Monash University Publishing titles pass through a rigorous process of independent peer review.

http://publishing.monash.edu/books/mma-9781925495188.html

Series: Australian History
Series Editor / Board: Sean Scalmer

Design: Les Thomas

Cover image: Gough Whitlam portrait illustration by Marc Nemorin

National Library of Australia Cataloguing-in-Publication entry:

Title:	Making modern Australia: the Whitlam government's 21st century agenda / Jenny Hocking, editor.
ISBN:	9781925495188 (paperback)
Subjects:	Whitlam, Gough, 1916-2014.
	Australian Labor Party--History.
	Social change--Political aspects--Australia
	Social change--Law and legislation--Australia
	Australia--Politics and government--1972-1975.
Other Creators/Contributors:	Hocking, Jenny, editor.

Printed in Australia by Griffin Press an Accredited ISO AS/NZS 14001:2004 Environmental Management System printer.

The paper this book is printed on is certified against the Forest Stewardship Council ® Standards. Griffin Press holds FSC chain of custody certification SGS-COC-005088. FSC promotes environmentally responsible, socially beneficial and economically viable management of the world's forests.

*'the changes we have made will remain
– like all great Labor legislation –
permanent landmarks in our history'*

Gough Whitlam

CONTENTS

About the contributors viii

PART I: GOVERNING FOR THE 21ST CENTURY 1

Chapter 1
An inquiry into the whole human condition?: Whitlam, sexual citizenship and the Royal Commission on Human Relationships (1974–77) 3
Michelle Arrow

Chapter 2
Buying back the farm: The Whitlam government and the Australianisation of mining 35
David Lee

Chapter 3
The regional and the local: Whitlam's 'quality of life' agenda 71
Lyndon Megarrity

Chapter 4
Reach of the imagination: The bold experiment of the Australian Assistance Plan 88
Melanie Oppenheimer, Erik Eklund and Joanne Scott

Chapter 5
Gough Whitlam's 1974 re-election: 'Government by double dissolution' 118
Jenny Hocking

PART II: FROM INSPIRATION TO IMPLEMENTATION 151

Chapter 6
Gough Whitlam and the re-imagined citizen-subject of
Australian social democracy........................ 153
Carol Johnson

Chapter 7
Labor reconstructs: The 1940s and the 1970s 181
Stuart Macintyre

Chapter 8
Furnishing the prime ministerial mind: Whitlam and the
national capital..................................... 210
Nicholas Brown

Chapter 9
Whitlam's transformation of the prime ministerial office,
its precursors and all that followed..................... 242
James Walter

Chapter 10
It's time: Spectrum's market research, modern campaigning,
and Whitlam's mandate.............................. 270
Murray Goot

Chapter 11
E G Whitlam: Reclaiming the initiative in Australian history 308
Greg Melleuish

ABOUT THE CONTRIBUTORS

Jenny Hocking is Research Professor and Australian Research Council Discovery Outstanding Researcher Award (DORA) Professorial Fellow at Monash University and the inaugural Distinguished Whitlam Fellow with the Whitlam Institute, Western Sydney University. She is an award-winning biographer and author of the two-volume biography of Gough Whitlam, *Gough Whitlam: His Time* (2012) and *Gough Whitlam: A Moment in History* (2008), winner of the 2014 Fellowship of Australian Writers' Barbara Ramsden Award and shortlisted for several literary awards including the Prime Minister's Literary Awards and the National Biography Award. Her other books include *Lionel Murphy: A Political Biography*; *Frank Hardy: Politics Literature Life* and *Terror Laws: ASIO, Counter-terrorism and the Threat to Democracy*. Jenny's latest book is *The Dismissal Dossier: Everything You Were Never Meant to Know about November 1975*, updated edition, 2016. She is currently working on an ARC funded project, *From Sarah Wills Howe to Thomas Wentworth Wills: An Australian Family Biography*. This biographical study will span three generations of the Wills family, a significant yet overlooked colonial family. From the economic success of its matriarch Sarah Wills who arrived in Sydney in 1798 with her convict husband, to the decline and suicide of her grandson the renowned sportsman and founder of Australian rules football, Tom Wills, their story will bring a new perspective to the early decades of colonial expansion.

ABOUT THE CONTRIBUTORS

Michelle Arrow is an Associate Professor in the Department of Modern History, Politics and International Relations at Macquarie University. Her books include *Friday on Our Minds: Popular Culture in Australia Since 1945* (2009) and *Upstaged* (2002) and she has published widely on post-war Australian history, the history of popular culture and history on film and television. Together with Catherine Freyne and Timothy Nicastri, Michelle won the 2014 NSW Premier's Multimedia History Prize for the radio documentary 'Public Intimacies: the 1974–1977 Royal Commission on Human Relationships'. In 2016, she held a National Library of Australia Fellowship for her current research project, a feminist history of the 1970s in Australia, which draws extensively on the records of the Royal Commission on Human Relationships.

Nicholas Brown is a Professor in and currently Head of the School of History, Australian National University. His *History of Canberra* for Cambridge University Press was published in 2014, and prior to that *A Way Through: The Life of Rick Farley* (NewSouth, 2011), co-authored with Susan Boden. With David Lee, Stuart Macintyre and Frank Bongiorno, he is currently working on a study of one of those figures who shaped Whitlam's 'great public service', Sir John Crawford.

Erik Eklund holds a Chair in Australian history and is the Director of the Centre for Gippsland Studies as well as a member of the Collaborative Research Centre in Australian History (CRCAH) at Federation University Australia. He recently completed a term as the Keith Cameron Chair in Australian History at University College Dublin from 2015 to 2016. He was a former Professor and Head of School at Monash University and has held appointments at the University of Newcastle, Georgetown University in Washington DC, and at the ANU as a visiting fellow. His major book publications include *Steel Town: the making and breaking of Port Kembla* (MUP, 2002), and *Mining Towns: making a living, making a life* (New South, 2012).

Murray Goot is an Emeritus Professor in the Department of Modern History, Politics and International Relations at Macquarie University. His most recent book is *The Conscription Conflict and the Great War* (2016), co-edited with Robin Archer, Joy Damousi and Sean Scalmer. He is currently working on the history of political campaigning (with Sean Scalmer) and the history of opinion polling.

Carol Johnson is a Professor of Politics and International Studies at the University of Adelaide. She has published extensively in the areas of Australian politics, ideology and discourse and the politics of gender and sexuality. Her books include *The Labor Legacy: Curtin, Chifley, Whitlam, Hawke,* Allen and Unwin 1989 and *Governing Change: From Keating to Howard* UQP 2000, 2nd edition 2007. She has also co-edited *Abbott's Gambit: The 2013 Australian Federal Election*, ANU Press, 2015 and *The Social Sciences in the Asian Century*, ANU Press, 2015. She is currently working on a book length study of how Labor governments have expanded their conception of equality beyond a traditional focus on the white, male, heterosexual working class breadwinner to address a much broader range of issues, including race, gender, sexuality, regional disadvantage, disability and technology – and the dilemmas that are involved in that expansion.

David Lee is an Adjunct Professor in History at Deakin University. He is a historian of Australian economic and political history and the history of Australian diplomacy. He is the author *inter alia* of *Australia and the World in the Twentieth Century*,

ABOUT THE CONTRIBUTORS

Circa, Melbourne, 2006 and *Stanley Melbourne Bruce: Australian Internationalist*, Bloomsbury, London and New York, 2010 and is the editor, with James Cotton, of *Australia and the United Nations*, Longueville, Canberra, 2012. His publications on the history of mining include *The Second Rush: Mining and the Transformation of Australia*, Connor Court Publishing, Redland Bay, 2016. He is working with Professors Stuart Macintyre, Nicholas Brown and Frank Bongiorno on a study of Sir John Crawford.

Stuart Macintyre is a professorial fellow at the University of Melbourne with interests in Australian social, political and intellectual history. His book on Post-War Reconstruction, *Australia's Boldest Experiment*, appeared in 2015 and he is currently working with Frank Bongiorno, Nicholas Brown and David Lee on a study of a particular reconstructionist, John Crawford. A study of a different and less happy reconstruction, that of Australian higher education in the 1980s and 1990s, will appear later this year as *No End of a Lesson*. With Jenny Gregory and Lenore Layman he also edited a volume of essays for Geoffrey Bolton published in 2017, *A Historian for All Seasons*.

Lyndon Megarrity completed his PhD in history at the University of New England (conferred 2002). He has subsequently worked as a researcher and tertiary educator. Megarrity has taught Australian and world history at the University of Southern Queensland (Springfield campus), and is currently an adjunct lecturer at James Cook University, where he has also taught history and political science subjects. As an historian, he has published widely on Queensland political history, race relations, Northern Australia, local government and international student policy. He was an Australian Prime Ministers Centre Fellow (2010-11) and was the inaugural Council of Australian University Librarians/Australian Society of Authors Fellow in 2014–15. Megarrity is the co-author of two books: *Made in Queensland: A New History* (UQP: 2009) and *A History of the Foundation for Australian Literary Studies 1966–2016* (2016).

Greg Melleuish is a Professor in the School of Humanities and Social Inquiry where he teaches political theory, Australian Politics and Ancient History. He has a substantial set of publications in the fields of Australian intellectual history and political ideas in Australia with a focus on the connections between political thought and religion. His books include *Cultural Liberalism in Australia* (CUP, 1995), *The Power of Ideas* (ASP, 2009) and *Two Traditions of Democracy in Australia* (ASP, 2014).

Melanie Oppenheimer took up the Chair of History at Flinders University in July 2013 after appointments at the University of Western Sydney and the University of New England. She is a former Dean of the School of History and International Relations and is currently serving a 3-year term on the ARC College of Experts. She has published seven monographs including the centenary history, *The Power of Humanity. 100 Years of Australian Red Cross* (HarperCollins, 2014) and with Bruce Scates, *The Last Battle. Soldier Settlement in Australia, 1916–1939* (CUP, 2016).

Joanne Scott is Professor of History; Executive Dean of the Faculty of Arts, Business and Law; and Pro Vice-Chancellor (Engagement) at the University of the Sunshine Coast. Across her career, she has published in the fields of Australian and Queensland history, labour history, gender and race relations, oral history, popular culture and higher education. She has a particular interest in communities and institutions.

ABOUT THE CONTRIBUTORS

James Walter is Emeritus Professor of Politics at Monash University, with interests in leadership, biography, policy deliberation and the history of ideas. His recent books include *What Were they Thinking? The Politics of Ideas in Australia* (2010), and (with Paul Strangio and Paul 't Hart), *Understanding Prime Ministerial Performance: Comparative Perspectives* (2013), *Settling the Office: The Australian Prime Ministership from Federation to Reconstruction* (2016) and *The Pivot of Power: Australian Prime Ministers and Political Leadership 1949–2016* (2017). He is working on a history of Australian government and patterns of policy deliberation between the late 1940s and the present.

Part I

Governing for the 21st century

Chapter 1

AN INQUIRY INTO THE WHOLE HUMAN CONDITION?

Whitlam, sexual citizenship and the Royal Commission on Human Relationships (1974–77)[1]

Michelle Arrow

In the commentary following the death of Gough Whitlam on 21 October 2014, the Royal Commission on Human Relationships was rarely mentioned as one of his government's achievements: indeed, it rarely figures in the historiography of the Whitlam era.[2] Shepherded

---

1   This research was supported by the National Archives of Australia through the 2012 Frederick Watson Fellowship. I would also like to thank Leigh Boucher, Barbara Baird and Robert Reynolds for the discussion and collaboration that has helped shape this research.

2   There are very few historical works which discuss the Royal Commission in depth, but it is given an incisive treatment by Geoffrey Bolton in his *Oxford History of Australia Volume 5: The Middle Way* (Melbourne: Oxford University Press, 1990), and briefly by Gough Whitlam in *The Whitlam Government: 1972–1975* (Ringwood: Penguin, 1985). Elizabeth Evatt offers an account of the Commission in 'Legislating for Social Change', in *It's Time Again: Whitlam and Modern Labor*, eds Jenny Hocking and Colleen Lewis (Melbourne: Circa, 2003). Sociologist Katie Wright places the Commission in the context of the rise of a 'therapeutic society' in *The Rise of the Therapeutic Society: Psychological Knowledge and the Contradictions of Cultural Change* (New Academia Publishing, 2011). Frank Bongiorno and Stephen Angelides both discuss the impact of the Commission's recommendations on sex education (Stephen Angelides, '"The Continuing Homosexual Offensive": Sex Education, Gay Rights and Homosexual Recruitment', in *Homophobia: An*

into existence by Whitlam's women's affairs adviser Elizabeth Reid (appointed as the first such adviser in the world in early 1973), and led by Justice Elizabeth Evatt, the Commission was not a long-planned part of Whitlam's famous 'program'. Instead, it emerged from a fractious parliamentary debate in 1973 over abortion. While many MPs were in favour of relaxing the law on the grounds of female autonomy and preventing the birth of children who would grow up neglected, many others (on both sides of the chamber) were strenuously opposed to any reform of the law, on both moral and religious grounds. The Royal Commission became a way to resolve the issue to neither party's disadvantage. The Commission was tasked not only with an examination of abortion, but also with examining the 'family, social, educational, legal and sexual aspects of male and female relationships' – terms of reference that Labor MP Race Mathews warned had the potential to balloon into 'an inquiry into the whole human condition'.[3]

The government appointed three commissioners, led by Chairman Justice Elizabeth Evatt, who had recently returned to Australia in 1973 to take up an appointment as the first female Deputy President of the Commonwealth Conciliation and Arbitration Commission.

Australian History, ed. Shirleene Robinson (Annandale: Federation Press, 2008), 172–191; Frank Bongiorno, *The Sex Lives of Australians: A History* (Melbourne: Black Inc, 2012). More recently, see Michelle Arrow, 'Public Intimacies: the Royal Commission on Human Relationships', in *Acts of Love and Lust: Sexuality in Australia from 1945–2010*, eds Lisa Featherstone, Rebecca Jennings and Robert Reynolds (Newcastle upon Tyne: Cambridge Scholars Publishing, , 2014), 23–43, and Michelle Arrow, Catherine Freyne and Timothy Nicastri, 'Public Intimacies: The 1974 Royal Commission on Human Relationships', *Hindsight*, ABC RN, first broadcast 28 April 28 2013, http://www.abc.net.au/radionational/programs/hindsight/public-intimacies3a-the-royal-commission-on-human-relationships/4646926.

3   Race Mathews, *Commonwealth Parliamentary Debates*, Vol. 85, 13 September 1973: 950, http://www.aph.gov.au/Parliamentary_Business/Hansard/.

CHAPTER 1

Evatt's fellow commissioners were Anne Deveson, a journalist with a strong interest in social justice, and Felix Arnott, the progressive Anglican Archbishop of Brisbane. Their terms of reference were extremely broad, necessitating investigations of sex education programs, medical training in sexuality, family planning, pressures on women in relation to children and family, the legal and medical status of abortion, and 'any other matters in relation to the family, social, educational, legal and sexual aspects of male and female relationships'.[4] Just as Elizabeth Reid had consulted widely with ordinary women across the country after she was appointed in 1973,[5] the Royal Commission created multiple opportunities for ordinary people to speak frankly about their intimate lives. The commissioners 'took steps to open channels of communication with all levels of the community ... we talked with many people of different ages, from the very old to the very young, with Aboriginals, migrant groups, people in cities and suburbs and with people in country towns and isolated places'.[6] The Commission received 1264 written submissions, conducted thousands of short informal interviews, and heard evidence from 374 people in public hearings in Sydney, Melbourne, Brisbane, Canberra, Adelaide, Bunbury and Hobart. People spoke or wrote of their private experiences of motherhood, fatherhood, sex education, homosexuality, disability, rape, child abuse, and domestic violence,[7] Evatt reflecting subsequently that the Commission 'was concerned with the [lives] of those who had no unions to speak

---

4   Elizabeth Evatt, Felix Arnott and Anne Deveson, *Royal Commission on Human Relationships Final Report Volume 1* (Canberra: Australian Government Publishing Service, 1977), ix.
5   Elizabeth Reid, 'The Child of Our Movement: A Movement of Women', in *Different Lives*, ed. Jocelynne Scutt (Ringwood: Penguin, 1987), 15.
6   Evatt, Arnott and Deveson, *Final Report Vol. 1*, 17.
7   Anne Deveson, *Australians At Risk* (Cassell Australia, 1978).

for them'.[8] Research projects into people's attitudes about sexuality, unwanted pregnancies, domestic violence, the needs of disabled children, sexual assault, and mothers in the paid workforce were conducted by Commission staff.[9] The public could also attend an 'open house' session and speak to a member of the Commission about issues of concern; one staff member recalls the Commission meeting people inside a shopping centre to hear their concerns.[10]

In these ways, the Royal Commission sought to provide a voice for citizens whose interests were not fully represented within the existing left-right political paradigm: most notably, women, children, gays and lesbians. It was particularly interested in the harms these groups suffered, typically behind closed doors and often in family settings. The Commission's 500-plus recommendations articulated emerging understandings of a new regime of protections and rights for these citizens, blurring and troubling the boundary between public and the private in ways that continue to transform Australian political life. At their core, the Commission's recommendations offered recognition of a new pluralism in family and intimate life, rather than seeking to assert absolute moral standards. They recommended law reform in the areas of age of consent, abortion, sexual assault, homosexuality, and they sought to better support families (and especially women) in the face of rapid social and cultural change, through better childcare, support for those experiencing family violence, and more thorough education in human relationships and sexuality. Yet while the Royal Commission was initiated and developed by the Whitlam

---

8   Elizabeth Evatt, in *Australians From 1939*, eds Ann Curthoys, A W Martin and Tim Rowse (Broadway: Fairfax, Syme and Weldon Associates, 1987), 413.
9   Evatt, Arnott and Deveson, *Final Report Vol. 1*, 19.
10 Faye Roberts in 'Public Intimacies'.

CHAPTER 1

government in 1974, the dismissal and subsequent election of the Fraser government in late 1975 meant that the meaning and reception of the Commission's final report was vastly different when it was released during the 1977 election campaign.

The Royal Commission's insistence on exposing the inequalities and harms of the private sphere dovetailed with the strategies of the feminist and gay rights movements of the 1970s. These movements could not be easily accommodated within the political contest between capital and labour: they articulated new ideas of the political.[11] Just as the women's liberation slogan suggested 'the personal is political', so the Royal Commission on Human Relationships placed personal experiences, particularly those that caused trauma and harm, on the political agenda. The Commission provided multiple opportunities for ordinary Australians to articulate their experiences of sex, intimate relationships (including same sex desires), violence, abortion and parenthood.[12] British scholar Jeffrey Weeks has described this deployment of private experience in public by women and homosexual activists in this period as making a claim to 'sexual citizenship'. He suggested that the women's and gay movements of the 1970s had two characteristic elements: first, a moment of transgression – where the self is invented and reinvented, and where previously exclusionary institutions and traditions are challenged. Second, he suggested, there was a moment of citizenship: a claim to inclusion, and to equal access and rights. The 'sexual citizen', he

---

11 Anna Yeatman, 'Women and the State' in *Contemporary Australian Feminism*, ed. K Hughes (Melbourne: Longman Cheshire, 1994), 178.
12 See Michelle Arrow, '"Everyone Needs a Holiday from Work, How About Mothers?" Motherhood, Feminism and Citizenship at the Australian Royal Commission on Human Relationships, 1974–1977', *Women's History Review*, 25, no. 2 (2016); Deveson, *Australians at Risk*.

suggested, was a 'hybrid being' produced by intimate life and involvement with the wider society: making public articulations of rights that hinge not on a universalist claim to citizenship, but are instead grounded in sexual or gender difference.[13] The Royal Commission, in responding to the inequalities of private life, articulated a politics of sexual citizenship. This enlarged understanding of the political informed the 500 recommendations contained in the Royal Commission's final report. Yet this new kind of politics was neither uncontested nor seamlessly incorporated in 1970s Australia.

While the historiography of the Whitlam era has highlighted his government's many policy landmarks towards greater equality for Indigenous people, migrants and women,[14] less attention has been paid to the ways that his government responded more fundamentally to a new politics of intimate and sexual life.[15] To date, the main body of scholarship to engage with questions of gender, sexuality and citizenship in the Whitlam government is the literature on Australian feminist bureaucrats or 'femocrats'.[16] Earlier debate focused on whether this engagement between the women's movement and the state represented a pragmatic strategy to advance women's rights or a co-option of liberationist energies. Recent assessments have examined

---

13 Jeffrey Weeks, 'The Sexual Citizen', *Theory, Culture and Society* 15, no. 3 (1998), 36–7.
14 For example, see Jenny Hocking and Colleen Lewis, *It's Time Again: Whitlam and Modern Labor* (Melbourne: Circa, 2003); and Troy Bramston ed., *The Whitlam Legacy* (Annandale: The Federation Press, 2013).
15 Although see Angelides, 'The Continuing Homosexual Offensive', and Carol Johnson 'From Morality to Equality: Labor's Sexuality Conundrum', paper presented at Australian Political Studies Association Annual Conference, 29 August 2014, http://papers.ssrn.com/sol3/papers.cfm?abstract_id=2440135.
16 Hester Eistenstein, *Inside Agitators: Australian Femocrats and the State* (Philadelphia: Temple University Press, 1996); Marian Sawer, *Sisters in Suits: Women and Public Policy in Australia* (Sydney: Allen and Unwin 1990); Anna Yeatman, *Bureaucrats, Technocrats, Femocrats: Essays on the Contemporary Australian State* (Sydney: Allen and Unwin, 1990); Suzanne Franzway, Diane Court, R W Connell, *Staking A Claim: Feminism, Bureaucracy and the State* (Sydney: Allen and Unwin, 1989).

the ways that feminists and the state shaped and reorganised each other: Merrindahl Andrew, for example, noted that Australian feminism was institutionalised relatively early because of receptive Labor governments.[17] This was in spite of the challenge feminism posed to traditional Australian Labor Party (ALP) identity and to laborist traditions that, as Marian Sawer noted, deemed feminism to be a 'middle class cause, disruptive of working class solidarity'.[18] Much of the ALP's women's policy direction under Whitlam came from activists and the bureaucracy outside the party.

However, Carol Johnson has argued that within the Labor tradition, Whitlam introduced a 'vastly expanded' conception of equality that encompassed women and migrants, who were often 'among the most vulnerable members of the working class … Whitlam saw himself as consolidating and extending conceptions of equality in ways that would benefit all Australians, including traditional Labor voters'.[19] Yet she also notes that Whitlam was slower to challenge the heteronormative citizenship models under which the ALP operated in postwar Australia, which relegated homosexuality to a matter of 'private' morality. Whitlam, she argued:

> may have been prepared to challenge the traditional gendered division which saw women's issues as issues confined to the private sphere of life, and not properly a matter for politics, but he did not challenge a similar division that appeared to be occurring in issues of homosexuality.[20]

---

[17] Merrindahl Andrew, 'Getting Pragmatic: The Women's Electoral Lobby on the Continuum of Radicalism', *Australian Feminist Studies* 29, no. 82 (2014).

[18] Marian Sawer, 'Reinventing the Labor Party? From Laborism to Equal Opportunity', in *It's Time Again: Whitlam and Modern Labor*, eds Jenny Hocking and Colleen Lewis (Melbourne: Circa, 2003) 375.

[19] Carol Johnson, 'Gough Whitlam and Labor Tradition', in *The Whitlam Legacy*, ed. Troy Bramston (Sydney: Federation Press, 2013).

[20] Johnson, 'From Morality to Equality', 3.

Yet the Royal Commission on Human Relationships *did* raise questions of gay and lesbian rights. Gay and lesbian activists made submissions and gave testimony. Most significant was the Commission's response to a challenge from the Catholic Church on the question of homosexuality. The Church challenged the Commission's authority to hear evidence from homosexual people on the grounds that that the 'human relationships' in the terms of reference referred only to 'human relationships of a man and woman together'.[21] The Royal Commission affirmed the inclusion of gays and lesbians in their terms of reference, arguing that it was not possible to exclude 'the effect of homosexuality on the individual's ability to form family, social and sexual relationships. These matters are themselves dependent to a large extent on current social attitudes to homosexuality and to the position of the homosexual in society.'[22] Thus the Whitlam government's receptiveness to the new claims for rights and protections made by feminist activists, granted legitimacy by acts such as the Royal Commission on Human Relationships, fractured the contours of Australian citizenship and began to reshape it: a reshaping that was foundational to the emergence of a new political culture in late twentieth century Australia. While the Royal Commission provided one site to articulate these new ideas of citizenship, the public reception of the Commission's final report revealed the ways that some of these ideas remained incompatible with contemporary political culture. Yet while the Royal Commission reinforced a new understanding of citizenship that sat outside dominant political allegiances, condemning it to controversy with the publication of its report and recommendations in

---

21 Commonwealth Reporting Service, *Official Transcript*, Vol. 8 (8 December 1975), 2554.
22 Elizabeth Evatt, Felix Arnott, Anne Deveson, *Royal Commission on Human Relationships, Interim Report 1* (Canberra: Australian Government Publishing Service, 1976), 8.

CHAPTER 1

1977, it nonetheless anticipated a more enduring shift in interpretations of Australian citizenship.

This chapter examines the furious reaction to the Commission's final report in the late 1970s. The outrage generated by the report demonstrates the ways that Australian political and public culture resisted many aspects of the emerging politics of sexual citizenship represented by the Royal Commission. First, I will briefly explain the emergence and operation of the Royal Commission and the ways that it underscored the importance of new understandings of citizenship and the state in 1970s Australia. Such forms of citizenship gave previously private identities political meanings that were crucial to the sexual and feminist movements of the period. I will then explain the fate of the Royal Commission at the hands of Malcolm Fraser's government and the press in the bitter politics of the 1977 Federal Election campaign. Finally, I will trace the ways that the Fraser government accounted for the report and its recommendations in the wake of their 1977 election victory. I argue that the Commission's determination to speak for those who were relatively powerless within conventional party politics left it without political champions in the post-dismissal world. However, while a political backlash against the Whitlam era may have immediately consigned the report to political oblivion in the late 1970s, many of the changes it recommended formed a template for policy changes enacted in subsequent decades.

Whitlam, the women's movement, and the establishment of the Royal Commission on Human Relationships

The election of the Whitlam government and the re-emergence of an active women's movement converged in the early 1970s to produce a unique political response to the problem of women's inequality.

Susan Ryan, Lyndall Ryan and others have pointed out the extent to which Whitlam's policy action on women's issues was a response to the women's movement, particularly the lobbying efforts of the Women's Electoral Lobby's (WEL) survey of all political candidates in the 1972 election.[23] The WEL survey exposed a clear difference between the two major parties on women's issues: Labor MPs (including Whitlam himself) performed very well, while Liberal and Country party members, with the exception of the Minister for Territories, Andrew Peacock, scored poorly.[24] WEL members reported that McMahon showed an 'outstanding lack of interest' in the survey.[25]

While Whitlam's policy program agitated for equal pay for women in line with United Nations and International Labour Organisation conventions, it was WEL's activism that exposed the absence of women's concerns from the agendas of all major political parties, and identified women as a new constituency for the ALP to pursue.[26] Historically, women had not been entirely ignored by the major parties: mothers, in particular, had long been viewed through the framework of maternal citizenship in terms of policy. However, by the 1970s, many women were campaigning for policies that promoted equal opportunity, rather than their maternal role. WEL, with its reformist goal of engaging in policy-making, capitalised on the

---

23 Susan Ryan, 'Women of Australia', in *The Whitlam Legacy*, ed. Troy Bramston (Sydney: Federation Press, 2013), 206–215; Lyndall Ryan, 'Feminism and the Federal Bureaucracy, 1972 – 1983', in *Playing the State: Australian Feminist Interventions*, ed. Sophie Watson (Sydney: Allen and Unwin, 1990) 71–82; Marian Sawer with Gail Radford, *Making Women Count: A History of the Women's Electoral Lobby* (Sydney: UNSW Press, 2008). Ch. 1.
24 Ryan, 'Women of Australia', 209.
25 'WEL Ratings Poor', *The Canberra Times*, November 20, 1972, 3.
26 Ryan, 'Women of Australia', 214.

CHAPTER 1

absence of women in the parliamentary Labor Party to influence the agenda of the new government.[27] The Whitlam-Barnard duumvirate immediately reopened the equal pay case and removed the sales tax on contraceptives.[28] Crucially, Whitlam appointed Elizabeth Reid to his office as women's affairs adviser in his office in 1973, which gave her considerable policy influence and made her a figurehead for women's liberation nationally.[29] The gradual influx of 'femocrats' into the bureaucracy after Reid's appointment was a visible sign of the closer interaction between feminists and the state. Finally, the attempt to change abortion law in the ACT also emerged from the Whitlam government's receptiveness to feminist claims on the state.

The Whitlam government's attempts at abortion law reform, as well as new support for childcare, women's refuges and welfare benefits, embodied new understandings of citizenship that took private sphere inequalities into account. As Carol Johnson pointed out, Whitlam wanted to expand not only traditional notions of equality, but also of 'the political', as he remarked at the opening of the Women and Politics conference in 1975:

> women are insisting more and more that concerns of the home be the concerns of politics, the personal be political. Child care, family planning, housework and so on are now becoming issues for the political arena. To this extent, women are in the process of trying to re-define and to re-describe, the political.[30]

---

27 Ibid., 210.
28 Ibid.
29 Elizabeth Reid, 'Creating a Policy for Women', in *The Whitlam Phenomenon*, Australian Fabian Society (Ringwood: Penguin/McPhee Gribble, 1986), 145–155.
30 Gough Whitlam, Speech at the Opening of the Women and Politics Conference, Canberra, 31 August 1975, 8, http://cem.uws.edu.au, cited in Johnson, 'Gough Whitlam and Labor Tradition', 359.

It was the convergence of women's activism (indeed, their willingness to engage with the state) and Whitlam's expansive vision of the Australian Commonwealth as a guarantor of 'positive equality' that proved remarkably productive for policy change for women. The Royal Commission on Human Relationships was just one outcome of this engagement.

It was also an unintended outcome. The Commission emerged from one of Whitlam's key promises to the women's movement: to introduce legislation to reform the laws governing abortion in the ACT. The Medical Practice Clarification Bill was introduced to the federal parliament on 10 May 1973 by Labor backbenchers David McKenzie and Tony Lamb. The McKenzie-Lamb Bill, as it became known, would have permitted women in the ACT to terminate a pregnancy in the first trimester, and established a national precedent. Any attempt to change the law was bound to be controversial (despite majority support for some relaxation of the law)[31] and thus the bill proved a potent tool for mobilisation. Right to Life groups descended on the Parliament for the debate (both in person and by sending more than 13 000 pieces of correspondence)[32] and on the day of the debate, women's groups set up a 'women's embassy' on the Parliament House lawn to protest the lack of women's voices within the House.[33]

The bill exposed cross-party fault-lines that fractured the Labor-Liberal divide. While two Labor MPs introduced the bill, many Labor members (as well as Liberal-Country party ones) were bitterly opposed to any change. The bill's co-sponsor, Tony Lamb emphasised abortion

---

31 Katharine Betts, 'Attitudes to Abortion in Australia: 1972 to 2003', *People and Place* 12, no. 4 (2004): 23.
32 P McElliott To G Yeend, 'Anti Abortion Campaign', 2 May 1973, in Papers of Elizabeth Reid, National Library of Australia MS9262, Series 16, Box 54.
33 Sawer, *Making Women Count*, 33.

CHAPTER 1

as a response to both individual women's needs and broader social problems: 'most unwanted pregnancies result in an unwanted child ... one more likely to develop into a deprived and unwanted child'.[34] Conservative Labor Minister Kim Beazley Sr also raised the spectre of the neglected child, but to oppose the bill: 'it is a tragedy, I think, that our attention is being diverted to how children can be eliminated when the attention of this parliament is very much needed to how they can be advanced'.[35] His arguments emphasising the 'sanctity of life' were also taken up by many of his colleagues on the other side of the house.[36] Others invoked the disruptive figure of the 'liberated woman': Country Party leader Doug Anthony feared that the bill posed a threat to the family, 'not an expression of the liberation of a woman but an affront to her womanhood'[37]. However, Liberal MP Harry Turner, while declaring he would vote against what he described as 'abortion on request', noted: 'here we are, a Parliament of all men; there is not a single woman in this chamber. Yet women are obviously intimately concerned with this matter.'[38] All parties allowed their members a conscience vote on the bill, which was emphatically defeated on 10 May 1973 by 98 votes to 23. Whitlam, Bill Hayden and Kep Enderby were among those in the ALP who voted for the bill; deputy prime minister Lance Barnard, Kim Beazley and opposition leader Billy Snedden were among those who voted against it. Whitlam did not speak during the debate, while Snedden argued against the bill that 'I do not believe that abortion

---

34 Tony Lamb, *Commonwealth Parliamentary Debates*, House of Representatives, Vol. 85, 10 May 1973: 1970, http://www.aph.gov.au/Parliamentary_Business/Hansard/.
35 Kim Beazley Sr, *Commonwealth Parliamentary Debates*, 10 May 1973: 1980.
36 See eg James Corbett, *Commonwealth Parliamentary Debates*, 10 May 1973: 1994–1997.
37 Doug Anthony, *Commonwealth Parliamentary Debates*, 10 May 1973: 1982.
38 Harry Turner, *Commonwealth Parliamentary Debates*, 10 May 1973: 1987.

can be seen as an extension of a contraceptive device'.[39] However, the issue was by no means settled and ALP members worked to approach the problem in another way.

What became clear during the debate was just how little was known about the extent of, and reasons for, abortion in Australia, prompting Labor MP Race Mathews to call for a Royal Commission into the subject. Matthews argued that; 'Royal commissions are a means of obtaining information which would otherwise be unavailable, of drawing to public attention facts which would otherwise be neglected, and of reconciling points of view which would otherwise remain opposed'.[40] This proposal was also defeated, but after an adjournment of some months, Matthews and Liberal MP Don Chipp moved a bipartisan proposal to hold a Royal Commission into 'the family, social, educational, legal and sexual aspects of male and female relationships'.[41]. After the terms of reference were amended by then-opposition leader Malcolm Fraser, who added that the investigation should have regard for the UN Declaration of the Rights of the Child and the 'sanctity and preservation of human life',[42] (probably to placate the well-organised and vocal Right to Life lobby), the proposal passed with bipartisan support.

The resolution to hold a Royal Commission on 'male and female relationships' appealed as a way for the parliament to circumvent the stalemate on abortion reform; women's liberationists saw it as a

---

39 Billy Snedden, *Commonwealth Parliamentary Debates*, 10 May 1973: 1991.
40 Race Mathews, *Commonwealth Parliamentary Debates*, 10 May 1973: 1983.
41 Evatt, Arnott, Deveson, *Royal Commission on Human Relationships Final Report Volume 1*, ix.
42 Malcolm Fraser, *Commonwealth Parliamentary Debates*, House of Representatives, Vol. 85, 13 September 1973: 951, http://www.aph.gov.au/Parliamentary_Business/Hansard/.

'consolation prize'.⁴³ While the parliament passed the bill establishing the Royal Commission on 13 September 1973, little progress was made for several months. By June 1974 – with the Commission still not formally established – Reid pressed Whitlam, insisting that a Royal Commission into male and female relationships could have a transformative effect:

> 'There have been many other commissions [overseas] looking into the more tangible problems of discrimination against women, [but] the significance of this commission is that it will be required to look into social problems the very existence of which we are reluctant to admit, the extent of which we have no knowledge but which affect, and in many cases quite adversely, ... almost every other person in our community.⁴⁴

Reid thus anticipated the ways in which the Royal Commission could enact – and endorse – a new kind of politics. This was a politics of sexual citizenship, one that troubled the boundary between the private and the public and which gave private identities new political purchase. Reid went on to oversee the establishment of the Royal Commission. Crucially, she renamed it the Royal Commission on Human Relationships, though the terms of reference directing an investigation into 'male female relationships' remained unchanged. Working with Whitlam and his other staff, Reid oversaw the appointment of Deveson and Evatt as commissioners. Together with Felix Arnott, they would undertake a three-year investigation, which

---

43 Sue Wills, interviewed by Michelle Arrow, 4 December 2012.
44 Elizabeth Reid to Prime Minister Whitlam, 5 June 1974, Papers of Elizabeth Reid, NLA MS 9262, Series 16 Box 68. Perhaps the most comparable Royal Commission (which received publicity in Australia) was the Canadian Royal Commission into the Status of Women (1967): see Joan Sangster, 'Words of Experience/Experiencing Words: Reading Working Women's Letters to Canada's Royal Commission on the Status of Women', in her *Through Feminist Eyes: Essays on Canadian Women's History*, (Athabasca University, Edmonton: AU Press, 2011).

they hoped would 'identify areas where social structures and legislation are lagging behind human need'.[45] In doing so, the Royal Commission become a platform for many Australians to articulate a new citizen identity through their private experiences in order to claim new rights and protections. In this way, the Commission was a significant, though contested, moment in the redefinition of the political in 1970s Australia.

'Little more than a giant talkback show': The Royal Commission begins

The Commission was formally established on 21 August 1974 and it began formal hearings in early November 1974. The terms of reference – the 'family, social, educational, legal and sexual aspects of male and female relationships' – were broad and interconnected.[46] Such diverse fields of inquiry demanded a range of research strategies. The Commission held a series of public hearings where witnesses gave testimony: often these witnesses had previously made written submissions. Many of these witnesses were recognised 'experts' such as doctors and social workers, but many were ordinary citizens whose authority to speak derived from their experiences (victims of sexual assault, gay men who had experienced discrimination). The public were invited to contribute: pamphlets and print and radio advertisements asked Australians 'what do you think?' about a range of social, cultural and sexual issues including abortion, sex education, marriage, parenthood and relationships.[47] The Commission received written submissions on a very wide range of issues, ranging from

---

45 Evatt, Arnott, Deveson, *Interim Report 1*, 3.
46 Ibid., 6–7.
47 Ibid., 45.

abortion, corporal punishment in schools, family violence, gay and lesbian life, rural isolation, disability, and parenting. 'Phone-ins' on specific issues, such as making the decision to terminate a pregnancy, were conducted as well as less formal 'open house' sessions.[48] Anne Deveson remembered that commission staff visited sports fields and community halls to speak to people about their experiences: they aimed for inclusiveness and diversity and sought to communicate the work of the Royal Commission as broadly as possible. The commissioners also initiated an ambitious research program, which was truncated after the 1975 election. These projects, undertaken by sociologists, included an investigation of the experiences of women living in Elsie, Australia's first women's refuge, attitudes towards sex and sex education, and the experiences of mothers in the paid workforce.[49]

The Royal Commission on Human Relationships was, in effect, tasked with auditing formations of Australian intimate life in the 1970s, with a particular focus on the problems created by family dysfunction, violence, poverty, and poor education. While some issues, such as abortion, were clearly defined within the Commission's remit from the outset others, such as the discrimination faced by gays and lesbians, emerged from submissions particularly from canny activists who used the platform the Commission provided to place these issues on the agenda.[50] Other issues, flagged from the outset, took on greater significance as the investigation progressed. Evatt recalled that investigating single issues in isolation often proved impossible:

---

48 Ibid, 11–14. On the Phone-in, see 68.
49 Ibid., 67–72.
50 CAMP NSW, *Homosexuals and Human Relationships: Submission to the Royal Commission on Human Relationships* (Sydney: CAMP NSW, 1975). Also see Evatt, Arnott, Deveson, *Interim Report 1*, 43–4.

for example, if a woman was seeking an abortion because she was living with a violent partner, then the commissioners felt compelled to investigate domestic violence as well.[51] It was clear that the Commission was succeeding in bringing private problems to broader public notice: a *Sun-Herald* story suggested that it was providing an 'attentive, receptive and above all, friendly ear' to many Australians facing hardship.[52] However, this new politics of private experience made the Commission a subject of controversy and even ridicule: a *Sydney Morning Herald* editorial suggested that the whole exercise had been 'little more than a giant talk-back show'.[53] For some commentators, the issues the Royal Commission was discussing should not be aired in public, nor were they a suitable subject for political debate.

Meanwhile, as the Commission was conducting its inquiry throughout 1974 and 1975, the Whitlam government was experiencing unprecedented political turmoil. First, the government had an extremely crowded policy program: to take just one example, the Royal Commission on Human Relationships was just one of thirteen Royal Commissions initiated by Whitlam in just three years of government.[54] The government faced a hostile Senate (which the 1974 double dissolution election failed to completely remedy), and deeply unfavourable economic conditions, including rising unemployment and fast-climbing inflation. By 1975, against a backdrop of scandals and extraordinary events (including the loans affair and Cyclone Tracy), the replacement of Snedden with the more

---

51 Elizabeth Evatt, interviewed by Michelle Arrow, 10 January 2013.
52 Martin Saxon, 'So Many in Need of Help', *The Sun-Herald*, February 29, 1976, 38.
53 'Royal Commission', *Sydney Morning Herald*, 27 February 1976, 5.
54 Australian Law Reform Commission, *Review of the Royal Commissions Act, Issues Paper 35* (Canberra: Commonwealth of Australia, 2009), 26.

CHAPTER 1

ruthless Malcolm Fraser as Opposition leader, and Fraser's decision to block supply, paved the way for the dismissal on 11 November 1975.[55] The timing could not have been worse for the Royal Commission on Human Relationships.

Horror and smut: the release of the final report

Initially, three years had been set aside for the Commission's work. Following the dismissal, just a little over a year after the Commission was established, the commissioners prepared an interim report for the new Fraser government in January 1976.[56] Amid ongoing funding uncertainty (on 28 January, Race Mathews claimed that the Commission could not even pay its telephone bill)[57], on 6 February, the Royal Commission was named as one of eight inquiries established under Whitlam that were ordered to curtail or finalise their reports by the end of the year.[58] The Commission's final, five volume report, with 500 recommendations on a wide range of aspects of family and private life, was presented to the Governor-General Sir John Kerr just three weeks before the 1977 elections, and it was read and discussed by Cabinet.

In a memo to the prime minister, Malcolm Fraser, A J Ayers, first assistant secretary to the Community Affairs Division, noted that the report contained many recommendations that 'would be welcomed by all sections of the community'. However, he also noted that 'on the other hand, there are some recommendations which will provoke an extreme reaction from some sections of the

---

55   Bolton, *Oxford History of Australia*, 227–241.
56   Evatt, Arnott, Deveson, *Interim Report 1*, 43–4.
57   'Inquiry "Hamstrung"', *The Canberra Times*, 28 January 1976, 7.
58   'Fraser to Apologise to Eight Inquiries', *The Canberra Times*, 6 February 1976, 3.

community'.⁵⁹ He highlighted a number of recommendations he deemed controversial, including abortion on demand, the decriminalisation of homosexuality and prostitution, and the replacement of the words 'man' or 'woman' with 'person' wherever possible in legislation and official documents, and replacing male and female pronouns with a word like 'id'. Ayers wondered whether the government should release the report at all, although he cautioned that 'the media will be aware that the report is controversial in parts and thus will be newsworthy. The media are already seeking access to it. The government runs the risk of being accused of censorship if the report is not released soon.'⁶⁰ On the other hand, he noted that releasing the report during the election campaign would produce a major distraction from the campaign itself. He also worried that even if the government could assure the public that the report did not necessarily reflect the views of the government, nevertheless the government would be 'pressed to express a view on some of the more controversial recommendations in the election campaign, particularly in NSW where the Rev Nile is a candidate'.⁶¹ He strongly advised holding off publicly releasing the report until it had been tabled in Parliament, after the election.

Yet just 10 days away from what Jenny Hocking has labelled 'one of the worst Labor election campaigns for decades',⁶² a selection of the most incendiary recommendations – particularly the decriminalisation of prostitution, homosexuality, incest between adults and making abortions available for girls over 14 – were leaked to the

---

59   A J Ayers, Memo to the Prime Minister 23 November 1977, National Archives of Australia (NAA): Series A1209 1977/503, Part 1.
60   Ibid.
61   Ibid.
62   Hocking, *Gough Whitlam*, 393.

CHAPTER 1

influential veteran reporter (and Whitlam critic) Alan Reid at *The Bulletin*.⁶³ Whoever leaked these first excerpts – Whitlam accused Fraser at the time, Elizabeth Evatt believed that it was Withers – they were highly sensationalized and deeply damaging.⁶⁴ Evatt responded with anger, suggesting that the report had been politicised and trivialised: 'I feel rather depressed that people in this community are not prepared to tackle seriously these issues and talk about them in a positive manner.'⁶⁵ Nonetheless, the *Mirror*'s front page story opened thus:

> The final report of the Royal Commission on Human Relationships has recommended vast and revolutionary changes to Australian laws and attitudes to almost every form of family and sexual relations. And the Minister for Administrative services, Senator Withers, who is responsible for releasing the $1 report, is horrified by it. [Withers declared that the report] will cause a lot of deep offence to the people in Australia – I think a majority of them.⁶⁶

Fraser declared – despite admitting he hadn't read the report – that there were things in it that would 'fill every family in Australia with horror'.⁶⁷ Whitlam retorted that Fraser was 'resorting to the politics of smut. You get the prefect and the fag getting a report, looking at it under the desk, and looking for the dirty bits. I want to see the lot before I comment'.⁶⁸ Both ALP sources and journalists believed that

---

63 Alan Reid 'Commission Recommends Legal Brothels, Abortions for Girls 14' *The Bulletin*, 3 December 1977, 38–9. On Reid's political influence, see Stephen Holt, 'The Ultimate Insider', *National Library of Australia News*, July 2006, 11–13.
64 Elizabeth Evatt, interviewed by Michelle Arrow, 10 January 2013.
65 'Report Critics Anger Judge', *The West Australian*, 2 December 1977, 1.
66 Brian White, 'New Pill, Abortion Laws', *The Daily Mirror*, 30 November 1977, 1.
67 David Broadbent, Stephen Nisbet and John Teerds, 'Sex Report Shocks PM', *The Age*, 1 December 1977, 3.
68 'Chipp Critical of PM Over Sexuality Report', *The Australian*, 2 December 1977, 2.

the government was responsible for the leak: Michelle Grattan suggested that it showed 'the extent to which politicians will, for their immediate needs, misuse a serious investigation into important social problems'.[69] Following this initial leak, Withers released volume one of the report to the press, and the following four were made public the following day.

In the debate that followed, the report was depicted as an illegitimate child, the product of an intimate encounter whom no one would now acknowledge. The *Advertiser* noted that both Whitlam and Fraser were 'at pains to deny either personal or party responsibility for establishing the commission'.[70] Whitlam, sagging badly in a dispiriting election campaign, obfuscated on the extent of his and Reid's involvement, declaring that '[my] administration had not appointed the Royal Commission on its own initiative' and emphasising that it had been established with bipartisan support. He continued: 'The Royal Commission was appointed by Sir John Kerr on the advice of the government pursuant to a resolution by the House of Representatives [… The parliamentary resolution] embodied an amendment by Mr Fraser and was supported by Mr Fraser'.[71] The ALP offered no defence of the report and it was too easily caricatured as a hangover of Whitlam-era permissiveness – in the words of the Sydney *Sun*, 'it was a typical smart political trick: leak some provocative points, recall that the commission was appointed in the Whitlam government's days and draw a wild conclusion that a vote

---

69 Michelle Grattan, 'Hypocrisy Too Much', *The Age*, 3 December 1977, 13.
70 'A New Hot Potato', *The Advertiser*, 2 December 1977, 5.
71 Geoff Walsh, 'Sex Report Stirs Up a Storm', *The Sun News Pictorial*, 1 December 1977, 1. While this was correct, it didn't account for Reid's change to the Commission's title from 'male and female' to 'human relationships'.

CHAPTER 1

for Labor is a vote for incest'.[72] The report's characterisation in the early press coverage as a mere 'sex report' obscured, and mocked, its significance.

The public discussion of the report revealed that Whitlam's new politics of gender and sexuality had found some social and cultural purchase, but they could still be easily characterised as highly partisan, permissive and outside the bounds of conventional politics without the backing of those willing to champion them. The debate around the final report revealed the persistence of normative family and gender roles and their accompanying political norms, and a questioning of the legitimacy of the sexual citizenship claims of women and homosexuals. The reactions reveal the ways that Whitlam's new politics – and conservative reactions to them – had both reorganised and reinstated partisan divides on questions of gender and sexuality in 1970s Australia.

After the five volumes of the report were publicly released, the tone of the media coverage softened somewhat. Many newspapers devoted several pages to sober discussion of the Commission's extensive recommendations and findings, particularly on issues like sexual violence, domestic violence, sex education and discrimination against women. Some reports endorsed the legitimacy of Australian's claims to sexual citizenship:

> While recognising that most human relations should be personal and private the commissioners agreed that at some point all personal and family relations are affected by government policies on education, employment, transport, health care as well as sex laws.[73]

---

72 'Humanity and Politics', *The Sun Herald*, 4 December 1977, 66.
73 David Broadbent, 'Public Rights and Private Morality', *The Age*, 2 December 1977, 12.

A woman dramatised these claims in a letter to the *Daily Mirror*, writing that the report's recommendations were:

> spot on to what is needed, I agree with every proposal they've put forward in particular the one on abortion. When I was 20 I had to get an abortion and I had to lie and crawl to get what I considered my right. The government has let Christianity rule it for too long and its time that these basic rights that belong to everybody should not be denied because of one particular creed.[74]

Some commentators identified the Commission's feminist orientation as part of the reason for the controversy: Brian White of the *Daily Mirror* argued later that the report was a 'catalogue of the abuse of man ... we can't have that in Man's Own Country now, can we?'[75] Just as 'liberated women' were positioned in the parliamentary abortion debate as a divisive social force, so too, they were framed as problematic in much of the popular response to the Royal Commission.

The frankness and range of the recommendations provoked the fiercest reaction: the idea that 'private' concerns could be the stuff of politics animated much of the outrage over the report. While there was some praise for the report's exposure of 'hidden' issues like family violence, there were others who sought to reinstate the primacy – and privacy – of the nuclear family. This was, after all, a report that focused on the inequalities, and at times the violence of family life, and many of the recommendations sought to expand the role of the state as a means of ameliorating these inequalities. Yet some sought to shield the family from political scrutiny: one letter writer to

---

74 Jane Garrow, '50-50 Phone-in Vote', *Daily Mirror*, 1 December 1977, 34.
75 Brian White, 'Silence is Deafening on Real Issues', *Daily Mirror*, 3 May 1978, 12.

CHAPTER 1

the *Courier-Mail* declared that 'several aspects of the Commission's report are against human nature, against the home and the family and particularly against women'.[76] Sir Charles Court, Premier of WA, said that he:

> believed that all decent Australians would reject the published recommendations. … the commission was trying to erode the whole of the family, he said. It wanted to usurp the position of parents and reduce any form of sexual activity to grossness without responsibility.[77]

The idea that the state was seeking to undermine the family was reflected in this letter to the *Daily Mirror*: 'I think is the basic right of the parents to instruct their children and I think it's a breaking down of the family laws and regulations as we know them and placing them in the hands of bureaucrats.'[78] Recognising the claims of sexual citizens, it was feared, might undermine the primacy of the family.

So what, then, was the report's meaning in the charged atmosphere of party politics in 1977? Clearly the Liberal/Nation party coalition had used the initial leak to their advantage in the election campaign. Many respondents seemed to either repudiate the politics of sexual citizenship or were at least taking stock of the changes that took place under his leadership. The United Church Reverend Alan Walker declared the report to be 'another example of the permissiveness of the Whitlam era,'[79] while a correspondent to the Hobart *Mercury* suggested that:

---

76 K Gilchrist, letter to the editor, *Courier Mail*, December 7, 1977, 4.
77 'Shocking is Court's view', *The West Australian*, December 2, 1977, 22.
78 Bray August in '50-50 Phone-in Vote', *Daily Mirror*, December 1, 1977, 34.
79 'Church and Women's Groups Split', *Daily Telegraph*, 1 December 1977, 4.

one is reminded of the freewheeling attitude on many of these moral issues which appeared during the time of the previous Federal government ... It would seem desirable to return Mr Fraser and his government on Saturday, if only to kill the intentions of this report and so retain our present community moral standards, which have already been eroded substantially in recent times.[80]

The commissioners and other supporters emerged to strongly defend the report: Evatt suggested that 'people should look at the whole of it – in particular the better program and support for the family. ... then they will see the parts that have been leaked to the Press in a proper sense of proportion'.[81] However, the report's initial framing as a scandalous embodiment of permissive social movements left it without political champions in the election campaign.

'Deliberate lack of speed': The Fraser government's response

Following the 1977 election, in which the Fraser government was convincingly returned to office, the report of the Royal Commission on Human Relationships in parliament was quietly, without comment or debate, tabled on 28 February 1978. The Minister for Home Affairs, Robert Ellicott, was tasked with co-ordinating the government's response. One of the most overwhelming problems for the government was the scale and scope of the recommendations. A Cabinet note estimated that of the 511 recommendations, 268 were state responsibilities, or those of non-government agencies. Of the remainder, it noted, '158 are considered implemented, 42 are under active consideration, 34 low

---

80   Jim Mooney, letter to the editor, *The Mercury*, 5 December 1977, 4.
81   'Fraser Unfair to Report: Evatt', *The Canberra Times*, 2 December 1977, 1.

CHAPTER 1

priority and aspects of 9 controversial' – that is, less than 10% of its 511 recommendations were 'under active consideration'.[82] Determining which recommendations to enact and which to set aside, was the task of an interdepartmental working group established by Ellicott. He requested comment from the State Premiers but only received material from NSW, WA and Tasmania – and only WA responded at any length, problematic for a report in which so many issues were the responsibilities of the states. The working group completed a report that was considered by Cabinet in May 1980, yet no decisions were reached. Ellicott drafted a lengthy statement outlining the government's response but it was never delivered to the Parliament,[83] and his successor in the portfolio, Ian Wilson, was 'disinclined to take the matter further'.[84] Daniel McVeigh replaced Wilson as Minister for Home Affairs in May 1982, and in a briefing note to the incoming minister, public servant D F McMichael wrote that while interest in the Commission had 'died down', 'unless instructed otherwise we will continue to work with deliberate lack of speed on our consideration of the recommendations which affect the ACT, as resources permit'.[85] McVeigh wrote to the prime minister in June 1982, suggesting that the government drop the question of a response to the Royal Commission's report. The prime minister agreed.[86] After a significant investment of time and resources, three years of

---

82 G E Rees, 'Notes on Cabinet submission no. 3989', 30 April 1980, National Archives of Australia (NAA) Series A10756, LC1781 Part 2.
83 'Questions Brief', undated, NAA: Series A1209 1987/1216 Part 8. Robert Ellicott, Draft Ministerial Statement, 15 April 1980, NAA: Series A10756, LC1781 Part 2.
84 Daniel McVeigh to Malcolm Fraser 16 June 1982, NAA: Series A1209 1987/1216 Part 8.
85 D F McMichael letter to Daniel McVeigh, 4 June 1982, NAA: Series A1209 1987/1216 Part 8.
86 'Questions Brief', undated, NAA: Series A1209 1987/1216 Part 8.

inquiries, and thousands of submissions, interviews and testimonies, this was an extraordinary response from the Fraser government.

Apart from the unwieldiness of the 511 recommendations themselves, the sticking points for the government was the ways the Royal Commission had treated those issues which were emblematic of the politics of sexual citizenship: among them legalising abortion, removing prohibitions on gay and lesbian people serving in the armed forces, expanding rights for de facto couples, particularly in relation to taxation and welfare benefits, and 'positive discrimination' in the public service.[87] Some of these recommendations were seen to be challenging the dominance of the nuclear family. Fraser, for example asserted his support for the heterosexual family, stating in Parliament on March 2 1978 in response to the question of whether the government would introduce a family policy (as recommended by the Commission):

> the platform and philosophy of the Government parties strongly emphasise the importance of the family as a cohesive force in society and as one of the most important elements in society. They emphasise also the need to strengthen that influence. I believe that in recent years we have seen some forces and some moves which almost seemed to be designed to weaken its influence. ... the government does take into account the effect on the family of a number of its policies. Indeed, a number of its policies have been designed quite specifically to enhance the family.[88]

In this view, expanding individual rights could not be achieved unless it was at the expense of the primacy and privacy of the family.

---

87 Robert Ellicott, Draft Ministerial Statement, 15 April 1980, NAA: Series A10756, LC1781 Part 2.
88 Malcolm Fraser, *Commonwealth Parliamentary Debates*, House of Representatives, Vol. 9, 2 March 1978: 341–2, http://www.aph.gov.au/Parliamentary_Business/Hansard/

CHAPTER 1

The Western Australian State Women's Council of the Liberal Party wrote in their response to the Royal Commission that

> The commissioners have shown great tolerance and understanding for those who are different. But in wishing to accommodate those minority groups, we think they have placed too much emphasis on them to the disadvantage of the Australian community at large. They have done nothing to uphold the accepted morals of our society or to defend or strengthen the family unit as we know it. ... We do not want government interference in all aspects of our life.[89]

Yet the report had shown that many Australians needed protection *within* the family. As Geoffrey Bolton noted, in practical terms, this meant increased government funding for services and support, yet 'this ran counter to the Fraser government's preference for stressing the virtues of self-help and self-reliance'.[90] A report that urged new interventions in private life on the part of the state was bound to provoke resistance from Liberal politicians, particularly in the context of the austerity politics of the late 1970s and the rise of neoliberal approaches to the role of the state.[91]

Liberal/National party unease with the Royal Commission's politics of private and sexual life was apparent well before the report was released. The Family Court of Australia, now widely regarded as one of the Whitlam government's most significant achievements, almost fell victim to the Fraser government's urge to undo their predecessor's reforms. The Court opened in January 1976 with Evatt as its

---

89 State Women's Council (WA), Liberal Party of Australia, 'Response to the Royal Commission on Human Relationships', 14 Nov 1980, NAA: Series A 1209, 1977/503 Part 7.
90 Bolton, *Oxford History*, 259.
91 Judith Brett, *Menzies and the Moral Middle Class* (Cambridge: Cambridge University Press, 2003), 162–163.

inaugural Chief Justice, but according to Jenny Hocking, the opening was stalled 'while some in the new government inquired whether it was possible to "un-proclaim" the legislation and to close the Family Court before it had even begun.'[92] Similarly, while Sara Dowse, head of the Women's Affairs Branch after Elizabeth Reid resigned in 1975, claimed that Fraser had been more supportive of women's policy than he has been given credit for, he nonetheless downgraded these issues when the branch was moved out of the Prime Minister's Department to the Office of Women's Affairs in December 1977, prompting Dowse's resignation.[93] While the Fraser government decriminalised homosexuality in 1976, the push for change had happened during the Whitlam government and gay activists did not support the legislation because it retained harsh penalties for some acts and maintained a higher age of consent for homosexuals.[94] The rise of moral conservatives in Australian politics like the Festival of Light and Fred Nile, who stood for election to the Senate for NSW in 1977,[95] almost certainly exerted pressure on the Liberal Party on questions of private rights and protections. Thus sexual citizenship had a somewhat tenuous purchase within the Fraser government's outlook well before the release of the Royal Commission's final report in 1977.

---

92 Hocking, *Gough Whitlam*, 385.
93 Dowse, 'The Prime Minister's Women', 400.
94 Graham Carbery, *Towards Homosexual Equality in Australian Criminal Law – A Brief History* (Parkville: Australian Gay and Lesbian Archives, 2010), 25, www.alga.org.au/files/towardsequality2ed.pdf.
95 Antony Green, 'The Christian Democrat Schism', November 11, 2009, http://blogs.abc.net.au/antonygreen/2009/11/the-christian-democrat-schism.html, Accessed 26 October 2015.

CHAPTER 1

Aftermath

In his 1975 election campaign speech, Malcolm Fraser asserted that 'we can have idealism, we can have reform, without handing control of our lives to politicians and civil servants'.[96] As Judith Brett suggested, socialism was no longer the enemy; conservatives now needed to stand against social democracy.[97] Yet within this ideology, what would be the place of those whom the Royal Commission on Human Relationships had identified as in need of the protection of the state, like women, children, and homosexuals? The Commission represented an attempt to expand the role of the state in order to address disadvantage and protect the vulnerable. In its endorsement of many key feminist issues, the report revealed the success of the women's movement push to reshape long-established norms around motherhood, citizenship and identity. The report's calls for state intervention ran counter to the Fraser government's insistence on reducing the role of the state, but the report also challenged heteronormative formations of citizenship and the primacy of the nuclear family. It was these challenges that provoked such a fierce reaction in the late 1970s on the part of the public and the Fraser government. Yet the report also challenged many in the ALP: while Fred Nile was hardly sympathetic to the Labor Party, he was probably right when he noted that the report 'will be an embarrassment to a lot of Labor men, particularly Catholics'.[98] The Royal Commission on Human Relationships dramatised the ways that Whitlam's 'new politics' cut across existing political divides, just as it forged new political

---

96 Malcolm Fraser, election speech, November 27, 1975, http://electionspeeches.moadoph.gov.au/speeches/1975-malcolm-fraser.
97 Brett, *Menzies and the Moral Middle Class*, 150.
98 'Trivialising Report Hit by Judge', *Hobart Mercury*, 2 December 1977, 3.

connections and alliances beyond party politics. It also formed a template for policy responses to many of the issues that it raised in subsequent years.[99] John Warhurst has suggested that Whitlam 'laid the foundation for Labor's successful adaptation of its policies to the needs of the social movements'. While these achievements were, in Warhurst's words, 'reactive rather than programmatic', they nonetheless effected a permanent change to the political agenda.[100] The polarising aspects of Whitlam's new politics of personal life in the 1970s have been obscured by the ways they have come to reshape contemporary political divides. The reception of the Royal Commission on Human Relationships reminds us of the political costs associated with this reshaping.

---

99   Evatt, 'Legislating for Social Change', 45.
100 John Warhurst, 'Transitional Hero: Gough Whitlam and the Australian Labor Party', *Australian Journal of Political Science* 31, no. 2 (1996), 250; Brett, *Menzies and the Moral Middle Class*, 148.

Chapter 2

BUYING BACK THE FARM

The Whitlam government and the Australianisation of mining

David Lee

One of the most ambitious policy objectives of the Whitlam government was its policy of 'buying back the farm'. This involved an effort to 'Australianise' the mining industry, an industry in which foreign ownership had made rapid progress following a decade of boom conditions for minerals after 1960. The policy borrowed from a phrase popularised by Country Party Trade Minister John McEwen in the 1960s when he warned of the dangers of uninhibited investment into Australia and coined the term 'buying back the farm'.[1] Early in 1973 Whitlam informed an annual dinner of the Australian Mining Industry Council that he would be introducing foreign investment rules that would require at least 50 per cent ownership in all resource projects.[2] In Tokyo in October, he announced that the government would be aiming at 100 per cent Australian ownership of

---

1 See Peter Golding, *Black Jack McEwen: Political Gladiator* (Carlton: Melbourne University Press, 1996). The development of Australia's mining industries in the period from 1972 to 1975 was addressed in a chapter of the author's general history of the development of mining in Australia from the early 1960s to 2012: *The Second Rush: Mining and the Transformation of Australia* (Redland Bay: Connor Court Publishing, 2016), 227-53.
2 Jenny Hocking, *Gough Whitlam: His Time: the Biography. Volume II* (Carlton: Miegunyah Press, 2012), 114.

energy projects (ie uranium, steaming coal, oil and natural gas) and a lesser degree of Australian ownership for mineral resource projects. The Whitlam government's *Foreign Takeovers Act* 1975 (eventually introduced by the Fraser government) later mandated 50 per cent ownership for key areas of the Australian economy, including new minerals and energy resource projects, and 75 per cent Australian ownership for new uranium projects.[3]

The adoption of these policies was inspired by the rapid rise of foreign ownership of the resources sector over the previous decade. The 1960s had been a period of extraordinary mineral development.[4] The end of a federal embargo of the export of iron ore in 1960 was followed by establishment of an iron ore industry in which foreign capital played a major part.[5] The discovery in the 1950s of bauxite in Queensland, the Northern Territory and Western Australia facilitated the creation of an integrated aluminium industry that was substantially foreign owned.[6] The black coal industry took rapid strides in exporting coal to Japan, first in New South Wales, and then in Queensland where the American mining company, Utah Development, and the Australian–American–Japanese consortium, Thiess Peabody Mitsui (TPM), became the dominant open-cut miners.[7] In the mid-1960s petroleum and natural gas were discovered

---

3   Barrie Dyster and David Meredith, *Australia in the International Economy in the Twentieth Century* (Melbourne: Cambridge University Press, 1990), 281.
4   Harold Raggatt, *Mountains of Ore* (Melbourne: Landsdowne, 1968).
5   David Lee, 'Reluctant Relaxation: The End of the Iron Ore Export Embargo and the Origins of Australia's Mining Boom', *History Australia* 10, no. 3 (2013): 149–170; David Lee, 'The Emergence of Iron Ore Giants: Hamersley Iron and the Mount Newman Company', *Journal of Australasian Mining History* (2013): 61–77.
6   Geoffrey Blainey, *White Gold: The Story of Alcoa of Australia* (St Leonards: Allen & Unwin, 1997); David Lee, 'The Development of Bauxite at Gove, 1955–1975', *Journal of Australasian Mining History* 12, (2014): 61–77.
7   Brian Galligan, *Utah and Queensland Coal: A Study in the Micro Political Economy of Modern Capitalism and the State* (St Lucia: University of Queensland Press, 1989);

CHAPTER 2

in Bass Strait from which extraordinary profits were reaped by the Broken Hill Proprietary Company (BHP) and American oil company, ESSO. Between 1963 and 1972 foreign ownership of the Australian mining industry rose from 34 to 48 per cent.[8]

Following the Labor Party's victory at the 1972 general election, Prime Minister Gough Whitlam appointed Reginald Francis Xavier (Rex) Connor as Minister for Minerals and Energy. Connor was born in 1907 in the coal-mining and steel-producing city of Wollongong in New South Wales.[9] Having joined the Australian Labor Party in the late 1930s, he narrowly won the State seat of Wollongong–Kembla and was a member of the New South Wales Parliament from 1950 until 1963, when the New South Wales coal industry was just beginning its first coking coal exports to Japan. In 1963 he left state politics to enter the House of Representatives as member for Cunningham.[10]

Although on the left of the Australian Labor Party, Connor aligned himself closely with Gough Whitlam when Whitlam was Deputy Leader and later Leader of the Opposition. This cost Connor his position on the ALP executive in the late 1960s when the left of his party failed to support him in a Caucus ballot. Although Connor lived in the shadows between 1969 and 1972, Whitlam never forgot

---

Chris Fisher, *Coal and the State* (North Ryde: Methuen, 1987).

8   Jeffrey D Wilson, *Governing Global Production: Resource Networks in the Asia–Pacific Steel Industry*, (Basingstoke: Palgrave Macmillan, 2013), 84. See also G L Crough and E L Wheelwright, *Australia: A Client State* (Ringwood: Penguin, 1982) and Humphrey McQueen, *Gone Tomorrow: Australia in the 80s* (Sydney: Angus and Robertson, 1982).

9   C J Lloyd, 'Reginald Francis Xavier 'Rex' Connor', in *Australian Dictionary of Biography, Volume 13*, ed. John Ritchie, (Carlton: Melbourne University Press, 1993), 486–488.

10 Ibid.

Connor's support.[11] He rewarded Connor's long-standing interest in mining by giving him the newly created portfolio of Minerals and Energy, which absorbed many of the functions of the old Department of National Development.[12] Many of Connor's statements in Opposition had indicated the trend of his thinking: to insist that Australian coal and other minerals be sold at world parity price; to construct a natural gas pipeline and assert national authority over the resources in the continental shelf; to stop 'principalities' being granted to companies like BHP and Burmah–Woodside in the North West Shelf; and fundamentally to oppose further foreign control of Australian industry and particularly the mining industry.[13] Connor immediately strengthened his department by appointing Sir C L (Lennox) Hewitt, formerly Secretary of the Prime Minister's Department under John Gorton, as his permanent secretary. In 1973 Connor and Hewitt set up a National Pipeline Authority to administer a national network to pipe natural gas around Australia. One of the ultimate objectives of the network was to be able to pipe the large amounts of newly found natural gas in the North West Shelf off the Western Australian coast to south eastern Australia where the main domestic demand for natural gas existed.

The Whitlam government failed to achieve the centre-piece of its policy, namely the establishment of a Petroleum and Minerals Authority (PMA), despite the passage of its enabling legislation in August 1974. The government was dismissed by the

---

11 Jenny Hocking, *Gough Whitlam: A Moment in History* (Carlton: Miegunyah Press, 2008), 276, 295.

12 For Whitlam's relationship with Connor during the Whitlam Government see Hocking, *Gough Whitlam: His Time*, 115, 200–203.

13 Michael Sexton, *Illusions of Power: The Fate of a Reform Government* (Sydney: George Allen and Unwin, 1979), 97.

CHAPTER 2

Governor-General in November 1975 following the Opposition's refusal to allow a vote on its supply bills in the Senate, in an atmosphere of crisis generated in part by an aborted attempt to borrow 'petrodollars' to help buy back the farm. This chapter argues that these failures notwithstanding, aspects of the Whitlam government's policy on mining were successful. Federal control of mineral exports helped Australia win higher prices for mineral exports such as coal and iron ore and assisted the government to persuade mining companies to set up Australian industry associations to negotiate with the Japanese Steel Mills. A sign of the value of the policies was that the Fraser government retained federal control for mineral exports and strengthened the policy of fostering Australian equity in new mining projects by establishing a Foreign Investment Review Board (FIRB). Connor and Whitlam had thus succeeded in bringing federal control and regulation of mining to the centre of Australian politics.

Revaluation, Australian equity guidelines and control of mineral exports

After the Whitlam government was elected on 2 December 1972, it was forced to act immediately to suppress the inflation that had accelerated in the last years of the McMahon government and that had been driven in part by the mining boom that had begun in the 1960s. Whitlam appreciated the Australian dollar unilaterally by seven per cent on 23 December 1972. In announcing this revaluation, Whitlam also gave notice that overseas-owned mining companies in Australia and oil explorers would not be able to bring investment funds into Australia for their activities unless they deposited 25 per cent of their capital with the Reserve Bank of Australia.[14] The main objective of the policy was to reduce domestic liquidity and to inhibit large inflows of foreign capital that impeded the government's ability to manage the economy. On 4 February 1973 the Australian dollar further appreciated when the Whitlam government decided not to follow the US government in devaluing. The aim of the collective revaluations was to restrict capital inflow, boost imports and check exports in an effort to bring inflation under control. Appreciation of the Australian dollar meant that exporters received less in the local currency for a given amount of exports, adversely affecting primary producers and the mining industry.[15]

The first reaction of the mining industry to the Whitlam government and to Connor in particular was negative.[16] Connor was scornful of mining executives responsible for writing mineral contracts in US dollars. Because many of the mining companies' contracts were written in US dollars, they were one of the major casualties of the realignment of the Australian currency in 1972 and 1973. One mining executive commented in January 1973 that the revaluation could reduce the gross profits of Australian iron ore companies by as much as 40 per cent. The Pilbara iron ore companies, for example, shared contracts totalling $6000 million, more than $5000 million of which were denominated in US dollars.[17] Connor displayed little sympathy for foreign-owned mining companies.[18] Moreover, in February 1973

---

14 'Foreign Explorers Await Cabinet Decision', *Australian Financial Review (AFR)*, 13 March 1973.
15 Alex Millmow, 'Australia and the Keynesian Revolution' in *The Seven Dwarfs: The Age of the Mandarins*, ed. Samuel Furphy, (Canberra: ANU Press, 2015), 76–77.
16 Editorial, 'The Miners and the Dollar', *AFR*, 3 January 1973; Trevor Sykes, 'Two Mines Face Currency Crisis', *AFR*, 19 February 1973.
17 *AFR*, 14 February 1973.
18 Article on Connor, *AFR*, 11 January 1973.

CHAPTER 2

he vented his anger when learning of the McMahon Government's eleventh hour approval of several uranium contracts to private interests worth $100 million. One of these contracts had placed ten per cent equity in mining Australian uranium in the hands of the Italian corporation *Ente Nazionale Idrocarburi* (ENI).[19] Connor believed in the imminence of a world energy crisis and questioned why the McMahon Government had been hurrying to sell uranium cheaply when prices for energy raw materials were about to rise steeply.

Despite Connor's occasional barbs against mining executives, he was a supporter of the mining industry, although he wanted it to be Australian-controlled. The mining industry, moreover, was not uniformly opposed to the Whitlam government's policies on mining. Early in 1973, parts of the mining industry actually lobbied the Whitlam government for strong federal intervention in the coal industry. One of the most significant voices urging action was B W Hartnell, Chairman of the Joint Coal Board, the joint Commonwealth–State regulator the New South Wales coal industry. For many years, Hartnell had criticised the failure of Australian coal mining companies to combine to negotiate with a cartelised Japanese steel industry and of foreign-dominated Queensland coal companies undercutting the price of the still substantially Australian-owned and underground New South Wales coal companies.[20] Hartnell and the New South Wales Coal Proprietors, including the American-owned Clutha Development, lobbied for the Australian government to intervene to regulate the coal mining industry. Hartnell recommended two possible options: to create a Commonwealth agency

---

19 Maximilian Walsh, 'Miners Anger Govt: Secretive Deal Threatens Uranium Contract', *AFR*, 4 May 1973.
20 Brian Toohey, 'Australian Coal Marketing Methods under Fire Again', *AFR*, 2 March 1973.

responsible for the marketing of all Australian coal overseas; or to leave individual contracts in the hands of private companies but to subject them to Commonwealth control.[21]

Connor heeded the advice from Hartnell and from the Department of Minerals and Energy and made two submissions to Cabinet in January 1973.[22] Both were based on the ALP's 1971 Platform, which stated that the party would only permit exports of minerals sold at full market price; and that it should not allow the depletion of fuel and energy resources needed for Australia's own national development. Connor argued that the rapid development of Queensland's open-cut coal mining posed the risk that Australia could deplete its easily mined open-cut coal, leaving the more costly underground coal with 'significant effects on future costs of Australian industry and long-term export capacity'.[23] He argued that the Japanese steel industry operated as a 'monolithic' buyer and was adept at playing one company off against another. Japanese steel companies based their purchasing policy, he argued, on the formula of 'cost plus a reasonable profit' and 'sought to profit by the competition created through excess capacity, which has been created, with their connivance, in the older sectors of the country, with supply at lower prices emerging elsewhere in Australia'.[24] Connor thought that Queensland mining companies could sell their coal at $US3 per ton higher and

---

21   Letter, B W Hartnell to Connor, 6 February 1973 and paper by Hartnell, 'Commonwealth Control of Coal Mining Industry', 19 December 1972, Papers of Rex Connor, Series 2, Box 8, D61 Joint Coal Board Controls part 2, University of Wollongong, Wollongong.
22   Submission from Connor to Cabinet, 'Export of Black Coal', 2 January 1973, Papers of Rex Connor, Series 2, Box 9, Export Controls Part 1, University of Wollongong, Wollongong.
23   Ibid.
24   Ibid.

CHAPTER 2

New South Wales coal producers at $US2 per ton higher than they were receiving. On this basis he predicted that Australia would be at least $A53 million better off in income earned from the sale of coal in 1972–73. The New South Wales Combined Colliery Proprietors' Association, the Miners' Federation, the Joint Coal Board and the Department of Minerals and Energy had all suggested the imposition of export controls to achieve orderly marketing of Australia's coal resources. Cabinet approved Connor's recommendation that the government should achieve 'balanced development' of Australia's black coal resources so that production of coal for export was in the best interests of Australia. Cabinet also agreed that new coal contracts, or expansion of existing ones, could only be approved if Connor and his department were satisfied that comparable coals at reasonable prices were not available from existing mines.[25]

Connor's submission on control of the coal industry was submitted in tandem with one for Commonwealth control of mineral exports generally.[26] At that stage there were already export controls on some minerals: a requirement to submit iron ore contracts to the Australian government was a legacy of the federal embargo of iron ore exports between 1938 and 1960; copper was controlled to ensure that Australian industry had adequate supplies; and natural gas to make reasonable provision for Australia's domestic needs. However, there were no controls in place for bauxite, alumina, nickel or coal. Connor argued that Australia's prices for mineral exports were being affected by combinations of overseas buyers presenting a united front to competing buyers as had been the case with coal and iron ore. He

---

25   Ibid.
26   Handwritten notes by Connor on reasons for export controls, n.d. 1973, Papers of Rex Connor, Series 2, Box 8, D61, University of Wollongong, Wollongong.

also pointed to foreign-owned companies exporting at the cost of production or some similar non-commercial basis as had happened with Queensland Alumina Limited, a consortium established to produce alumina from Weipa bauxite. Connor also advised his colleagues that he was particularly concerned that the Commonwealth had no systematic knowledge of commercial arrangements for the sale of Australia's mineral exports other than for iron ore. Embarrassingly, the federal government had to rely on public or semi-public sources, the state governments, private companies and the press. This lack of basic data in the critical resources domain led the government to institute the Fitzgerald Review into the minerals and energy sector and associated ownership and taxation levels, discussed below. To help achieve the government's policy objectives, Connor obtained Cabinet's approval to apply export controls to all minerals, including alumina, but not aluminium metal and refined lead and zinc. The operation of federal controls on mineral exports would prove to be an enduring legacy of the Whitlam government's policies on mining, being retained by the Fraser government in the late 1970s and early 1980s and by the Hawke government for much of the 1980s.

The Australian Industry Development Corporation, the Fitzgerald Review and the Petroleum and Minerals Authority

In seeking to give effect to its policy of encouraging more Australian ownership of mineral projects, the Whitlam government began by using machinery that was already in existence. These included the McMahon government's *Foreign Takeovers Act* 1972, which allowed the Treasurer to veto foreign takeovers not in the national interest,

CHAPTER 2

and the Australian Industry Development Corporation (AIDC).[27] The AIDC was a government corporation established by Liberal Prime Minister John Gorton and John McEwen, Leader of the Country Party and Gorton's deputy prime minister, in 1970. They established the AIDC to marshal funds, mainly from foreign sources, to provide assistance to Australian companies which requested the AIDC to invest in them. Whitlam and Connor wanted the AIDC to be able to raise risk capital to allow Australian companies to invest in one of the sectors that most needed it – Australia's mineral resources.

In March 1973 Whitlam announced a vision for an enhanced AIDC. He sought to remove restraints on the corporation's activities and to establish a National Investment Fund to raise capital in Australia for its work.[28] Under Whitlam's plan, the AIDC would be required to prioritise the goal of assisting Australian ownership of resources and their development. The Labor government introduced legislation into the parliament in August 1973 to strengthen the corporation. This legislation aimed at expanding the functions of the AIDC and enhancing its money-raising powers in the Australian capital market. The amending legislation, however, irritated business groups and the Opposition-controlled Senate, which suspected that the initiative was designed to help the government control private industry. The opposition to the bill resulted in the amending legislation to the AIDC being held up in the Senate in 1973 and 1974.[29]

In the meantime, Whitlam's ministers differed about how the AIDC would actually work. On the one hand, Connor argued for

---

27 Golding, *Black Jack McEwen*, 258–60, 300.
28 *AFR*, 2 March 1973; Robert Haupt, 'The AIDC to be Development Spearhead', *AFR*, 7 March 1973.
29 'AIDC Bill Contrary to Free Enterprise', *AFR*, 18 October 1973.

the prohibition of future equity investment by foreign corporations in new Australian mining projects.[30] Connor pressed Whitlam to notify the State Premiers 'that the States must not continue to usurp the rightful functions of the Australian government by their indiscriminate allocation of huge tracts of land as mining leases without regard to national planning'.[31] The Minister for Overseas Trade, Jim Cairns, however, advocated partnerships between foreign and overseas interests and the Treasury strongly opposed a complete prohibition on foreign investment in new mining ventures.[32]

On a visit to Japan in October 1973, Whitlam sought to end the uncertainty within the government by issuing a comprehensive statement on foreign investment policy. Whitlam announced that the government required equity in new energy projects – coal, oil, gas and uranium – to be in Australian hands while looking for foreign participation in some ways 'though access to technology, loans and long-term contracts'. As to non-energy resources, the Whitlam government's policy was more flexible. The prime minister announced that '[w]e desire partnership between Australian and foreign equity capital. I want to make it quite clear that there is no proscription of foreign equity participation in mining'.[33] Under the new system announced by Whitlam, all foreign investment in Australia would be screened and require approval by the Treasury.[34]

---

30   Report of speech by Connor at Twelfth General Meeting of the American Chamber of Commerce in Melbourne, *AFR*, 26 March 1973.
31   Letter, Connor to Whitlam, 15 August 1973, Papers of Rex Connor, Series 2 Box 45, D61/2/534, University of Wollongong, Wollongong.
32   Gary Smith, 'Minerals and Energy' in *From Whitlam to Fraser: Reform and Reaction in Australian Politics,* eds Allan Patience and Brian Heads, (Melbourne: Oxford University Press, 1979), 238.
33   Fred Brenchley. 'New Mineral Rules – Whitlam Gives the Details', *AFR*, 30 October 1973.
34   Wilson, *Governing Global Production*, 88.

CHAPTER 2

By the time that Whitlam made this statement in Tokyo, planning was well advanced for another corporation much more powerful than the AIDC to assist the government in the field of minerals and energy. This was the Petroleum and Minerals Authority (PMA), the brain-child of Connor who in March 1973 had sketched an idea for legislation to create a government corporation to perform three functions: it would be a government oil company capable of undertaking the full range of activities from exploration to distribution of petroleum and natural gas; it would also be a government mining company empowered to undertake the full range of mining activities from exploration for ore to refining metal; and it would be an entity which was also able to assist Australian companies undertaking any of the activities which the new petroleum and mining company had the power to undertake. In April 1973, Connor advised Whitlam that the enterprise he had in mind could best be thought of in terms of the Italian state-owned venturer, ENI, which had recently purchased Australian uranium.[35] In 1953 Italy had established the ENI as a state-run energy corporation which over the next 20 years would set up 180 subsidiary and associated companies operating in about 30 countries, employing 80,000 people and with gross sales of $2500 million in 1973. ENI acted as a state holding company for its wide-ranging subsidiaries which were supposed to act as private companies under Italian law.[36]

Connor's idea was that the legislation establishing the PMA would also proscribe new foreign equity participation in mining exploration and development by using the Commonwealth's corporations power

---

35 Letter, Connor to Whitlam, 11 April 1973, Papers of Rex Connor, Series 2 Box 45, D61/2/534, University of Wollongong, Wollongong.

36 Brian Toohey, 'State Ownership Italian Style Could be Model for Petroleum Authority', *AFR*, 10 December 1973.

which the High Court had construed generously in the *Concrete Pipes* case of 1971. In the absence of foreign investment, the PMA would take up the slack by investing in private Australian mining companies or engaging in exploration and mining in its own right. As Connor argued to Cabinet in June 1973 'we would generally not grant exploration permits other than to Australian interests and we would ask the States not to grant exploration permits other than to Australian interests pending the introduction of the new legislation'.[37] The exception for Connor was that the new authority might allow foreign exploration and exploitation of some areas which the authority might discard or in areas, such as deep sea drilling, which required foreign expertise.[38]

> I conceived of the Authority both as a vehicle for increased Australian ownership and control of our resources and also as a revenue producer for Australia. A major national objective of the Authority is the creation and exploitation of opportunities for participation in future discoveries which will lead to financial returns for Australia as well as to increased ownership of the industries based on these discoveries.[39]

When Connor introduced the Petroleum and Minerals Authority Bill (PMA Bill) into Parliament in 1973, the mining industry was strongly opposed to the legislation. The Leader of the Country Party, Doug Anthony, represented feeling in the mining industry when he labelled the PMA Bill 'a monstrous piece of legislation ... tainted with socialism' and accusing Connor of being 'driven by his open

---

37   Submission 488 from Connor to Cabinet, 27 June 1973, Series 2 Box 45, D61/2/534, Papers of Rex Connor, University of Wollongong, Wollongong.
38   Ibid.
39   Letter, Connor to Crean, 22 July 1974, Papers of Rex Connor, Series 2 Box 45, D61/2/534, University of Wollongong, Wollongong.

CHAPTER 2

hatred for free enterprise and his obsession with foreign companies'.[40] While the mining industry recognised that the Whitlam government had a mandate to create a Petroleum and Minerals Authority, the Australian Mining Industry Council (AMIC) argued that such a body should compete on equal terms with private mining companies and be subject, as private companies were, to state mining legislation.[41] For AMIC the bill gave the PMA 'authority, against the wishes of the occupier, to explore, occupy and mine anywhere in Australia including exploration areas under leases already held and worked by mining companies'. The PMA, the AMIC feared, would become the 'overriding Mines Department of Australia with the power to act, as it saw fit, over any land regardless of prior rights'.[42] In February 1974, the peak Australian mining body, working through the Country Party, was pressing for a complete rewriting of the bill.[43]

Resistance to the PMA Bill continued in 1974 until, with the Senate's failure to pass it for a second time, the bill became one of the grounds on which Whitlam advised the Governor-General, Sir Paul Hasluck, to dissolve and hold elections for both Houses of Parliament. After Labor won the election on 18 May 1974, an historic joint sitting of both houses of parliament passed the PMA legislation, along with all six 'trigger bills' which had precipitated the double dissolution election. Speaking in favour of the bill, Connor defended the authority's not being subject to state laws on the ground that its powers flowed from the Constitution and that it would be a

---

40 Quoted in Hocking, *Gough Whitlam: His Time*, 181.
41 Comments on the Petroleum and Minerals Authority Bill, n.d. Papers of Rex Connor, Series 2 Box 45, D61/2/534, University of Wollongong, Wollongong.
42 Ibid.
43 Minute, Bob Sorby to Connor, 17 February 1974, Papers of Rex Connor, Series 2 Box 45, D61/2/534, University of Wollongong.

denial of the Constitution to make the exercise of its powers subject to any state. He argued that the creation of the PMA would not result in an impractical and massive takeover of the minerals industry. It would not be the end of private enterprise, Connor insisted, but the beginning of a partnership between government and private enterprise that would lead to a great expansion of the petroleum and minerals industry under the aegis of the federal government in the national interest.[44]

Connor's arguments on the need for public involvement in mining were bolstered by the conclusions of the Fitzgerald Review, which Connor had commissioned to inquire into the Australian mining industry and taxation. Fitzgerald reported that between 1967 and 1972 federal government assistance to the mining sector exceeded tax payments from mining companies by $40 million.[45] The report found that Utah Development had paid only about 5 per cent of its profits in tax from 1969 to 1973, Hamersley Holdings 0.2 per cent tax from 1966 to 1973, Western Mining Corporation 0.6 per cent tax from 1967 to 1973, and Alcoa of Australia and Queensland Alumina Limited had paid no tax at all between 1968 and 1972.[46] Released on the eve of the 1974 election, the Fitzgerald Review attracted widespread publicity and caught the peak mining lobby, AMIC, flatfooted. The Fitzgerald Review was grist to the mill for Connor's arguments about the PMA. Despite the PMA Act being passed by the Joint Sitting of the House of Representatives and the Senate, to Connor's chagrin, the High Court later invalidated the

---

44 'Minerals Bill Passed Challenges Likely', *Sydney Morning Herald*, 8 August 1974.
45 Sarah Burnside, 'Mineral Booms, Taxation and the National Interest', *History Australia* 10, no. 3, (2013): 180.
46 See Hocking, *Gough Whitlam: His Time*, 200.

legislation.[47] The High Court did not decide that the legislation was *ultra vires* but rather found that the requisite three months had not elapsed, between the first time and the second time that the Senate failed to pass it, to make the bill a legitimate double dissolution 'trigger' bill eligible to be passed at a joint sitting of both houses of parliament.

Connor and the coal and iron ore industries

Although the Whitlam government was thwarted in its attempt to establish the PMA, other aspects of its policies on mining were more successful. The biggest success came with its management of mineral export controls. Paradoxically, these controls assisted foreign-owned companies such as Utah as well as Australian companies, such as Western Mining Corporation and the Colonial Sugar Refining Company (CSR). But the Whitlam government's introduction of the controls also gave Connor powerful leverage to persuade sectors of the mining industry to present a united front against Japanese buyers. The mineral export controls met with strong resistance from the Japanese government, which claimed that the controls were causing 'uncertainty and anxiety' and would force it to reconsider its position in undertaking further mining investments in Australia.[48] In 1966 and 1967 the Japanese Steel Mills had forced the Holt government to withdraw guideline prices on iron ore exports by threatening to give further iron ore business to Australia's competitors in South America. After the Whitlam government's introduction of export

---

47 George Williams, 'The Whitlam Government and Constitutional Reform' in *It's Time Again: Whitlam and Modern Labor*, eds Jenny Hocking and Colleen Lewis, (Armadale: Melbourne Publishing Group, 2003), 205–206.
48 Wilson, *Governing Global Production*, 90.

controls on all minerals, Japanese steel firms tried the tactic again by threatening to shift their coal imports to the Soviet Union, South Africa and Canada.[49]

By 1973, however, Australian miners of coking coal and iron ore had established themselves as the lowest cost and largest suppliers of the Japanese steel industry. Consequently, the Whitlam government was able to withstand the threat of trade reprisals.[50] In 1973 Connor persuaded Australian iron ore companies to negotiate as a united front in Japan. With Connor's backing they secured a 17.5 per cent price increase in 1973 to compensate for revaluation and a further 20 per cent price increase in 1974 to make up for inflation and rising costs. Iron ore miners thus earned a 40 per cent price increase from the depressed price levels of 1973.[51] In part the price increase resulted from the Japanese steel industry's recognition of the hardship that appreciation of the Australian dollar was causing the miners. But the degree of the price increase won by the miners was not anticipated by the Australian iron ore companies and had much to do with the federal controls instituted by Connor over the negotiations by mining companies with the Japanese steel industry. These controls, the encouragement of a united front against the Japanese Steel Mills and the backing of the Australian government gave the Australian mining companies greater bargaining power in negotiations with the Japanese.

In 1973 export controls helped Connor achieve another objective for which the Joint Coal Board had long been striving. In July of

---

49 Ibid.
50 Ibid.
51 John McIlwraith, 'Iron Ore Miners Calculate Solid Gains on New Japanese Prices', *AFR*, 17 September 1974.

CHAPTER 2

that year, New South Wales Coal Proprietors' Association and the Queensland Coal Owners' Association agreed to establish a national coal industry through the vehicle of the Australian Coal Association (ACA), an organisation representing New South Wales and Queensland producers. The association, whose chairman was Edward Ryan of Bellambi Coal, appointed a delegation, including representatives from mining companies, Coalex, Utah and Thiess Bros, to work out a timetable for industry to industry discussions in Japan.[52] Most of the New South Wales coal producers' contracts with the Japanese were due for renewal in 1974, negotiations for which would commence as early as the second half of 1973.[53] In persuading coal producers to unite in an ACA, Connor was contributing to his goal of 'Australianisation' by achieving the formation of Australian industry organisations to argue for Australian positions with the Japanese steel industry.

In 1974 producers of hard coking coal in New South Wales and Queensland negotiated with the Japanese as representatives of a unified Australian coal industry working under federal oversight. Coal negotiations were conducted separately by coal producers in 1974 but were nonetheless under guidelines set by the Department of Minerals and Energy and approved by Connor. The first approach was by Ryan who left for Japan to negotiate on behalf of the South coast of New South Wales producers – Bellambi, Kembla Coal and Coke and Clutha Development – in the early part of

---

52 'Coal Industry's United Front to Overseas buyers', *AFR*, 2 July 1973.
53 Discussions between S. Nagano, Chairman, Nippon Steel Corporation, Inayama, Representative Director and President, Nippon Steel Corporation, S. Tanabe, Managing Director, Nippon Steel Corporation, and B W Hartnell, Chairman, Joint Coal Board, in Tokyo, 26 July 1972, Papers of Rex Connor, Series 2, D61, Box 8, University of Wollongong, Wollongong.

1974.[54] On 28 March 1974 the ABC reported that Australian government intervention had compelled the Japanese Steel Mills to offer New South Wales South Coast producers spectacular increases for Australian coking coal, reportedly after Connor had threatened the Japanese with banning the export of coking coal if prices were not improved.[55]

The price increases secured by New South Wales and Queensland coal producers in 1974 improved the value of Australian coal contracts from $A290 million in the year ending in March 1974 to well over $A500 million in the year ending in March 1975.[56]

Connor's success in helping the mining industry achieve higher prices for mineral exports earned him praise from unlikely quarters. The *Australian Financial Review* observed in 1974 that Connor had transformed minerals and energy, previously a 'rather dull, administrative area of little consequence', into a 'top policy portfolio'.[57] The paper further assessed that:

> Because he was obdurate on energy exports and because he was proved right by the dramatic turn of events in the international scene, Mr Connor presided over a radical change in public acceptance of government involvement in energy policy … Anybody who considers that Australian fuel policy should return to the laissez faire days of a few years ago is sadly misreading the changed relationship any government anywhere in the world must have to the energy industry.[58]

---

54   Minute, R J Gray to Connor, 11 March 1974, Papers of Rex Connor, D61, Series 2, Box 8, D61/2/100, University of Wollongong, Wollongong.
55   Transcript of ABC radio broadcast, *AM*, 28 March 1974, Papers of Rex Connor, D61, Series 2, Box 8, D61/2/100, University of Wollongong, Wollongong.
56   Ibid.
57   'Building Energy Plants or Just Monuments', *AFR*, 14 May 1974.
58   Ibid.

CHAPTER 2

The long-term contracts between the Japanese coal industry and the coal producers in the 1970s made provisions for annual negotiations on prices taking place before April. The negotiations on coal prices in 1975 for the Japanese fiscal year 1975 to 1976 were critical because the Japanese mills were now dealing with a unified national industry backed by Connor and the Department of Minerals and Energy. On 10 March 1975 Connor and Hewitt met with representatives of the Australian Coal Association in Sydney to discuss negotiating tactics. There were two schools of thought within the new association. One voiced by Bellambi and Utah was that it was realistic to aim at prices of between $US50 and $US52 per tonne for Australia's high quality hard coking coal.[59]

The other more optimistic view, pressed by Kembla Coal and Coke and Clutha Development, was that that the Australian coal exporters should ask for a $20 per tonne increase so that Australian high quality coal could reach a price of about $US57 per tonne. This was near the level which US coal exporters had just secured. Connor chose the higher price of $US57 as the guideline price at which Australia should aim for high quality coking coal (from Queensland and the South Coast of New South Wales) and $US40 per tonne for soft coking coal from the Newcastle area. But the Japanese steel industry, which was contemplating a decline in steel production in the forthcoming year, adopted a tough approach with the Australian negotiators. By that time, Australia was the leading exporter of metallurgical coal to Japan, having contracted to export 32 million tonnes of coal to Japan in the Japanese fiscal year 1975–76, amounting to in excess of 45 per

---

59   Department of Minerals and Energy Brief for discussions with Australian Coal Association – Prices for April 1975, 10 March 1975, Papers of Rex Connor, Series 2, Box 57, D61/2/668, University of Wollongong, Wollongong.

cent of Japanese imports of foreign coal. The Japanese steel industry was determined to keep the price of Australian coking coal down, aiming at a price of around $US45 per tonne for South coast hard coking coals and around $US32 per tonne for the Newcastle area soft coking coals.[60]

As was the case in 1974, Edward Ryan, the President of the ACA, opened the negotiations in March 1975 in association with Clutha Development. Bellambi and Clutha negotiated for New South Wales hard coking coals, which were expected to set the benchmark for the entire Australian coal industry. While Clutha pressed for a price increase amounting to $US20 per tonne, the Japanese mills indicated that they would go no higher than $US42 per tonne on the grounds that Japanese steel production was depressed. The Japanese Steel Mills argued that the Australians should not have the benefit of both long-term contracts and market prices but should accept the formula of 'costs plus a reasonable profit'.[61]

Ryan objected that the low price which Japan had paid for Australian coals over the previous decade had helped the Japanese steel industry become the third biggest steel industry in the world. Ryan informed Hewitt that the stand taken by the mills reflected that they knew about the agreement between Connor and the ACA on 10 March 1975 on prices and were reacting harshly to what they regarded as 'unwarranted interference by Government in normal commercial relationship between buyer and seller'.[62] In these circum-

---

60 Department of Minerals and Energy Brief for discussions with Australian Coal Association – Prices for April 1975, 10 March 1975, Papers of Rex Connor, Series 2, Box 57, D61/2/668, University of Wollongong, Wollongong.
61 Memorandum by G F Clarke, Counsellor (Minerals), Tokyo, 26 March 1975 conveying telex from Ryan to Hewitt drafted in the Australian Embassy, Tokyo, Papers of Rex Connor, Series 2, Box 57, D61/2/668, University of Wollongong, Wollongong.
62 Ibid.

CHAPTER 2

stances, Ryan sought to persuade Connor to let the industry try to settle for lower coal price increases than Connor had stipulated on 10 March 1975. But after speaking to Frank Duval, an experienced Australian businessman resident in Japan, Hewitt advised Connor to let the Australian negotiators return to Canberra. Having asked for a $US20 per tonne increase and only being offered $US8 per tonne, the Australians, Duval thought, should certainly press for a higher increase. In addition, Duval criticised the coal proprietors for telling the mills that Connor was behind their initial bid for a $US20 per tonne increase.[63]

The price negotiations remained stalemated until Connor made a visit to Japan in June 1975 to discuss a range of matters with government and industry, including coal liquefaction and uranium enrichment. In discussions in Tokyo, Saburo Tanabe, Managing Director of Nippon Steel, explained to Connor that American coal exporters were putting the Japanese steel industry under pressure by demanding excessive spot prices for their coal and that Australia should not attempt to link its coal prices, under long-term contracts, to these American spot prices. Connor replied to Tanabe that the Australian government did not want to intervene in the coal negotiations but that protracted negotiations were not good for either Australia or Japan.

In the end, the two men brokered a deal in which Connor agreed to allow the Australian coal exporters to settle for prices of around $US50 per tonne for hard coking coal and $US38 for soft coking coal. These prices were less than Connor had initially sought. But in return for this concession, Connor received from the Japanese steel

---

63 Note for File by Hewitt, 1 April 1975, Papers of Rex Connor, Series 2, Box 57, D61/2/668, University of Wollongong, Wollongong.

industry an assurance about its intent to increase its coal purchases from Australia in the longer term. The assurance came in the form of a letter to Connor from Yoshihiro Inayama, Chairman of Nippon Steel, to the effect that Japan intended to increase its coal purchases from between 27–29 million tonnes in the mid-1970s to between 44 and 49 million tonnes by 1980, an increase of some 20 million tonnes per annum. This had been based on a formal assurance from the Australian government, through Connor, that Australia could meet the Japanese requirements for Australian coking coal. Connor hailed the Inayama letter and the associated price increases up 71 per cent by comparison with the prices that prevailed a year earlier. He announced that the value of Australia's coal exports should increase from $A400 million in the current year to as much as $A1700 million per year by 1980. Connor described the arrangements resulting in earnings to Australia of about $A7000 million over five years as 'the highest commercial value agreement in Australian history, and that they 'gave the guarantee of stability to the Australian coal industry for production and employment throughout a period of world economic uncertainty'.[64]

During the course of 1974 the Japanese steel industry had become anxious to secure from Australia another approximately 20 million tonnes of coking coal annually from Australia by the end of the 1970s. This was necessary to meet the needs of its steel industry, which though affected by the economic adversity of the early 1970s, was still internationally competitive and maintained a thirst for low-cost Australian coals. The Japanese steel industry wanted three particular projects to be developed: Utah's planned mine at Norwich Park, Thiess Peabody Mitsui's project at Nebo, and a consortium of mainly

---

64   S'Lots of Holes in Coal Agreement', AFR, 17 July 1975.

CHAPTER 2

Australian producers wishing to mine at Hail Creek in Central Queensland. Connor agreed on the need to increase Australia's coal exports which he aimed to increase by 28 million tonnes annually within five years.[65] However, he delayed approving any of the three new projects on the basis that the extra tonnages required by Japan could be obtained by existing mines in Queensland and New South Wales.

By the middle of 1975 the Premier of Queensland Joh Bjelke-Petersen and his Treasurer, Sir Gordon Chalk, were voicing such strong criticisms of the Whitlam government's coal policy, that Bill Hayden, the Queenslander who had replaced Jim Cairns as Treasurer in June 1975, wrote to Connor and Whitlam urging them to place Norwich Park and Nebo before the Foreign Investment Review Committee.[66] At the bottom of Connor's opposition, was a deep dislike of multinational corporations in general and Utah in particular.[67]

Utah had approval from the Queensland government to export 300 million tonnes of coal from the North Bowen Basin and 100 million tonnes from its Blackwater lease in the south of the region. In 1975 Utah was asking the Queensland government to waive the limit of 300 million tonnes on its exports from the North Bowen Basin and also to open its fifth open-cut mine at Norwich Park. Instead, the company was seeking permission to export up to 30 per cent of its mineable reserves in the North Bowen Basin, which the company had now established to contain some six billion tons. In a press release, Connor objected that:

---

65 Rockhampton *The Morning Bulletin*, 14 July 1975.
66 Letter, Hayden to Connor, 10 July 1975, Papers of Rex Connor, Series 1, D/61/2/8, University of Wollongong, Wollongong.
67 Quoted in Galligan, *Utah*, 128.

> Despite its reserves from four existing mines, [Utah] was pressing to open up another shallow open cut at Norwich Park ... without any further concessions or increased Australian shareholding. It is claiming the right to rip out and export 1600 million additional tonnes of Australia's best coking coal, valued at current prices at around $A60,000 million. Utah will gain over 53 per cent of Australia's coal export profits during the forthcoming year.[68]

Connor was therefore strongly predisposed against approving Norwich Park. He was also inclined to temporise over Thiess Peabody Mitsui's (TPM) Nebo project. This was in the hope that a legal battle in the United States would result in Peabody's owner, Kennecott, divesting itself of coal properties in the United States and would result in Peabody's stake in TPM being taken up by Australian interests. He was most favourable to Hail Creek, a deposit 60 kilometres southwest of Mackay in the same general area but nearer the coast than the Goonyella, Peak Downs and Saraji fields. An Australian consortium, Associated Australian Oilfields and Interstate Oil, had discovered the field in 1969 with indications that it contained 800 million tonnes of coal. In mid-1971 a syndicate known as Hail Creek Associates formed to develop the deposits consisting of Australian Associated Oilfields and Interstate Oil with 60 per cent equity, Western Mining Corporation with 25 per cent, making up total Australian equity of 85 per cent in Australian hands, and the residual 15 per cent taken up by Marubeni Corporation and Sumitomo Shoji Kaisha.[69] Because, however, the $227 million project was premised on

---

68 Statement by Rex Connor, Papers of Rex Connor, Series 1, D61/2/8, University of Wollongong Wollongong.

69 Synopsis of Hail Creek Coking Coal project prepared for Rex Connor, 14 February 1973, Papers of Rex Connor, Series 1, D61/2/8, University of Wollongong, Wollongong.

CHAPTER 2

sharing infrastructure with Nebo, it was held up by Connor's delay on approval of Nebo.

Connor's opposition to any change in the Whitlam government's foreign investment policy throughout 1974 and 1975 bolstered his case against supporting new coal projects. But in September 1975 Connor was beaten in Cabinet on the issue of foreign investment in mining after which Whitlam announced a more 'open-door foreign investment policy'.[70] The government now set a 50 per cent maximum ceiling on foreign ownership and control for new development projects and merged the Foreign Investment Committee and the Committee on Foreign Takeovers into the Foreign Investment Advisory Committee. In the following month Whitlam announced that the government had given approval for the planned projects at Hail Creek, Nebo and Norwich Park in Queensland on the basis of giving the Japanese steel industry the security of an additional 15 to 20 million tonnes of coal annually and that additional iron ore business from Japan might also be dependent on the new coal contracts being approved.[71] By 14 October 1975 Connor had been forced to tender his resignation as Minister for Minerals and Energy for misleading Parliament over his role in the attempt of the government to borrow petrodollars.[72] Despite the Whitlam government's defeat in the General Elections of December 1975, the modified September 1975 foreign investment policy continued to be implemented by the Fraser Liberal–National Party Coalition and carried on in the early years of the Hawke Labor government.

---

70   'Whitlam Creates a Big Brother – The Catch in the New Foreign Investment Policy', *AFR*, 26 September 1975.
71   'Coal go ahead', *AFR*, 13 October 1975.
72   Hocking, *Gough Whitlam: His Time*, 230–236.

It was under this bipartisan foreign investment policy that Utah's Norwich Park mine was eventually approved. While the new Coalition Minister for Trade, National Party leader Doug Anthony, insisted on 50 per cent Australian equity in Norwich Park, he acceded to a request from Utah and the Queensland Government that this equity could be spread across all of the leases of its Central Queensland Coal Associates (CQCA) coal mines. A 50 per cent Australian equity in Norwich Park translated into an increase in Australian equity from 10 to 20 per cent across the four CQCA mines and the port of Hay Point. In March 1976 the Fraser Coalition government announced approval for the $240 million Norwich Park project on the basis of 55 per cent Australian equity spread across all Utah's northern Bowen Basin projects and Hay Point. To bring this policy into effect, Utah announced that the Australian Mutual Provident Society (AMP) and Utah Mining Australia Limited (UMAL) would take up shares of 7.75 and 4.0 per cent in the CQCA joint venture. This combined 11.75 per cent stake added to UMAL's existing 10.8 shares in Utah Development Company (equating to 9.2 Australian ownership of CQCA) brought total Australian ownership of CQCA to 20 per cent.[73]

Uranium and the Loans Affair

In the emerging uranium industry Rex Connor had what he thought was the perfect vehicle for implementing the Whitlam government's policies on minerals and energy in full measure.[74] Since most of Australia's uranium deposits were in the Northern Territory, they were a federal rather than a state responsibility and the Menzies-era

---

73   Galligan, *Utah*, 136–137.
74   See Alice Cawte, *Atomic Australia, 1994–1990* (Kensington: University of New South Wales Press, 1992).

CHAPTER 2

Atomic Energy Act vested all the Northern Territory's uranium in the Commonwealth. The industry was mainly Australian-owned and it was in an earlier stage of development than industries such as the coal, iron ore and aluminium industries. Connor refused to approve further uranium contracts besides those approved at the eleventh hour by the McMahon government. With Whitlam's approval, he ensured in September 1974 that all sales of Australian uranium would be marketed by the Commonwealth.[75] In the same month he predicted to the House of Representatives that Australia would be providing the Japanese market with 300,000 short tons of uranium by 1980. Connor estimated that merely exporting as yellow cake would earn $7 billion while exporting as enriched uranium would earn Australia $35–40 billion.

Frustrated by the High Court's striking down of the PMA Act as not having fulfilled the temporal requirement for a double dissolution 'trigger bill', Connor sought other means of implementing the PMA's core functions. At the end of 1974 he persuaded Whitlam and other senior ministers to approve the government seeking international funds to invest in Australia's minerals and energy sector in partial compensation for the adverse economic effects in Australia of the rise in the price of oil engineered by the Organisation of Petroleum Exporting Countries (OPEC). The fourfold increase in the price of oil in 1973 produced economic malaise in Australia that was manifested in higher unemployment and slower economic growth. But higher oil prices had also meant that oil-producing countries were earning large amounts of 'petrodollars' from the sale of their

---

75 Wayne Reynolds, 'Australia's Quest to Enrich Uranium and the Whitlam Government's Loans Affair', *Australian Journal of Politics and History* 54, no. 4 (2008): 571.

oil. These petrodollars were available in copious amounts to lend to other countries and international organisations. The International Monetary Fund borrowed petrodollars in 1974 as did Japan, France and the United Kingdom.[76] Connor wanted Australia to avail itself of the same opportunity.

At a meeting of the Executive Council on 13–14 December 1974 Whitlam, Cairns (Deputy Prime Minister and Treasurer), Connor and Lionel Murphy (Attorney-General) agreed to borrow US$4 billion. Funds for the development of uranium mining and milling featured in the initial list of items to be financed. The list also included a natural gas pipeline from the Cooper Basin to Perth and below the sea from Dampier to North Rankin, the government's share of a petro-chemical plant at Dampier, rail electrification and the upgrading of coal exporting harbours.[77] The authority to seek $4000 million was vested in Connor and the Department of Minerals and Energy and specified that the loan was for 'temporary purposes'.[78] Attorney-General Murphy argued in a legal opinion that the loan was 'temporary' because it was for a twenty-year term and in response to the energy crisis that had started to unfold in 1973. The loan, he argued, was necessary to:

> deal with exigencies arising out of the current world situation and the international energy crisis, to strengthen Australia's external financial position, to provide immediate protection for Australia's supplies of minerals and energy and to deal

---

76 Hocking, *Gough Whitlam: His Time*, 202.
77 Wayne Reynolds, 'Australia's Quest to Enrich Uranium and the Whitlam Government's Loans Affair', *Australian Journal* of Politics and History 54, no. 4 (2008): 564–565.
78 Hocking, *Gough Whitlam: His Time*, 204.

CHAPTER 2

with current and immediate foreseeable unemployment in Australia.[79]

The 'temporary purposes' path allowed Whitlam to argue that the loan would not need to come before the Loan Council, the organisation consisting of Commonwealth and state officials that had oversight of major borrowings. Whitlam's view was that the borrowing of $4000 million, being for temporary purposes, was exempt from immediate consideration by the Loan Council.[80] Connor's authority from the Executive Council was to finalise a loan, which Whitlam would then forward to the Loan Council for approval.

Connor and Hewitt thereupon pursued the possibility of accessing Middle East funds through the London-based Pakistani commodities dealer, Tirath Khemlani. But only weeks after the original 13 December 1974 decsion to authorise Connor to borrow $4000 million, his authority was revoked by acting Prime Minister Jim Cairns on the advice of the Secretary to the Treasury, Sir Frederick Wheeler, who was adamantly opposed to the method of loan raising. When Whitlam returned from overseas in January 1975, he restored Connor's authority to borrow but limited the amount to $2000 million.[81] This second authority remained in force until 20 May 1975 until finally revoked by Whitlam on the advice of Treasury.[82] After Whitlam recalled Parliament for a special sitting on 9 July 1975 to defend the attempted transaction, public controversy over what was being dubbed the 'loans affair' subsided. But evidence that Connor

---

79   Explanatory Memorandum, Minute Paper for the Executive Council, 'Proposed Borrowing' 14 December 1974, A571 1975/96.
80   Hocking, *Gough Whitlam: His Time*, 205.
81   Ibid., 222.
82   Ibid.

had attempted to raise money after the revocation of his authority led to his resignation on 14 October 1975.[83] Thereafter Opposition Leader Malcolm Fraser used the attempted loan raising as the justification for the Senate blocking supply to the government. This led, in turn, to Sir John Kerr's dismissal of the Whitlam government on 11 November 1975.

Historian Wayne Reynolds argues that Connor in late 1974 and early 1975 came to be concerned with applying borrowings of petrodollars to uranium enrichment. Connor was discussing uranium enrichment with the Japanese around the same time as the Executive Connor gave him authority to borrow $4000 million. In a letter to R W Boswell on 12 December 1974, Connor emphasised the necessity for the establishment of uranium enrichment facilities in Australia, that US4 billion was available to be borrowed, and that 'this amount should be borrowed by the Australian Atomic Energy Commission', an agency for which the Department of Minerals and Energy had responsibility.[84] Selling enriched uranium was immensely more profitable to Australia than selling yellowcake and Connor had visions of a fully Australianised uranium industry.

Connor knew that the French had made an agreement with the Shah of Iran to enrich uranium under which the Shah would lend the French $US1 billion for a ten per cent share in the output of uranium form an enrichment plant in the Rhone Valley.[85] After the OPEC-engineered spike in oil prices in 1973 and Hewitt's visit to Japan in September 1973, the Japanese agreed to explore with

---

83   Ibid., 234–236.
84   Letter from Connor to Boswell, 12 December 1974, A571/144, 1974/96 part 2 quoted in Reynolds, 'Australia's Quest to Enrich Uranium', 565.
85   Ibid.

CHAPTER 2

Australia the possibility of developing a joint programme to enrich uranium.[86] Although unable to formalise this cooperation with the Japanese, Connor pressed ahead with his plan to establish a uranium enrichment plant in Australia in 1975. After deciding on the site of a plant at Lake Phillipson in South Australia, the AAEC persuaded him that the site needed to be in Central Australia to support the Ranger and Mary Kathleen uranium deposits.[87] On 28 May 1975 Connor announced to the House of Representatives that Australia had made substantial progress on uranium enrichment and that it might be possible for Australia to 'go it alone' without the help of American technology by using the centrifuge process to enrich uranium. The United States government, however, ruled out any US support for Connor's program and the Japanese government appeared to succumb to US diplomatic pressure in telling Connor when he visited Japan in 1975 it would be 'premature' to go ahead with a joint project on enriched uranium.[88] Following the defeat of the Whitlam government in 1975, no future Australian government would be successful in fostering the enrichment of Australia's uranium. Commenting on this failure, a taskforce advising the Howard government in 2006 stated that 'for Australia to possess such a large proportion of the world's uranium resources – approximately 40 per cent of the global total – and not to have taken up opportunities over the past 35 years to develop uranium enrichment industries is highly regrettable'.[89]

---

86   Reynolds, 'Australia's Quest to Enrich Uranium', 571.
87   Ibid, 572.
88   *National Times*, 4 July 1975.
89   *Review of Uranium Mining, Processing and Nuclear Energy in Australia*, June 2006 quoted in Reynolds, 'Australia's Quest to Enrich Uranium', 562.

Conclusion

The Whitlam government's attempt to 'buy back the farm' is most commonly associated with failure: particularly the striking down of the PMA legislation, the demise of Connor's grand plan to pipe natural gas from the North West Shelf to the eastern states (the gas field was ultimately developed for export) and the role of the loans affair in the fall of the government. Another way to look at the policies, however, is to examine how the successor Liberal–National Coalition government dealt with the legacy left by Whitlam and Connor. Not long after taking office, the Fraser government outlined a policy to 'restart' the mining industry, promising a lesser role for government and a greater role for private enterprise. But notwithstanding its free-enterprise philosophy, the Fraser government 'elected to formalise, codify – and in some areas advance – the resource nationalist agendas during the late 1970 during the late 1970s and early 1980s'.[90]

The Fraser government retained the Whitlam government's 50 per cent local ownership guideline for new mining project and set up an independent review agency, the Foreign Investment Review Board (FIRB), as a successor to Whitlam's Foreign Investment Advisory Committee to advise the Treasurer on the *Foreign Acquisitions and Takeovers Act* 1975. The FIRB was given the role of assessing foreign investment applications against a set of 'national interest' criteria including whether the proposed project would produce a 'net economic benefit' (through the introduction of new technology or the creation of new export markets); whether the project would serve 'Australia's best interests' (through local processing of minerals, involvement of Australians in management, etc.); and whether 'sufficient' Australian

---

90 Wilson, *Governing Global Production*, 94.

CHAPTER 2

ownership had been achieved, and whether greater scope for Australian ownership existed. In other words, there remained for more than a decade after Connor's resignation in 1975, bipartisan support for a policy of 50 per cent participation in ownership and control of 'key areas' including minerals and energy and bipartisan support for a Foreign Investment Review Board (FIRB) has continued to the present day. The establishment of the FIRB allowed the Fraser government to institute a cooperative process whereby foreign investors could bargain over the degree of Australian ownership. A higher degree of foreign ownership could be bargained against other benefits a new minerals project might bring such as infrastructure spending or locals minerals processing. The policy of mandating a proportion of Australian equity in new mining projects was ultimately jettisoned in 1992 when the cost of investment in mining operations proved beyond the capacity of local finance. This, in turn, gave retrospective justification for a body like the PMA, one of whose tasks was to finance large mining projects.

In 1974 and 1975 the Whitlam government seriously contemplated an initiative of buying back the farm by buying back Australia's largest mining house, Conzinc Riotinto of Australia (CRA), from its British parent Rio Tinto Zinc (RTZ). The initiative, pursued largely by Secretary of the Department of the Prime Minister and Cabinet John Menadue, was overtaken by the dismissal of the Whitlam government but the 'Australianisation' of CRA was later advanced by a more gradual process. In 1978 the Fraser government announced a policy under which foreign-owned firms would be exempted from screening requirements for new projects if they committed to increasing Australian ownership of their existing operations to 50 per cent over a timetable negotiated with the FIRB. Under this policy

CRA began the naturalising process in 1978 and achieved 50 per cent Australian ownership in 1986. By that time, following the recession of 1981 and 1982 and more troubled times for the global coal trade, BHP had acquired Utah's coal operations in Queensland and Australian diversified company, CSR, had acquired the coal operations of Thiess Brothers, thus considerably adding to Australian ownership of the mining industry. In iron ore, CRA bought out the American Kaiser Steel's position in Hamersley Iron and Australian miner, Peko-Wallsend took over the management of the Robe River iron ore project. Consequently large parts of the Australian mining industry were Australianised in the 1980s with the assistance of policies initially implemented by Whitlam and Connor. The Fraser government also retained Connor's mineral export controls despite vigorous efforts by the Japanese Steel Mills and state governments such as the Bjelke-Petersen government in Queensland and the Court government in Western Australia to persuade Fraser to dismantle them. Whitlam and Connor helped transform what was perceived as the dull administrative backwater of National Development into the top portfolio of Minerals and Energy. They also succeeded in making the issue of how Australians should benefit from their mineral resources a vitally important issue for government and for national politics. The government's fall on an issue connected with mining has attracted far more attention than the important historical legacy that it left behind.

Chapter 3

THE REGIONAL AND THE LOCAL

Whitlam's 'quality of life' agenda

Lyndon Megarrity

Gough Whitlam once said that he wanted 'every kid to have a desk, with a lamp, and his own room to study'.[1] This was just one expression of Whitlam's conviction that it was the right of all Australians to experience the same opportunities for cultural, economic and social betterment, no matter where they lived. As leader of the ALP, Whitlam developed policies during the 1960s and 1970s aimed at ensuring an improved quality of life for those in the suburbs, regional centres and remote areas and which also provided opportunities for the ambitious. As well as catering for individual growth, Whitlam's attention to quality of life issues was an attempt to emphasise the importance of community life in Australia and to strengthen it through Commonwealth support of local and regional activities. This paper

---

This research was supported by the Australian Government under an Australian Prime Ministers Centre Fellowship, an initiative of the Museum of Australian Democracy.

[1] Stuart Macintyre, *A Concise History of Australia,* 3rd edition (Port Melbourne: Cambridge University Press, 2009), 237.

will explore a forgotten element in Whitlam's 'quality of life' agenda: the Whitlam government's substantial local and regional policies.

Local government before Whitlam: Curtin, Chifley and Menzies

The Whitlam government's local and regional policies were the product of several decades of debate about the role of local government in the federation. Some discussion of the broader historical context in which these policies were developed is useful in understanding Whitlam's quality of life agenda.

By the 1940s, the traditional responsibilities of local councils, such as road maintenance, had to be balanced with increasing public demands to provide community services such as libraries, recreational facilities and crèches. In their search for financial support for their enlarged mission, local governments were especially keen to see their relationships with the Commonwealth expand.[2]

In theory, the Commonwealth had no constitutional power to directly fund local government, as local authorities were the sole legislative responsibility of state governments. However, by the Second World War, the federal balance of power in financial terms was shifting in favour of the federal government. Crucially in this regard, from 1942 the Commonwealth became the sole collector of Australian income tax following the States' agreement to relinquish their right to collect it.[3]

---

2   See M. Bowman, 'Historical Perspectives' in *Getting the Numbers: Women in Local Government*, eds A. Sinclair with M. Bowman and L. Strahan (North Melbourne: Hargreen Publishing Company, 1987), 15; A. Bundy, 'Case-study: Public Libraries – Books, Bytes, Buildings, Brains' in *Paper Empires: A History of the Book in Australia 1946–2005*, eds C. Munro and R. Sheahan-Bright (St Lucia: University of Queensland Press, 2006), 373–377.

3   R T Fitzgerald, *Through a Rear Vision Mirror: Change and Education: A Perspective on the Seventies from the Forties* (Hawthorn: Australian Council for Educational

CHAPTER 3

While pragmatic considerations underscored local government lobbying of the Commonwealth, ideological considerations also took centre-stage. Groups such as the Local Government Association of New South Wales argued that local government, as the unit of government closest to the people, must be given greater power and autonomy in a decentralised postwar Australia. Local government groups pushed for greater control over town planning, housing, child welfare, hospitals and other services which could be classified as specific to each local government area. The resulting decentralisation of social services, they argued, would be more responsive to local nuances and thus create a more democratic federal system of government.[4]

The Curtin Labor government's postwar agenda echoed parts of the local government push for decentralisation. The Pacific war had focused attention on Australia's tendency to concentrate population and industry within a handful of metropolitan centres, making it vulnerable to attack and limiting its options. John Curtin's government consequently believed that a postwar program of decentralisation was necessary to enhance national security while increasing overall prosperity and community well-being.[5]

Following an agreement between the premiers and Prime Minister Curtin in 1944 to initiate regional planning, each state defined its own regional boundaries for planning purposes. This resulted in the theoretical creation of nearly 100 regions across Australia. New South

---

Research, 1975), 257.

4   Local Government Association of New South Wales, *Local Government in the Future: Statement of Policy*, Local Government Association of New South Wales (LGANSW), 28 April 1944 [pamphlet], in [Personal Papers of Prime Minister Curtin] Correspondence 'L', A1415 379, National Archives of Australia (hereafter NAA). See also A. Mainerd (Secretary, LGANSW), to J B Chifley, 8 November 1945, in Local Government, A461 P327/1/1, NAA.

5   See Lyndon Megarrity, '"Necessary and Urgent"?', *Journal of the Royal Australian Historical Society* 97, no. 2 (2011): 137.

Wales, Victoria and Tasmania established Regional Development Committees which included state and local government representatives. While many Regional Development Committees surveyed their region's resources and submitted plans to their state governments, no tangible Commonwealth or state action was taken to bring these plans to fruition.[6]

Federal Labor's interest in collaborating with local authorities rapidly lost steam in 1945, following the death of John Curtin. Unenthusiastic about unproven experiments in participative democracy, the new Labor Prime Minister Ben Chifley was happy for the states to maintain their tight grip on local government matters. Chifley's successor as prime minister, the Liberal party's Robert Menzies, shared much the same attitude.[7]

The impact of limited Commonwealth interest in local and regional matters can be seen in a draft 1951 memorandum by the Regional Development Division of the federal Ministry of National Development. Prepared under the direction of Acting Director Grenfell Rudduck, the memo noted that despite the lip service paid to the need for decentralisation and regionalism since 1944, capital cities were increasingly becoming congested and rural areas were rapidly losing population. The memo also suggested that given the Commonwealth's high postwar immigration program, the Commonwealth was contributing to centralisation and thus needed to take some responsibility for creating more rigorous regional policies

---

6   Lyndon Megarrity, 'Local Government and the Commonwealth, 1943–75', *Public Policy* 7, no. 1 (2012): 10–11.

7   Francis Thomas Hurley, 'An Event that Never Happened: The History and Politics of Decentralisation in Victoria and New South Wales 1885–1985', PhD thesis, (Melbourne: Deakin University, 1989), 151–154; H C Coombs, *Trial Balance*, (South Melbourne: Macmillan, 1981), 65–66.

in cooperation with state and (by implication) local authorities. If this memo eventually made it to the Prime Minister's office, it cannot have had much impact. In Menzies' eyes, local government matters were state government matters and nothing to do with the Commonwealth government: the regional development committees instituted by Curtin and Chifley were allowed to die.[8]

The Menzies government's relative lack of engagement with regional development allowed Labor, then radically rebuilding its platform from Opposition, to reinvent itself as the champion of local government. This transformation occurred largely as a result of the persistence of Gough Whitlam, who used the issue of local government to illustrate his ideas about quality of life and community in modern, postwar Australia.[9]

Whitlam, local government and 'quality of life': 1945–1960

Whitlam's personal background made him predisposed to take the issue of local government seriously. As a young family man in the 1940s and 1950s, he had lived in the southern and western suburbs of Sydney, where the population was growing much faster than social amenities and basic infrastructure such as hospitals and schools. Whitlam knew that the enjoyment of a good quality of life

---

[8] See memo attached to Grenfell Rudduck (acting director of the regional development division of the Ministry of National Development) to G C Watson (Department of Immigration), 8 February 1951, in Regional Development – General Policy, A439/1 1951/11/269, NAA. For Menzies' views, see *Deputation from Australian Council of Local Government Associations to meet Prime Minister and Treasurer* [report], in 'Australian Council of Local Government Associations – General', A463 1956/922, NAA. See also Geoffrey Blainey, *A Shorter History of Australia* (1994) (Milsons Point: Vintage, 2000), 233.

[9] Andrew H Kelly, Brian Dollery and Bligh Grant, 'Regional Development and Local Government: Three Generations of Federal Intervention', *Australasian Journal of Regional Studies* 15, no. 2 (2009): 174–77.

in the suburbs was not an unreasonable goal, having spent much of his youth in the well-planned city of Canberra. As Whitlam later wrote:

> I was able to absorb the great advantages of a planned city, especially one built by a single authority under the control of national Government ... Every home [in Canberra] was well serviced by properly paved footpaths and roadways. Every home had adequate access to kindergartens, parks, schools, shopping centres and health centres.[10]

Prior to winning the western suburbs seat of Werriwa in 1952, Whitlam had stood unsuccessfully for office in the Sutherland Shire Council. His early speeches as the Member for Werriwa, however, seriously discounted the capacity of local government and the states as then constituted to achieve much for the public good. Instead of a federal system, Whitlam advocated the Canadian system, whereby:

> All new powers are automatically taken by the national parliament, and all the powers given to the provinces are specified. At best federation is a compromise, a temporary stage in our political evolution. The States are neither flesh nor fowl nor good red herring; neither national bodies nor local government bodies. They have not the means to be national and have not the time to be provincial.[11]

In his Chifley Memorial Lecture (1957), Whitlam advocated the abolition of the states in favour of a system of metropolitan and regional councils. Such councils, concerned with local matters like town planning, would complement the national interest work of a

---

10 Gough Whitlam, *The Whitlam Government 1972–1975* (Ringwood: Viking, 1985), 371–372. See also Jenny Hocking, *Gough Whitlam: A Moment in History* (Carlton: Melbourne University Publishing Limited, 2008), 111, 132, 149–152.
11 Whitlam, *Commonwealth Parliamentary Debates*, 8 October 1953, 1180.

CHAPTER 3

Commonwealth unfettered by the legal and political barriers imposed by the states.[12]

Regional and local policies: Whitlam 1960–72

Whitlam's preference for a radical constitutional overhaul which transformed local authorities into larger regional units was a consistent element of his policy towards local government. However, as his profile grew in the 1960s, first as Deputy Opposition leader and then as Labor leader, Whitlam's rhetoric necessarily shifted as he moved closer to his ultimate goal: the Prime Ministership. A realist, he instinctively understood that a future Whitlam government would have to accept the reality of the states as powerful players within the federal system.[13] But while local governments had no direct constitutional links with the Commonwealth, Whitlam saw no reason why local and regional authorities could not play a key part in his emerging 'quality of life' agenda. Through his regular speeches and public statements, Whitlam argued that local government could and should play a larger role in improving social amenities and infrastructure within their own communities. He advocated federal financing of local government to support these objectives. Increased funding was highly attractive to cash-strapped councils, which were struggling to provide the parks, civic beautification, sporting facilities and other 'quality of life' services increasingly expected of local authorities.[14]

---

12 E G Whitlam, 'The Constitution versus Labor', Chifley Memorial Lecture, University of Melbourne, 1957, reprinted in his *On Australia's Constitution* (Camberwell: Widescope International Publishers Pty Ltd, 1977), 33–44.

13 See Graham Freudenberg, 'Confessions of a Reformed but Unrepentant Centralist: From Whitlam to Wran', in *Issues in Contemporary Australian Politics*, Occasional Paper 3, Australian Studies Centre (Humanities and Social Sciences), University of Queensland, 1983, 14–20.

14 To trace the intellectual origins of Whitlam's local government policies would be beyond the scope of this paper. It should be noted, however, that Whitlam and his

During the 1960s and 1970s, Whitlam railed against what he once described as 'NewSydneyGong', a partial reference to the possibility that Newcastle, Sydney and Wollongong would join up to become one sprawling mass.[15] In its wider sense, 'NewSydneyGong' was a resonant description of the way in which Australian cities were becoming larger and more anonymous because of unregulated urban sprawl, congestion and a neglect of social amenities. Gough Whitlam tapped into a concern that in the modern city, people were gradually losing a sense of community because of a civic culture that prioritised commercial activities over the needs of residents. Country towns were also suffering a loss of community as young people left for the city. In late 1971, one year before his election victory, Whitlam insisted that:

> We must abandon the notion that if people want occupation, accommodation or recreation, particularly if they are young people, they have to go to the State capitals. One of the saddest things in Australia is that whenever one goes to the country one finds in the local newspapers a report of a farewell for some teenager ... who is leaving for the city, by which is meant the State capital.[16]

---

office were influenced in the area of local government and city development by the ideas and concerns of Australian-based academics such as Patrick Troy and Max Neutze. Patrick Troy to Lyndon Megarrity, 6 April 2011, email in possession of the author. For local government's increasing social and community role, see for example John R Robbins, 'An Outline of South Australian Local Government' in *The Flinders History of South Australia: Political History*, ed. Dean Jaensch (Netley: Wakefield Press, 1986), 403; Barbara Buchanan, 'Bringing the Bush Back to the City: The Re-greening of Lane Cove North in the Early 1970s', *Australasian Parks and Leisure* 9, no. 4 (2006): 20. See also 1972 correspondence between Whitlam's office and local governments in Richard Hall Papers, series 15, folder 20, MS 8725, National Library of Australia (hereafter NLA).

15 'Decentralisation – E.G. Whitlam: Yass – 7th September [1966], in [Personal Papers of E G Whitlam] Decentralisation Yass 7.9.1966, M170 66/11, NAA.
16 Whitlam, *Commonwealth Parliamentary Debates*, 9 December 1971, 4405.

CHAPTER 3

Underpinning Whitlam's thinking was the notion that no matter where a person lived they were entitled to the same social and economic opportunities. This was combined with a commitment to investing in regions outside the capital cities to make them more 'liveable' and thus prevent congestion and social problems in the larger urban areas. At the same time, Whitlam wanted the Commonwealth to help build community life within the potentially fragmented suburban areas of the cities. He advocated stronger, better financed local authorities to help deliver these social and economic goals, believing that a strong local government served to strengthen democracy itself.[17]

Whitlam envisaged a system whereby individual states and local authorities could create detailed plans for urban and regional priorities such as roads, entertainment facilities and recreation areas, and then submit them to the Commonwealth for possible funding. Whitlam's position on local government, however, was ambiguous. On the one hand, Whitlam as Opposition leader (1967–72) railed against Commonwealth and state neglect of local government; on the other, he was pessimistic about the existing sector's capacity to realise his urban and regional goals.

Whitlam condemned the states for failing to amalgamate Australia's large number of local authorities, which had reached a total of some 890 by 1972.[18] He reasoned that municipalities with larger geographical areas were preferable because of their enhanced revenue base and ability to 'implement rational urban planning'.[19] Moreover,

---

17 E G Whitlam, 'Future of Australian Federalism', Address by the Leader of the Opposition, Mr. E.G. Whitlam, Q.C., M.P., to the Academy of Social Sciences – Australian National University Seminar on Inter-Governmental Relations, 8 November 1971, in Richard Hall Papers, series 15, folder 20, MS 8725, NLA.

18 R J K Chapman and Michael Wood, *Australian Local Government: The Federal Dimension* (North Sydney: George Allen & Unwin, 1984), 38.

19 E G Whitlam, 'Regional Representation and Development', Address to the Shires' Association of New South Wales to be delivered by E.G. Whitlam, Q.C., M.P. on

as much as Whitlam presented well-researched speeches on local government issues, he was clearly more interested in discussing fresh plans for selective, Commonwealth supported decentralisation. Whitlam's vision of decentralisation involved the establishment of a concentrated number of new regional cities to take the pressure off congested capital centres, thereby creating a better quality of life for Australian citizens.[20] Toowoomba City Council's Deputy Town Clerk, Eric Thorne, was one of many state and local Council players who viewed Whitlam's penchant for grand regional visions as a threat to local autonomy. Thorne wrote:

> [Whitlam] is saying – more finance to State and Local Authorities, but let us do away with the States anyhow and have large regional areas, which also means the doing away with the structure of Local Government as we know it to-day. We see the chocolate-coated lolly being given to the little boy – but what is under the chocolate[?][21]

Whitlam in office: 1972–75

As prime minister between 1972 and 1975, Whitlam could legitimately claim that he had massively expanded the Commonwealth–local

---

Wednesday, 5 June 1968', copy held at NLA.

20 'A New Decentralisation', Address by Mr E.G. Whitlam, Q.C., M.P. ... to the National Development Conference, Park Royal Motor Inn, Canberra, 8.00 PM 19 August 1971, in [Personal Papers of Prime Minister E G Whitlam], "A New Decentralisation", Canberra 19.8.71, M170 71/69, NAA; Policies of Decentralisation: Statement made by Mr. E.G. Whitlam, Q.C., Albury, 28 April 1972, in [Whitlam Papers] Decentralisation Albury 28.4.72, M170 72/141, NAA. Initiated by the Whitlam Government, the Albury-Wodonga National Growth Centre Project was inspired by the notion of selective decentralisation. See Bruce Pennay, *Making a City in the Country: The Albury-Wodonga National Growth Centre Project 1973–2003* (Sydney: UNSW Press, 2005).

21 Eric Thorne, 'Dangers to Local Control', in *Dunkirk for Local Government: Two Papers Presented at a Seminar Organised by the New England Electors' Association* (Tamworth: New England Electors' Association, 1972) [copy in NLA].

government relationship and secured outcomes which improved the basic standard of living and quality of life in numerous local areas:

> The Federal Government's payments to and for local government authorities increased from $7 500 000 in 1972–73 to $165 372 000 in 1975–76 ... local government programs which the Government financed through the States included senior citizens' centres ... sewerage backlog, leisure facilities ... urban transport and tourism.[22]

Much of the Commonwealth funding of the local government sector under Whitlam was through grants given to the states for distribution to local authorities, a prudent measure given that there was no constitutional basis for direct federal grants to local government. However, the Whitlam government created a number of specific Commonwealth funding programs for which a variety of organisations, including local government authorities, were deemed eligible to apply, such as the Regional Employment Development scheme. In such cases local councils often received direct funding.[23]

There is no doubt that Whitlam viewed support for the 'local' as a vital part of his concept of the national interest. He stated that what the Whitlam government wanted was to:

> enliven and invigorate people's lives, to make sure that the rewards and satisfactions of the arts, and decent opportunities for sport and recreation and holidays, are shared by as many people as possible ... It's surprising how much can be done with small sums applied carefully for local purposes. It's not necessarily a matter of building vast stadiums ... mainly it's helping

---

22 Whitlam, *The Whitlam Government*, 724.
23 Commonwealth Government, *Australian Government Assistance to Local Projects: A Guide to Sources of Funds and How to Apply for Them* (Canberra: Australian Government Publishing Service, 1975), 1, 28–29.

local groups and authorities improve existing facilities – a new changeroom, an extra tennis court, floodlighting for an oval.[24]

Whitlam remained convinced that the 'local' was best tackled by regional forms of governance, through a mix of local government and regional planning. At the same time that he was increasing funding for local government, Whitlam was implementing ideas that reflected his goal of a decentralised Australia which privileged the creation of moderate to large regional units over existing local government arrangements. The Whitlam government created 76 regional organisations across the nation as a means of administering Commonwealth grants to local authorities. Each region consisted of several existing local governments, although as Geoffrey Sawer noted, the regional organisation was 'little more than a post office for transmitting applications from the member local governments'. The successful applicants for those grants still had their Commonwealth funds transmitted via the states.[25] Whitlam, however, hoped that local governments would use the new regional organisations to further the cause of decentralisation. He believed that Australia had 'far too few genuine regions and far too many local government bodies; far too little regionalism and far too much parochialism'.[26]

---

24 Prime Minister's Queensland Broadcast No. 20: 'Quality of Life' – Sunday, 3 August 1975, in Press Releases, Speeches and Transcripts folder 3 Aug 1975–31 Aug 1975, M163 39, NAA.
25 Geoffrey Sawer, *Federation Under Strain: Australia 1972–1975* (Carlton: Melbourne University Press, 1977), 22. See also J M Power and R L Wettenhall, 'Regional Government Versus Regional Programs', *Australian Journal of Public Administration* 35, no. 2 (1976): 122.
26 'Local Government and the National Government', Speech by the Prime Minister, Mr E G Whitlam … Opening the Annual Conference of the Australian Council of Local Government Associations, at Alice Springs, on Monday 11 November 1974, document held at the Whitlam Institute (University of Western Sydney) http://www.whitlam.org/

CHAPTER 3

Whitlam also introduced a competing form of regionalism in the form of the Australian Assistance Plan (AAP). The AAP provided regional funding for social welfare projects, with a strong focus on the involvement of local voluntary organisations. The administrative machinery included the creation of Regional Councils for Social Development across the states. This form of regionalism troubled some local authorities, as they feared that the Commonwealth's creation of additional regional bodies was at the expense of the status and profile of local government within the federal system and among the community at large.[27]

The need for the Commonwealth to find ways around the Constitution to avoid 'states rights' issues in its dealings with local government frustrated Whitlam. Section 96 of the Australian Constitution empowered the Commonwealth to 'grant financial assistance to any State on such terms as the Parliament sees fit'. Whitlam made effective use of section 96 to provide indirect federal funding for local government programs via the states. This enabled linking of Commonwealth funds to specific local projects but did not allow a direct Commonwealth–local government financial relationship. To clarify this issue, it became the subject of one of four referenda put to the Australian people at the May 1974 double dissolution election. Specifically, the referendum sought to change the Constitution in order to give the Commonwealth the power to 'borrow money for, and grant financial assistance to, local

---

27 Melanie Oppenheimer, 'Voluntary Action, Social Welfare and the Australian Assistance Plan in the 1970s', *Australian Historical Studies* 39, no. 2 (2008): 167–182; Graham Miles (Secretary, Local Government Association of NSW), 'Is the Honeymoon with Labor over?', *Australian Financial Review* Local Government Feature, 9 June 1975, 10; Frank Hornby, *Australian Local Government and Community Development: From Colonial Times to the 21st Century* (North Melbourne: Australian Scholarly Publishing Pty Ltd, 2012): 176.

government'.[28] The referendum was strongly opposed by the Liberal/Country party Opposition and the states and, like all the referenda put that day, it failed. Possible reasons for its failure include the historic tendency of Australian voters to reject constitutional changes that lacked bipartisan support, as well as the government's decision to conduct three other referenda and a federal election for both houses of parliament on the same day.[29] But the referendum result also suggests that there was limited voter appetite for the radical transformation of local government and its relationship with national government which Whitlam implied in his statements on regionalism.

In any event, the Whitlam government ultimately failed to adequately present a consistent local government policy. The central message which Whitlam had presented was that his government wished to 'elevate' local government within the federal system. However, this was somewhat contradicted by the prime minister's own statements, which suggested that the Commonwealth–local government partnership was focused on creating regionalism on a national scale. Whitlam asserted in 1974 that 'More direct co-operation between the national government and local government can help end state centralism by giving the chance for the growth of genuine regionalism'. The prime minister saw this as a 'choice imposed upon us by necessity, by the inevitability of Australian history'.[30]

28　Cheryl Saunders, 'Constitutional Recognition of Local Government in Australia', in *The Place and Role of Local Government in Federal Systems*, ed. N Stelyer (Johannesburg: Konrad-Adenauer-Stiftung, 2005), 49.

29　I McAllister, M Mackerass and C B Boldiston, *Australian Political Facts: Second Edition* (South Melbourne: Macmillan Education Australia Pty Ltd, 1997), 111–112.

30　'Local Government and the National Government', Speech by the Prime Minister, Mr E G Whitlam, Monday 11 November 1974, document held at the Whitlam Institute (University of Western Sydney) http://www.whitlam.org/

CHAPTER 3

Statements such as this allowed the Opposition to portray Whitlam's regional policies as an insidious form of 'imposed regionalism' from the centre that would lead to the destruction of the states and less, not more, power for local governments:

> We recognise that there is a natural tendency for regions to develop as the community grows and expands. Labor does not want to encourage or build on this natural evolution. It wants to tear down the structure that developed and impose a new scheme which suits its centralist tendencies. We [the Liberal/Country Party coalition] are committed to support Local Government ... but we will work in partnership. Labor will impose its solution.[31]

Local government bodies, furthermore, were not interested in new organisational structures. While the President of the Local Government Association of New South Wales, H. Greg Percival, welcomed the symbolism of Commonwealth funding as a sign that local government was 'entitled to a share in the national wealth', he was not prepared to embrace structural change along with it.[32] Percival's speech to the Institute of Municipal Administration (1974) indicated that local authorities sought to enhance existing arrangements rather than significantly alter the federal system:

> My Association, along with all the other Local Government Associations in Australia, want Local Government to retain its basic relationship with the States ... We are not ... looking for independence from the States, but we are looking for more independence in managing our own affairs.[33]

---

31 Liberal–Country Party Coalition, *The Way Ahead with a Liberal Country Party Government: Local Government* (Canberra: Liberal Party of Australia, 1974), 3.

32 H Greg Percival, 'The Place of Local Government in the Australian Scene', *Bulletin* (Local Government Association of NSW), no. 1 (1975): 7.

33 Ibid., 8–9.

Conclusion

During its time in office, the Whitlam government increased the status of local government within the federal system, only to produce political confusion by creating larger regional schemes which challenged state and local government assumptions about their respective roles within the federation. Partly as a result of this perceived threat to the established system, Whitlam's regional projects and structures were dismantled or watered down during the Liberal-Country Party government (1975–83) led by Malcolm Fraser.[34] However, 'big picture' regionalism has remained an important feature of Commonwealth policy-making, sometimes overshadowing local government debates. Indeed, the Commonwealth since Whitlam's era has often expressed a preference for supporting aspects of local government which lend themselves to a 'regional' approach, such as infrastructure and economic sustainability.[35]

There is some capacity for local government to serve the cause of national social cohesion through 'place-shaping': that is, creating

---

[34] Dismantled programs included the Australian Assistance Program and the regional organisation of local governments for funding purposes. Whitlam's major symbol of his decentralised cities agenda, the Albury-Wodonga growth centre project, continued for several years, but the regional growth centre idea lost momentum and no further projects were established after 1975. See Charles P Harris, 'Local Government and Regional Planning', in *Australian Regional Developments: Readings in Regional Experiences, Policies and Prospects*, eds Benjamin Higgins and Krzysztof Zagorski, (Canberra: Australian Government Publishing Service, 1989), 109–112.

[35] While the Commonwealth Roads to Recovery program initiated under the Howard Government assisted individual local councils with the maintenance, upgrade and replaced of local roads, it was arguably a program which was as much about making a collective contribution to 'regional and rural Australia' as it was about strengthening individual local governments. For a general overview of Commonwealth–local government interactions since the Whitlam years, see Lyndon Megarrity, *Local Government and the Commonwealth: An Evolving Relationship* (Canberra: Parliamentary Library, 2011); Kelly, Dollery & Grant, 'Regional Development', 184–186; Michael Wood, 'The "New Federalism" of Whitlam and Fraser and their Impact on Local Government', *Politics* 12, no. 2 (1977): 104–115.

a bond between people and local areas through local democratic processes and initiatives.[36] However, the goal of 'place-shaping' is perhaps undervalued by the Commonwealth because it cannot politically 'own' specific localities. Certainly, it is easier to develop 'big picture' policies when one is dealing with larger, more anonymous 'regions'.

The 'quality of life' problems of today are similar to those identified by Whitlam in the 1960s. Controversies over the fair provision of public amenities and the prioritisation of business wishes over community values are as prevalent today as they were in 1965.[37] However, there are few, if any, contemporary politicians, who are willing or able to follow Whitlam's example of turning regional and local quality of life issues into a major national issue and political cause.[38] 'Public needs and public convenience must take priority over private property rights', Whitlam wrote in 1965, 'There is no alternative if city living is to be made bearable'.[39] In an age when public policy treats citizens as consumers, Whitlam's thoughts on the local and regional in national life still stand out as a challenge to the status quo.

---

36 For a discussion of 'place-shaping', see Brian Dollery, Bligh Grant and Sue O'Keefe, 'Local Councils as 'Place-shapers': The Implications of the Lyons Report for Australian Local Government', *Australian Journal of Political Science* 43, no. 3 (2008): 481–494.

37 See 'Light Rail and the Transport Challenge', *Canberra Times*, 13 July 2015, 2; Melanie Kembrey, 'Parramatta Risks Being "Glass Boxes and Concrete"', *Sydney Morning Herald*, 20 May 2015, 13; Jason Dowling, 'Developers Say Stick to Plans, Locals Don't Need Input', *Age*, 12 March 2015, 15.

38 In 2015, new Liberal Prime Minister Malcolm Turnbull appointed a Minister for Cities and the Built Environment, Jamie Briggs. However, the Turnbull Government's justification for greater Commonwealth involvement in urban areas appears (at first glance) to centre around the notion of extracting economic productivity gains from public transport reforms rather than securing a better quality of life for all. See Mark Kenny, 'Leaders Argue Over Transport Planning', *Sydney Morning Herald*, 13 October 2015, 9; Jacob Saulwick, 'More Federal Power Flagged in City Projects, *Sydney Morning Herald*, 9 October 2015, 3.

39 Gough Whitlam, 'Cities in a Federation' [1965], *Australian Planner* 49, no. 2 (2012): 19.

Chapter 4

REACH OF THE IMAGINATION

The bold experiment of the Australian Assistance Plan[1]

Melanie Oppenheimer, Erik Eklund and Joanne Scott

A largely forgotten, yet highly original social policy program of the 1970s, the Australian Assistance Plan (AAP) sought to reframe citizens' participation in their communities, stimulate voluntary organisations and transform earlier models of engagement amongst all levels of government and the emerging voluntary sector. Influenced by both domestic and international programs and approaches, this 'pioneering experiment in community development' directed federal funding to community groups through a new mechanism, Regional Councils for Social Development (RCSDs), instead of the traditional avenue of State governments.[2] The AAP epitomised Prime Minister Gough Whitlam's ideas on federalism – where 'any function or

---

1. This paper was originally presented at the Australian Historical Association's conference in Sydney, 8 July 2015 as part of a thematic panel on 'The Whitlam Government, 1972–75: a foundational moment'. We have received funding from the Australian Research Council for this project. 'Bold Experiment: An Historical Evaluation of the Australian Assistance Plan' (DP150103022).
2. E G Whitlam, 'Power and People – Community Participation in Federal Government', *The Australian Quarterly* 47, no. 2 (June 1975): 36. For an overview of the AAP, see Melanie Oppenheimer, 'Voluntary Action, Social Welfare and the AAP in the 1970s, *Australian Historical Studies* 39, no. 2 (June 2008): 167–182.

CHAPTER 4

activity which can be hitched to the star of the Commonwealth grows in quality and affluence'.[3] As part of his 'avalanche of social reform'[4] to address poverty and inequality in Australian society, the AAP attracted plaudits and condemnation in almost equal measure.

During the 1960s and 1970s, there was a shift in western democracies towards an evidence-based approach to social policy reforms and an increase in community engagement and consultation. The formation of the Whitlam government's Department of Urban and Regional Development (DURD) in December 1972, with similar policy and ideological origins to the AAP, was a major Commonwealth response to the groundswell of grass roots activism in a range of areas including planning, urban amenities, ethnic affairs, heritage protection and citizen participation.[5]

The innovative suite of reforms had a direct impact on regionalism and voluntary action that extended beyond the period of the Whitlam government itself. As a 'major mechanism for regionalisation', the AAP was central to this core government mission.[6] In its approach to social policy the AAP sought to foster a regional focus and encouraged local input, to deliver services to diverse communities

---

3 E G Whitlam, 'ALP Policy Speech, 1972', quoted in Deborah Brennan, *The Politics of Australian Child Care: From Philanthropy to Feminism* (Melbourne: CUP, 1994): 70.

4 Brian Howe, 'Social Policy' in *The Whitlam Legacy*, ed. Troy Bramston (Sydney: The Federation Press, 2013), 198.

5 For a history of DURD the best is CJ Lloyd and Patrick N Troy, *Innovation and Reaction. The Life and Death of the Federal Department of Urban and Regional Development* (Sydney: George Allen and Unwin, 1981). See also Melanie Oppenheimer, *Volunteering. Why We Can't Survive Without It* (Sydney: UNSW Press, 2008).

6 Letter from David Hall, Member of Task Force, Royal Commission on Australian Government Administration to Mrs E V Knight, Chairman, Loddon-Campaspe RCSD, 24 June 1975, File 8/10 (ii) Royal Commission on Government Administration, Box 8, M07587, MS 11455, State Library of Victoria (hereafter L-C RCSD).

through new forms of funding and participatory methods.[7] The AAP was an innovative administrative policy that provided a 'bridge' between Commonwealth government programs and local communities' expectations and aspirations.

In this way the AAP goes to the heart of the Whitlam project, articulated in the ALP's 1972 policy speech. Whitlam declared:

> Our program has three great aims. They are to promote equality; to involve the people of Australia in the decision-making processes of our land; and to liberate the talents and uplift the horizons of the Australian people.[8]

The AAP certainly strove to meet all of these aims. It broke new ground and, perhaps not surprisingly, was highly controversial. It sought to reframe citizen involvement at a local level through the promotion of a new approach to community development and the dissemination of social welfare. Emphasising greater recognition for voluntary activity and community engagement, the AAP attempted to create vehicles 'for developing a community soul'.[9] Bypassing the State governments (the traditional custodians of such funding streams and responsibilities) and side-lining local government structures, funding for the scheme came directly from the Commonwealth government to the newly instituted RCSDs. Thirty-five RCSDs were established across Australia, administered by the (also newly established) Social Welfare Commission, led by Marie Coleman, the first woman to head a Commonwealth statutory authority.

---

7 Erik Eklund, Melanie Oppenheimer and Joanne Scott, '"Developing a Community Soul": A Comparative Assessment of the Australian Assistance Plan in Three Regions, 1973–1977', *Australian Journal of Politics and History* 62, Issue 3 (September 2016): 419–434.

8 Whitlam, 'Power and People', 36.

9 L Tierney et. al., *Victorian Evaluation of the Australian Assistance Plan* (Department of Social Studies, University of Melbourne, 1975).

CHAPTER 4

In an Australian first, the RCSDs were given a 'planning function', an attempt by the Social Welfare Commission to decentralise social planning to a regional level. As Whitlam himself later noted, 'The AAP represented an attempt to regionalise welfare services and return administrative power to a grassroots level where welfare needs are best assessed'.[10] Coleman argued that the AAP focused on 'opening up the process of planning and decision-making to the poor and disadvantaged', an approach that dismayed many of the scheme's critics.[11] A feature of the AAP was that it was heavily evaluated, both internally and externally, using evidence-based research techniques.

The extensive literature generated about the AAP in the 1970s reveals that its values and structures were hotly contested. It certainly challenged the orthodoxies of the day. Key individuals in social welfare circles disputed the AAP's rhetoric of community participation, empowerment and democracy.[12] Others dismissed its potential and decried the Commonwealth government's encroachment into areas traditionally the preserve of the States.[13] In 1974, Victoria unsuccessfully challenged the AAP's constitutional validity in the High Court. Arguing that the Commonwealth had exceeded

---

10   Gough Whitlam, *The Whitlam Government, 1972–1975* (Ringwood, Victoria: Penguin, 1985), 364.

11   Marie Coleman, 'Social Planning and its Consequences' in *Social Work in Australia: Responses to a Changing Context* eds Phillip J Boas and Jim Crawley (Melbourne & Balmain: Australia International Press & Publications, 1976), 47.

12   See, for example, Peter E R Jones, 'The Australian Assistance Plan – Welfare (?) on the Cheap', *Australian Journal of Social Issues* 10, no. 1 (1975): 63–74; R J K Chapman, 'Australian Assistance Plan: A Study of Ineffective Planning', *Australian Journal on Social Issues* 10, no. 4 (1975): 283–298.

13   See, for example, G Starr, 'Federalism as a Political Issue: Australia's Two "New Federalisms"', *Publius. The Journal of Federalism* 7, no. 1 (Winter 1977): 7–26; R Sackville, 'Social Welfare in Australia: The Constitutional Framework' in *Perspectives in Australian Social Policy. A Book of Readings*, ed. Adam Graycar (South Melbourne: Macmillan, 1978), 49–66; and A Graycar & J Davis, *Australian Assistance Plan. An Evaluation Report, No 2* (Canberra: AGPS, 1979).

its powers under Section 51 of the Constitution, the case was narrowly defeated.[14]

Following his victory in the December 1975 election and despite having promised that he would retain the AAP, incoming Prime Minister Malcolm Fraser announced that Commonwealth funding would cease from mid-1977. This was one of the reasons why the former Minister for Social Security during the caretaker phase after the dismissal, Don Chipp, left the Liberal Party in March 1977 and formed the political party, the Australian Democrats. Chipp was enthusiastic about the AAP and had supported it as the Shadow Minister for Social Security and Welfare. In his resignation speech to parliament, he regretted:

> the abolition of the Australian Assistance Plan which I, with the full authority of the joint Parties had previously commended in this House as being one of the most exciting and progressive social reforms ever undertaken.[15]

In this chapter, after situating our analysis within a conceptual framework that recognises voluntary action as a core theme for understanding Australia's past, we examine how the Australian Assistance Plan operated locally through a case study of the Loddon-Campaspe Regional Council for Social Development in Victoria.[16]

---

14 Victoria was joined by New South Wales and Western Australia. The case was defeated by four votes to three. See Oppenheimer, 'Voluntary Action, Social Welfare', 179.

15 'Don Chipp resigns from the Liberal Party', http://australianpolitics.com/1977/03/24/don-chipp-resigns-from-the-liberal-party.html, accessed 20 December 2015.

16 To date, we have found the surviving records of seven RCSDs, a rich and largely untouched archive. In addition to the Loddon-Campaspe RCSD, they are the Hunter RCSD, the Illawarra, and Inner City RCSD (NSW); Mackay Council for Social Development (Qld); Western RCSD, Footscray (Victoria) and Western Adelaide RCSD (SA).

CHAPTER 4

Voluntary action and volunteering

Both the number and diversity of voluntary organisations increased significantly during the 1970s, stimulated, we argue, by Commonwealth funded programs such as the Australian Assistance Plan.[17] As Whitlam stated in a speech to an Apex Convention in Albury in March 1975:

> The Australian Assistance Plan is a pioneering experiment in community involvement. Its essential purpose is to seek out and meet areas of social need hitherto either ignored or unidentified by the existing welfare agencies – national, state, local or voluntary. Its essential characteristic is that its work is based on regions, on regional communities and that its work and planning is to be done by genuinely independent, genuinely community based groups of concerned citizens who know the special needs of the community of which they are a part.[18]

Voluntary action (or in more recent discourse 'social capital' or 'civil society') can be defined as that space between governments and the voluntary sector. It is, as William Beveridge declared in his landmark 1948 British report *Voluntary Action*, 'everything that citizens do outside their duties to the State, to improve the conditions of life for themselves and others'.[19] The history of voluntary action, encompassing the third sector or civil society, has been described by American historian Kathleen McCarthy as including a 'broad range of institutions and activities falling between the family and the state'.[20] Lester Salamon suggests it is that 'lost continent on the social

---

17 Oppenheimer, *Volunteering*.
18 Whitlam, 'Power and People', 39.
19 William Beveridge, *Voluntary Action. A Report on the Methods of Social Advance* (London: George, Allen & Unwin, 1948).
20 Kathleen McCarthy, *American Creed. Philanthropy and the Rise of Civil Society, 1700–1865* (Chicago: University of Chicago Press, 2005).

landscape of our world', while acknowledging the work of Robert Putnam, as well as scholars from the British voluntary action history network.[21]

Voluntary action also concerns the practice of volunteering, defined by the Australian Bureau of Statistics as 'unpaid help in the form of time, service or skills, through an organisation or group, and carried out willingly without coercion'. Together, voluntary action and volunteering are integral to our western democratic tradition and largely occur within that 'loose and baggy monster', the third sector.[22] Voluntary action relies on people acting individually or in association with each other for the common good. Such freedom of association is fundamental to social, cultural, political and economic life in Australia. At the centre of the voluntary principle are civic pride and virtue, a duty to one's community, and a concern about contributing to society overall and acting co-operatively through altruism, charitable endeavour and reciprocity.[23]

British historian Geoffrey Finlayson describes the relationship between the voluntary sector and the state as 'a moving frontier', conveying the idea of a shifting balance between these two domains as they interact with each other and within a changing landscape.[24] In Australia, the frontier 'moved' significantly during the Second

---

21 Lester M Salamon, 'Putting the Civil Society Sector on the Economic Map of the World', *Annals of Public and Cooperative Economics* 81, no 2 (2010): 167–210. See also Melanie Oppenheimer & Nicholas Deakin, eds. *Beveridge and Voluntary Action in Britain and the Wider British World* (Manchester: Manchester University Press, 2011).

22 See Jeremy Kendall and Martin Knapp, 'A Loose and Baggy Monster. Boundaries, Definitions and Typologies' in *Introduction to the Voluntary Sector*, eds J Davis Smith et. al. (London: Routledge, 1995), 65–92.

23 Frank Prochaska, *The Voluntary Impulse. Philanthropy in Modern Britain* (London: Faber & Faber, 1988).

24 Beveridge, *Voluntary Action*; G Finlayson, *Citizen, State and Social Welfare in Britain, 1830–1990* (Oxford: Clarendon Press, 1994).

CHAPTER 4

World War, with heightened civic engagement, during the immediate postwar era, and then again in the Whitlam years.[25] Two key periods for the development and implementation of labor policy – the 1942–49 Curtin and Chifley governments and the 1972–75 Whitlam government – are characterised by major changes in the relationship between the State and voluntary sector.[26] Thus, one prism through which to view the 1970s and the longer-term impact of the Whitlam era, is the transformation of volunteering and the 'volunteering impulse' in Australia, drawing on Finlayson's 'moving frontier' thesis.[27]

From the beginning of the 1970s, there was a notable increase in the number of self-help groups such as tenants' rights movements. Marie Coleman and others identified a change in the 'range and character of voluntary welfare organisations' especially around women's rights, with such associations as the Women's Electoral Lobby, the Nursing Mothers Association, Women's Health Centres and the Abortion Counselling Service. Coleman suggested that 'the Australian Assistance Plan, by bringing people together, has facilitated the development of many of these new special agencies'. She also noted that older and well established organisations responded to the changing landscape, extending or revising their programs.[28] The AAP and other social welfare policies of the Whitlam era effected a fundamental and in some respects unanticipated shift in the practice

---

25   For a discussion of these concepts, see Melanie Oppenheimer, *All Work. No Pay. Australian Civilian Volunteers in War* (Walcha: Ohio Productions, 2002); Melanie Oppenheimer, 'Voluntary Action and Welfare in Post-1945 Australia: Preliminary Perspectives', *History Australia* 2, no. 3 (December 2005): 82.1–82.15.

26   For a detailed study of the Curtin and Chifley period, see Stuart Macintyre, *Australia's Boldest Experiment: War and Reconstruction in the 1940s* (Sydney: NewSouth Publishing, 2015).

27   See, for example, Oppenheimer, *Volunteering*, especially 121–150.

28   Coleman, 'Social Planning and its Consequences', 47.

of voluntary action in Australia. The outcome was an increase in voluntary organisations and a reshaping of the relationship between governments and volunteering that outlasted both the AAP and the Whitlam government.

The expansion of the social work profession during the Whitlam period and the involvement of social workers in the AAP also influenced the practice of voluntary action. Social workers occupied leading positions in the Australian Public Service, most notably Marie Coleman as the head of the Social Welfare Commission, as well as roles within the AAP itself. By mid-1974, the Department of Social Security employed 146 social workers and 22 welfare officers.[29] Many recently qualified social workers found their first employment opportunities as Community Development Officers within RCSDs across the country. Social workers' attitudes towards the AAP varied and sometimes changed, further complicating the moving frontier of voluntary action. Leonard Tierney, a social work academic from the University of Melbourne, initially welcomed the AAP as 'a potential vehicle' for social workers to be involved not only in 'social protection' but also in policy and planning. The 'novel and imaginative structure' of the AAP, he wrote in 1975, offered social workers the chance to combine 'planning perspectives with perspectives related to ordinary people ... choosing not to have certain services in favour of other services; and of releasing the energies of ordinary people for societal purposes'.[30] His initial enthusiasm waned, however, and he later described the AAP as 'confusing' and 'a collage of ideas' that was not

---

29 This compared with 26 social workers in 1957 and 50 ten years later. See John Lawrence, 'Australian Social Work: In Historical, International and Social Welfare Context', in Boas & Crawley, *Social Work in Australia*, 34.

30 L J Tierney, 'The Next Twenty Years in Social Work' in Boas & Crawley, *Social Work in Australia*, 256.

CHAPTER 4

'systematically put together and grounded in practical knowledge'.[31] Many critiques of the AAP, especially those published in the late 1970s after the Fraser government withdrew funding, were damning.[32] This, no doubt, contributed towards the 'forgetting' of the AAP in subsequent decades and its absence from much of the literature on the period of the Whitlam government.[33]

At the heart of the AAP was the idea that active citizens within their local communities should and could be involved in the planning and execution of their specific social policy and welfare needs. Whitlam had been developing and refining arguments about the interconnected concerns for inequality, living standards, education, access to services and location for some time prior to coming to office. Regional disparities existed within major capital cities as well as rural Australia, and Whitlam focused on 'the availability and accessibility of the services which the community alone can provide and ensure' as the key to his notion of 'positive equality'.[34] The implementation of some of these ideas was facilitated through the establishment of the Social Welfare Commission, a government body designed to integrate these new planned welfare services. It was, as Whitlam's first Minister for Social Security, Bill Hayden, suggested, 'the midwife to an election promise called the *Australian Assistance Plan*' [his italics] that 'aimed at helping to develop a social welfare system' and which,

---

31 Leonard Tierney with Helen McMahon, *From Vague Ideas to Unfeasible Roles* (Canberra: AGPS, 1979), 1.
32 For a comprehensive list and discussion, see Oppenheimer, 'Voluntary Action, Social Welfare and the AAP in the 1970s'.
33 References to the AAP are generally missing from survey histories such as Geoffrey Bolton, *The Middle Way, 1942–1988* (Melbourne: Oxford University Press, 1993, 1990); Stuart Macintyre, *A Concise History of Australia* (Melbourne: Cambridge University Press, 1999).
34 Quoted in Brennan, *The Politics of Australian Child Care*, 72.

'together with a new social security benefits system, place this country once again in the forefront of social advancement'.[35]

RCSDs were to be established across the country and along broadly defined local government boundaries, with sufficient flexibility to accommodate regional variations across the States; they would advise, evaluate and monitor the needs of each region, and deliver the funds of the AAP. This was part of the Whitlam government's innovation in regional and urban policy. Creating the AAP 'regions', however, was problematic. Concurrently, the Department of Urban and Regional Development was establishing its own regions; additionally there were both long-established State government-defined regions and the development of new regional definitions. In 1974, for example, the Victorian government adopted the concept of regional boundaries. In Loddon-Campaspe, these boundaries were similar but not identical to the RCSD, with the Victorian government including the Shire of Gisborne. Furthermore, the Victorian 'regions' did not always align with the boundaries used by such State agencies as the Police, Country Fire Authority, Electricity and Water Commissions, the Country Roads Board and Agricultural Department.[36]

Despite the State Coalition government's hostility, it was in Victoria that the AAP's ideas were most fully adopted and implemented. Perhaps the size, geography and demography of Victoria lent themselves to such a program. Or perhaps it was because in Geelong, 'an Australian Assistance Plan type program had commenced before Labor took office'.[37] As Executive Director of the Victorian Council

---

35   Bill Hayden, 'Planning and Integration of Welfare Services: An Australian Government Viewpoint', *Australian Journal of Social Issues* 9, no. 1 (1974): 6.
36   See 'Regions', File 6/4 (i) Report prepared on the social resources of the region, 'From here to there [where?]', 1976–1977, Box 6 – M07585, L-C RCSD.
37   *The Future of the Australian Assistance Plan*, Committee of Inquiry into the AAP and its Future, (March 1977): 6.

CHAPTER 4

of Social Service, Marie Coleman, along with the State government and the Geelong Community Chest, had been involved in a community-based social survey that prefigured core elements of the AAP. By mid-1974, five RCSDs (Outer Eastern, North Western, Loddon-Campaspe, Westernport and Inner Southern) had received approval for annual funding. By mid-1975 there was an RCSD in each region across the State, a total of eight. A Victorian Association of Regional Councils was also established to coordinate efforts.[38]

The Loddon-Campaspe RCSD

The first public meeting for what became the Loddon-Campaspe Regional Council for Social Development was held on Friday 15 February 1974. It attracted over 120 people, including representatives from non-government organisations, local government authorities, state government departments, trade unions and employer groups. The meeting elected an interim voluntary management committee, led by the dynamic local councillor and social work administrator, Elaine Knight. As President of the Loddon-Campaspe RCSD, Knight became an active supporter of the AAP and later led the unsuccessful campaign to save the program after the demise of the Whitlam government.[39] The RCSD was based around three major towns in north-western Victoria: Bendigo, St Arnaud and

---

38   See Loddon-Campaspe RCSD, Interim Committee, *First Annual Report*, 1974–75, Box 1, M07580.
39   Elaine Knight joined the ALP at 18. She stood unsuccessfully as an ALP candidate for the Legislative Council in the 1976 Victorian State elections. She tried her luck again in the 1979 election when she stood for the seat of Bendigo. See Australian Women's Register, http://www.womenaustralia.info/biogs/AWE3840b.htm, accessed 31 December 2015. Elaine Knight/McNamara was the first woman elected as a Councillor for the Marong Shire from 1972–1994. She also served as Mayor. Her other community engagements included the position of long time secretary of the Golden Square Football League, Bendigo. Elaine remains active in the Bendigo community.

Castlemaine. Its geographical reach encompassed 26 municipal areas, more than 23,300 square kilometres, and 133,000 people. It extended from Maryborough in the south to Echuca in the north, and from St Arnaud in the west to Romsey in the east.

Figure 4.1 'A basic, hand drawn map, typical of many in the RCSD files, outlining the main sub-regions of the Loddon-Campaspe region. From the front page of the Loddon-Campaspe Annual Report 1974-1975, Box 1 M07850 File 1:1. The original image has been enhanced to improve legibility.

The Council was formally constituted, with a volunteer management committee. Its seven objectives were:

> To devise plans for welfare services provision to meet the needs of the region, in consultation with and having regard to the autonomy of Australian, State, Local Government and Statutory and voluntary organisations

CHAPTER 4

To encourage the provision of personal welfare services which may attract grants

To promote co-operation between all organizations and persons involved in the field of Social Welfare in the Region

To relate to and co-operate with any appropriate regional planning body

To promote and assist the education and training of persons in the field of Social Welfare

To encourage people in the Region to contribute towards and participate in the work of the Council

To promote and assist the development of all aspects of Social Development in the Loddon-Campaspe Region.[40]

The interim committee's priority was to get the RCSD off the ground. Its first action was to apply to the federal government for AAP funding. After representations from the Federal Member for Bendigo, Liberal John Bourchier, to the Minister Bill Hayden, the RCSD secured an initial grant of $2000 in May 1974, followed by $20,000 (later increased to $40,000) for the period to June 1975 to employ four Community Development Officers (CDOs). They were appointed to the 'sub-regions' of Castlemaine and Maryborough, Echuca and St Arnaud, Bendigo, and Kyneton. Murray Taylor was seconded from the Department of Social Security to become the Director of Social Planning. Until Commonwealth monies arrived, local government provided rooms and secretarial services for the committee. Volunteer sub-committees for 'staff & office establishment', 'publicity, information and liaison', and 'research and project

---

40   Loddon-Campaspe RCSD, Interim Committee, *First Annual Report*, 1974–75, Box 1, M07580.

development' were formed. Capitation grants of $132,340 for the 6 months to 30 June 1975 and $264,680 to 30 June 1976 were also received, and the RCSD invited submissions for funds. It allocated funds to 31 projects, approved by the minister.

Never before had Commonwealth funds been available to such an array of grassroots organisations, thus empowering the local citizens who ran these groups to execute projects. This was the radical element of the AAP. Analysis of the records of the Loddon-Campaspe RCSD reveals how much it stimulated volunteers across this region. Our ongoing analysis of other RCSDs across the country suggests a similar effect on the voluntary sector during the period of the Whitlam government. This impact on voluntary and community-based organisations also helps to explain the popularity of the AAP at a local level.

Local community welfare and co-ordinating committees run by volunteers were created throughout the region. These 17 committees provided 'an important source of local knowledge and experience' for the RCSD and offered 'opportunities for local citizens to become involved in planning for their own community needs'.[41] In their respective communities of Bendigo, Cohuna, Dunolly, Maldon, Pyramid Hill, Rochester, Korong Vale, Lockington, Boort, Echuca, Castlemaine, Cobaw, Maryborough, St Arnaud, Inglewood, Charlton and Wedderburn, these often small but 'energetic' committees initiated diverse projects. In mid-1975, for example, the Cohuna Community Welfare Committee developed a funding submission for teaching aids for use in a remedial reading workshop at the local high school. The Korong Committee facilitated the cooperative

---

41   Loddon-Campaspe RCSD, *First Annual Report*, 1974–75, Box 1, M07580.

CHAPTER 4

use of the primary school as a venue for childcare services, a youth club, a senior citizens club and creative leisure activities for adults.[42]

Key roles for the Loddon-Campaspe RCSD included gathering and disseminating information and facilitating workshops. For example, in St Arnaud a 'group of local women' conducted a pilot survey of childcare needs, and in Bendigo a survey of the needs of elderly people and their carers was undertaken. In Maryborough, there were surveys of aged person's welfare, childcare, and community education needs; the last two were funded by the AAP. In October 1976 the RCSD assisted the Victorian Association of Youth Clubs with a workshop on 'adolescence' designed for paid youth workers and volunteers.[43] The AAP also contributed funding for seminars such as the Combined Inner Wheel & Business & Professional Women's Committee's seminar on Education, Family Law Act and Women in Society in March 1976.[44]

The local community welfare and co-ordinating committees lobbied the RCSD for specific services, embracing the AAP's model of working from the bottom up, thereby empowering local communities and promoting 'true democratic participation'.[45] For example, having identified an absence of training facilities for Infant Welfare Sisters and Pre-School Directors in country Victoria, the Bendigo Development Committee lobbied the RCSD to advocate for courses

---

42 Social Planners Report for the period July 25th to August 15th 1975, Murray Taylor, Director of Social Planning, File 3/4, Box 3, M07582.
43 Letter from Phil Butcher, Youth Worker, Victorian Association of Youth Clubs to Nan Muir, 25 August 1976, File 1/3, Box 1 – M07580.
44 Letter from Murray Taylor, Director of Social Planning, L-C RCSD to Mrs E Levecke, 4 March 1976, File 1/3, Box 1, M07580.
45 Again, this was hotly contested both during and after the period in which the AAP was active. See Oppenheimer, 'Voluntary Action', 178–179.

to be held at teachers' colleges, such as the one in Bendigo, thus avoiding travel to Melbourne.[46]

Efforts to localise training extended to the CDOs employed under the AAP, with courses for new recruits held in Bendigo as well as Melbourne. The CDOs performed central roles in enabling communities to pursue their agendas. In Loddon-Campaspe, Nan Muir was employed as a CDO in March 1975. Based at Castlemaine, she also served the municipalities of Maldon, Newstead, Metcalfe, Maryborough, Bet Bet and Tullaroop. Muir worked closely with local welfare committees advising them on funding sources and assisting with the dissemination of the rationale and work of the AAP. Access to such expertise was especially useful in small rural communities such as Dunolly (west of Bendigo in the heartland of the former goldfields) where a local group wanted to establish a Kindergarten and Child Minding Centre. In this instance, Muir helped the group to prepare a successful $30,000 submission to the Children's Commission. She considered that, with its 'catalytic approach', the role of the Community Development Officer had 'unlimited potential within a community to assist in all areas of development, educating isolated and inarticulate groups of the tasks required to achieve their aims'.[47]

The Loddon-Campaspe RCSD recognised and sought to respond to issues and shortcomings pertaining to rural and regional Australia during the 1970s. Those issues included migration to the cities, especially by younger people; problems with the agricultural industry;

---

[46] Letter from RW Martin, Executive Officer, Bendigo Development Committee to Murray Taylor, Director of Social Planning, L-C RCSD, File 6/6, Box 6, M07585.

[47] Letter from Nan Muir to Senator the Hon Margaret Guilfoyle, undated, circa March 1976, 1/3, Box 1, M07580.

CHAPTER 4

and inflation, land usage and the impact of hobby farmers. Problems relating to social welfare and social disadvantage in this region included shortages of preschool teachers; a lack of welfare workers and child foster carers; scarcity of visiting services for senior citizens; and unemployment.[48] Amongst a diverse array of concerns and responses, the Loddon-Campaspe records reveal a particular focus on children and youth; services to and advocacy for the disabled; and the efforts of the RCSD network to save the AAP.

Children and youth

The focus on facilities for children and youth is especially striking. Applications were received and funded by the AAP for holiday programs; pre-schools; play groups/play centres; adventure playgrounds; youth drop-in centres; youth clubs and sporting equipment as well as projects that focused on education and employment. In 1975–76, the Youth Development Group in Bendigo received $3,059 to establish a Drop-In Youth Centre; the Castlemaine Youth Drop-In Centre and Maldon Drop-In Centre each received $1,000 for equipment; the Epsom/Huntly Pre-School Committee received $5,000 to purchase land for a Pre-School & Infant Welfare Centre; $2,000 was received by the Maryborough Historical & Wildlife Co-op for an Adventure Playground; the Campaspe Valley Youth Group received $938 to meet rental and equipment costs; and the South Castlemaine Kindergarten received a grant of $500 for outdoor equipment. The Honorary Secretary of the kindergarten, Mr W. Carter, wrote to Elaine Knight in June 1976, stating that the support was 'much appreciated by both the children and their

---

48 'New Faces on Board of Social Council', *Riverine Herald*, 1 December 1976, 4, in File 2/5, Box 2, M07581.

parents'.[49] The Marong & District Play Group Association received a grant of $271 for 26 weeks of hall hire and the purchase of a record player, records, blackboard, cupboards, and First Aid Kit.[50] In many instances, these community-based initiatives would not have eventuated when they did without the stimulus of AAP funding. As V E Watts, Honorary Secretary of the Dunolly Youth Club, wrote, 'without this grant [$1,000] we of the Club would never have got off the ground'. Watts reported that the equipment 'is being well used by the Youth of the shire of Bet Bet and the visitors we get in holiday time'.[51]

The four CDOs in Loddon-Campaspe were particularly busy with children and youth projects. In mid-1975, Clem Frost negotiated with the local community to assist the Eaglehawk Drop-In Centre to find a suitable space in which to operate. He assisted the Axedale Play Group (a group of mothers in the Axedale and Longlea area) to organise a playgroup, held in a disused primary school. Frost convinced the Bendigo Regional Office of the Education Department that local citizens with 'any bonefide (sic) activity' could use disused school buildings. Tom Parsons, based at Echuca-St Arnaud, assisted an informal club in Boort that had been operating for three years to help young people identified as 'socially deviant or drop-outs' to establish itself. Laurie Barrow assisted the Kyneton Play Group, a small group of mothers who were meeting in a church hall, to apply for equipment, children's toys and funds to assist with operating costs.[52]

---

49 Letter from Mr W Carter, Hon Sec, South Castlemaine Kindergarten to Councillor E Knight, Shire of Marong, Victoria, 7 June 1976, File 1/3, Box 1, M07580.
50 Letter from Taylor to Mrs J Watts, Marong & District Playgroup Association 13 May 1976, File 18/8, Box 18, M07597.
51 Letter from V E Watts to LCRCSD, 16 May 1977, File 19/1, Box 19, M07598.
52 Social Planners Report for the period July 25th to August 15th, 1975, Murray Taylor, Director of Social Planning, File 3/4, Box 3, M07582.

CHAPTER 4

Historians and childcare experts such as Deborah Brennan suggest that it was the *Child Care Act of 1972*, initiated in the dying days of the McMahon Coalition government, that led to the introduction of Commonwealth subsidies to non-profit organisations to run childcare services for working mothers.[53] With funding by the Whitlam government, the number of facilities to care for pre-school age children such as day nurseries, occasional care playgroups, family day care and student co-operatives, had increased significantly. Brennan views the Whitlam era as 'a turning point in the politics of child care' where 'crucial lessons about policy making, policy implementation and bureaucratic politics were learned'.[54] The philosophy of the AAP, she contends, with its community focus and grassroots approach, was influential in determining Labor's childcare policies. The Whitlam government's childcare policy focused on a 'community management of services' approach with a 'community initiation of projects' at its core.[55] For the first time, the Commonwealth government was directly involved in areas such as childcare, and during a period when the idea of community childcare and its benefits were being widely discussed and implemented.[56]

The experiences of the Loddon-Campaspe RCSD confirm Brennan's argument. The sub-regional records are full of applications for funding for projects for children and youth. A majority of the services that were funded through the AAP in this region involved

---

[53] Deborah Brennan, 'Children and Families: Forty Years of Analysis and Commentary in the Australian Journal of Social Issues', *Australian Journal of Social Issues* 40, no. 1 (Autumn 2005): 74.
[54] Brennan, *The Politics of Australian Child Care*, 71.
[55] Ibid., 92.
[56] See, for example, 'Community Child Care', Children's Action Group, *Social Development* vol. 1, no. 3 (September 1975), Albury Wodonga RCSD, File 21/2, Box 21, M07600.

young children, including the provision or extension of the work of Infant Welfare Sisters (Bendigo) and the establishment of play groups, childcare centres, and mobile libraries.[57] Drop-in centres and social clubs for youth were also popular.

The demand for such services continued to exceed supply. An RCSD evening seminar on childcare, held in Bendigo on 7 April 1975, attracted people from across the region. With a focus on financial assistance available for childcare and the specific types of services that could be established in the region, the speakers included Ms Barbara Spalding, a member of the Commonwealth government's newly established Children's Commission Interim Committee; a pre-school adviser for the Victorian Department of Health; and experts on community childcare. The seminar 'hammered home the fact that the Loddon-Campaspe region lacked many amenities for children' such as 'preschools, day child minding centres, after school recreation programs, facilities for mothers and toddlers, and facilities to help working mothers'. Replies to a questionnaire circulated during the seminar confirmed the unmet demand. Even in large centres such as Bendigo with 'the best facilities in the region', the demand for pre-school, kindergarten and crèche facilities far outstripped supply; what was available was situated only in the city centre. There were no play centres or mother-toddler groups. Towns such as Echuca had pre-school facilities but required crèche and day-care centres for working mothers as well as play centres and mother-toddler groups. Smaller towns, such as Rochester and Maryborough, reported a dearth of child-minding facilities of all types especially for working

---

57   The Infant Welfare Sisters provides an example of the RCSD working closely with local municipal councils and lobbying politicians for increases in subsidies for wages. Letter from Murray D Taylor to all LBAs, 29 October 1974, File 4/3, Box 4, M07583.

CHAPTER 4

mothers. There was consensus that in the Loddon-Campaspe RCSD most towns had some pre-school or kindergarten facilities but they were insufficient to meet demand.[58]

This lack of childcare extended to the school aged children of working parents coming home from school to an empty house. In July 1975, a group of 'concerned citizens' including parents and student teachers established an 'After School Activities' Group' for 'latch-key' children in Bendigo. It was set up in a pavilion in the show grounds. The local newspaper described 'an invasion. One hundred and thirty school-age children poured into the flower pavilion and each set about doing their own thing with right good will'. The once a week pilot project soon received AAP funding to operate full time. It became a model for other communities.[59]

Services and advocacy for people with disabilities

The Loddon-Campaspe files reveal a strong emphasis on services to and advocacy for the 'handicapped'.[60] There had been some policy movement in the disability sphere from the late 1960s. In 1968, the Coalition Gorton government amended the *National Health Act* so the Commonwealth could pay $1.50 per person per day to charitable or religious organisations offering institutional care for handicapped children under 16 years. The Gorton government extended the Commonwealth's new role in this sphere, providing further funding for special training facilities and accommodation

---

58 Replies to Questionnaire submitted to people attending regional child care seminar in Bendigo, 7 April 1975, File 10/4, Box 10, M07589.
59 'Group Meets the Need of "Latchkey Kids"', *Bendigo Advertiser*, 14 July 1975. File 10/1, Box 10, M07589.
60 We are conscious that the language of the records in this section reflects prevailing views and concepts of the early 1970s.

for handicapped children. The Whitlam government continued this policy direction and in 1974 introduced the *Handicapped Persons Assistance Act* which provided capital expenditure and subsidies for sheltered workshops, hostels, and training and activity centres for disabled people. Funding was also available for staff subsidies and maintenance costs.[61]

There was some differentiation of support in terms of physical versus mental disabilities. When physically disabled children turned 16 they were no longer eligible for funding under the state-based Home Help for the Physically Handicapped Service. By contrast, no age limit was applied to mentally disabled children. One of the first pilot projects undertaken by the Loddon-Campaspe RCSD within the Bendigo Municipal area was home help for persons caring for the physically handicapped. In December 1974, the Loddon-Campaspe RCSD sent a submission to the Victorian government's Minister for Health, Hon A H Scanlan, MLA, arguing that the current scheme was inequitable as it did not help those caring for the physically handicapped. The submission explained the difficulties faced by carers and recommended that eligibility 'not be affected by the age of the handicapped person'.[62]

The Victorian Association of RCSDs supported Loddon-Campaspe's submission, declaring that 'the differentiation between parents of the mentally retarded, and parents of the physically

---

61   Rob Linn, *Perseverence. The Story of the Spastic Centres of SA* (Adelaide: Spastic Centres of SA, June 1994): 98–99. For a discussion of children and disability in Australia, see Dave Earl, '"A Group of Parents came Together": Parent Advocacy Groups for Children with Intellectual Disabilities in Post-World War II Australia', *Health and History* 13, no. 2 (2011): 84–103.
62   'Submission regarding home help for parents of the handicapped', Loddon-Campaspe RCSD, 10 December 1974, File 4/7, Box 4, M07583.

CHAPTER 4

handicapped that exists under present arrangements is totally unjustified'.[63] The scheme should also be flexible enough to allow parents and home help supervisors the choice of home-based or institutional care. In January 1976, the RCSD convinced the Victorian state government to test the initial Bendigo model pilot in Ballarat City and Shire, Sunshine and Diamond Valley in addition to Bendigo.[64] From January 1977, the Victorian government agreed to fund home help for the physically handicapped.

In what was probably an Australian first in terms of government funding, using AAP capitation monies, the Loddon-Campaspe RCSD provided voluntary organisations, local shires and individuals with emergency funding for the transportation of handicapped children. For example, $234 was allocated to assist with travelling expenses for a family in Serpentine. For over eight years the parents of a disabled boy had transported him for regular surgery at Yooralla Hospital; they subsequently took their son twice weekly to the Bendigo Spastic Centre for special education. The regular travel, along with other household demands, imposed pressures on the family, especially the mother.[65] Similarly, $200 was allocated to assist in the provision of transport for handicapped children in the Korong Shire to the Peter Harcourt Centre in Bendigo. Two families in straitened circumstances benefitted from this funding.[66]

---

63   Letter from P Bartholomeusz, Secretary, The Interim Committee for the Central Gippsland RCSD to Hon A H Scanlon, MLA, Minister for Health, 16 July 1975, File 4/7, Box 4, M07583.
64   See memo from Murray Taylor, 12 January 1976, File 4/7, Box 4, M07583.
65   Letter from TJ Rudkins, Shire Secretary, Shire of East Loddon to Mr Taylor, Director of Social Planning, L-C RCSD, 3 March 1976, and letter from Taylor to Rudkins, 23 June 1976, File 15/2, Box 15, M07594.
66   See File 20/1, Box 20, M07599.

Saving the AAP

The third and final key feature of the Loddon-Campaspe RCSD records demonstrates the efforts of local community members to try to 'save' the AAP; the extant contemporary evaluation literature of the AAP did not acknowledge those efforts. By 1976, 85 regions had been mapped out across Australia. Fourteen RCSDs including Loddon-Campaspe had received grants; 23 had received administration ($40,000 per annum) and CDOs ($12,000 per annum) funds. Most of the other regions had received only $2,000 initiation grants. Despite announcements to the contrary, and a pre-election pledge to continue the AAP, the Fraser government abolished the AAP by withdrawing funding. As the Minister for Social Security, Margaret Guilfoyle stated, 'In the context of our belief in the Federal system, we are convinced that this type of program is a totally appropriate one for administering at the State and local government level'.[67] This decision, viewed by some as a 'short term, short-sighted economy measure', also reflected a philosophical and political stance.[68] The Commonwealth government agreed to provide RCSD administration and CDO funding until 30 June 1977 only. It was left to the States to determine whether to continue the AAP or some variation of it.

Although Victoria and NSW State governments pledged to support the AAP, they were unwilling or unable to provide replacement funding for what was in essence a federally conceived and implemented scheme. Beverley Long was a member of the Interim Committee

---

67 Minister for Social Security, Press statement, 21 May 1976, in First Annual Report on the Hunter Regional Council for Social Development, July 1976, Appendix, Box C750, Hunter Regional Council for Social Development records, University of Newcastle archives.

68 See 'The Australian Assistance Plan', 12 July 1976, File 9/3, Box 9, M07587.

CHAPTER 4

of the North-West Regional Council for Social Development, which included the working class areas of Broadmeadows, Brunswick, Coburg and the Shires of Bulla and Gisborne. She commented that, despite the Australian Assistance Plan offering 'a very real opportunity for local people to be involved in identifying and expressing their social needs and in planning to meet those needs' it was 'unlikely that any similar program could be implemented for many years'.[69] The overriding concern of some of the conservative States, that 'the AAP bypasses the constitutional and statutory responsibilities of the State' with 'insufficient account' of the 'responsibilities of municipalities' called into question the 'legitimacy of Regional Councils'. The scheme was scrapped.[70]

The Loddon-Campaspe RCSD was prominent in the rear-guard action to save the AAP. From Elaine Knight to local community members of voluntary organisations that had benefitted from AAP funding, individuals fought to save the AAP. Sustained pressure was applied to try and persuade the Fraser government to honour its original commitment to the AAP. A Survival Task Force was established by the Victorian Association of RCSDs led by Elaine Knight, with Sid Spindler (who was later instrumental in creating the political party, Australian Democrats, with Don Chipp), Pat Bartholomeusz (Central Gippsland) and John Zeleznikow. The Task Force's 'survival kit' included template petitions; 'fill in the blank' letters to be sent to local representatives of Federal and State parliaments as well as local government representatives; a list of State and Federal politicians and their contact details; examples of draft press releases; and

---

69   See File 21/5 North West RCSD Part 1, Box 21, M07600.
70   Letter from W V Houghton, Victorian Minister for Social Welfare to Mrs Beverley Long, North-West RCSD, 6 March 1975, File 21/5, Box 21, M07600.

talking points for media interviews. The Task Force even lobbied unfunded regions highlighting the positive features of the AAP and the achievements of the RCSDs.[71] The message was clear:

> Unless the Australian Assistance Plan ... is continued and fully and permanently funded at all levels hundreds of communities and organisations and thousands of people throughout Australia will suffer unnecessary social disadvantages ... the Australian Assistance Plan has given Australians ... a real say in their community & positive method of overcoming basic social problems and needs.[72]

A Peoples Conference on the Australian Assistance Plan in May 1976 was attended by over 200 people. The Australian Social Welfare Union and the Victorian Council of Social Service supported the campaign. The Save Access AAP Action Group, which included the Outer Eastern RCSD, submitted a petition signed by over 3000 people from the Casey electorate on the outskirts of Melbourne's eastern suburbs in support of a federally funded AAP. The petition stressed the contested issues surrounding the AAP and models of 'co-operative federalism', and specifically mentioned the 'estimated 60,000 hours of work from voluntary helpers and organisers'. The 'motivation and morale of this no-cost work force' was threatened by the uncertainty surrounding the AAP, risking future 'community involvement in self-help projects' if the Commonwealth walked away from the AAP before State and local governments were ready to pick up the pieces. The newly elected Liberal member, Peter Falconer, presented the petition to the prime minister in August 1976.[73] It was

---

71   See File 9/3, Box 9, M07587.
72   Sample Petition (undated circa 1977), File 8/4, Box 8, M07587.
73   'Save AAP Access Action Group', 12 August 1976, File 9/3, Box 9, M07587. Peter Falconer held the seat of Casey for the Liberals from 1975–1983 when the seat was

CHAPTER 4

too late. Commonwealth funding ceased the previous month, with interim funding for RCSDs expended by mid-1977. The five-year experiment that had been embraced by so many Australians was gone. This 'program of such potential' as Marie Coleman suggested, was no more.[74]

Conclusion

Although the AAP was finished politically, the same cannot be said for the voluntary sector and the new generation of 'active community politics' it spurred. In those years of the AAP's mix of regional, local and community activity, voluntary action across the country had also been transformed. In 1978 Ronald Henderson, who had chaired the 1975 Commission of Inquiry into Poverty, noted that it 'would be difficult to refute the conclusion that the sum of $6.6 million granted to Regional Councils of Social Development in 1975–76 promoted a very large amount of constructive welfare activity because it was spent in support of local and often voluntary effort'. Henderson predicted, correctly, that 'many of these ongoing ventures will probably survive, whatever happens to the AAP'.[75] Commonwealth AAP grants were used to create local infrastructure, provide services and help the disadvantaged. Funds were expended 'to underwrite emergency relief payments, assist Housing Commission and private tenants to organise, establish a woman's refuge, employ welfare rights officers, assist women workers particularly migrants' as well as supporting voluntary self-help groups such as the Lone Supporting Fathers

---

won by the ALP.
74 *Grassroots: Newsletter of the Australian Assistance Plan*, no. 17 (1976): 4.
75 Ronald F Henderson, 'Social Welfare Expenditure', in *Public Expenditures and Social Policy in Australia Volume 1: The Whitlam Years, 1972–75*, eds R B Scotton & Helen Ferber (Carlton: Longman Cheshire/University of Melbourne, 1978), 173.

Association.[76] From community radio stations to community health centres, AAP monies flowed directly from Commonwealth coffers to underpin and enable the ideas, energies and actions of local communities. The stimulation to the voluntary sector and volunteers was significant and should not be underestimated. It generated 'greatly increased voluntary involvement by providing the initial impetus and minimal administrative support which enables voluntary groups to continue their work'.[77]

The AAP also contributed to the professionalisation of local government services and practices. Despite many local councils 'being highly suspicious' of the AAP, they reaped the benefits of this new stream of federal government funding. Finally, the most successful RCSDs, such as Loddon-Campaspe, became catalysts for change in their regions. They provided organisational expertise, brought communities together, and facilitated a range of services and programs that made a significant difference to people's lives.

The rich archival records of the RCSDs provide us with an additional lens through which to view the Whitlam government and its legacy, especially in relation to the moving frontier and voluntary action. We can transcend the traditional focus on politics and legislative innovation, and consider how programs such as the AAP interacted with communities. This is particularly important when such programs had, at their heart, a commitment to participation and engagement and when they were not enshrined in legislation. The AAP experience reveals that examining the relationship of governments with the voluntary sector extends our understanding of our past. As one of many innovative programs and policies introduced by

---

76   Committee of Inquiry into the AAP and its Future, 13.
77   Committee of Inquiry into the AAP and its Future, 14.

CHAPTER 4

the Whitlam government, the AAP was a reach of the imagination for ordinary Australians, and its impact offers further evidence that the Whitlam period constituted a foundational moment in the history of Australia.

Chapter 5

GOUGH WHITLAM'S 1974 RE-ELECTION

'Government by double dissolution'

Jenny Hocking

'The 1974 election is in danger of taking its place in Australian political memory as the election that never was'.

Gough Whitlam

One of the Whitlam government's most decisive and effective actions of reform came not from its enduring policy innovations, but from a parliamentary and constitutional feat. This was the 1974 double dissolution, called under the intriguing, far-sighted, provisions of section 57 of the Constitution. The double dissolution election of 18 May 1974, Whitlam's historic second election victory, was central to the success of his government's reform agenda. It was the third use of section 57 and the first full use of its intricate provisions, with the Joint Sitting of both Houses of parliament on 6–7 August that followed the government's re-election. It was at the Joint Sitting that the critical elements in the Whitlam government's program, Senate representation for the mainland Territories, 'one vote one value' and universal health insurance (Medibank), were enacted, when the 6

CHAPTER 5

'trigger bills' which had precipitated the double dissolution were finally passed. It remains a unique example of what Sawer has termed 'government by double dissolution'.[1] Yet despite its undoubted significance, the election itself is frequently overlooked, and at times entirely forgotten. Whitlam called it 'the election that never was'.[2]

Section 57 is a unique, innovative, means of resolving repeated Senate obstruction of government legislation. It allows for any bill which has twice been passed by the House of Representatives and which has twice 'failed to pass' the Senate to become a 'trigger' for a double dissolution.[3] If the government is returned at the subsequent election and the bills are again passed by the House and again fail to pass the Senate, they may then be presented at a Joint Sitting of both Houses of parliament. The bills must pass at the Joint Sitting with an absolute majority of Members and Senators combined, voting as one.[4] With the Whitlam government facing a defiantly obstructive Opposition, section 57 offered a high risk and protracted means of passing six key bills that had twice 'failed to pass' the Senate: bills to establish Medibank; bills to introduce electoral equity or 'one vote one value' and to grant Senate representation to the Northern Territory and the Australian Capital Territory; and a bill to establish the Petroleum and Mineral Authority.[5]

---

1 Sawer, G. *Federation Under Strain: Australia 1972–1975* (Carlton: Melbourne University Press. 1977), 42.
2 Whitlam, E.G. *The Whitlam Government 1972–1975* (Ringwood: Penguin Books Australia. 1985), 730.
3 See Appendix I Section 57 Disagreement between the Houses: 'if after an interval of three months ... the Senate rejects or fails to pass it'.
4 Because of the nexus between the numbers in the House of Representatives and the numbers in the Senate, in all but the narrowest of government victories, the trigger bills would be expected to pass at such a Joint Sitting.
5 By the time of the proclamation dissolving Parliament there were 6 trigger bills: two bills to do with the establishment of the universal Health Insurance scheme, Medibank: *Health Insurance Bill 1973* and *Health Insurance Commission Bill 1973*;

The antecedents of the 1974 double dissolution can be found in Whitlam's formative political years in Canberra, his familiarity with the essential role of public administration in government, his awareness of the inevitable tensions and synergies between the arms of government, and his knowledge of the Constitutional possibilities for reform as well as the difficulties. It is impossible to overstate the significance of this personal and intellectual background for Whitlam's institutional innovations in government, exemplified firstly by his formation of the 'government of two' – the duumvirate – in the earliest days of the government and second by his decision to call the 1974 double dissolution election.[6] It instilled in him a deep understanding of the structures of government, their powers, their intersections and, most significantly, of the mutual respect between them and for their different roles, without which parliamentary democracy in practice cannot function. In this he mirrored his father, Fred Whitlam's, view that 'parliamentary democracy provides the best political system for the ordering of a humane organised community life', driven by key values of equity, tolerance and self-determination.[7]

Gough Whitlam once said, 'no-one who knew my family could ever imagine that I could be anything other than a Labor man'.[8] Fred Whitlam was one of Australia's leading public servants, Deputy

---

three bills relating to matters of electoral equity and parliamentary representation: *Commonwealth Electoral Bill (No 2) 1973, Senate (Representation of Territories) Bill 1973* and the *Representation Bill 1973*; and a bill to establish an authority to undertake and manage the exploration and development of petroleum and minerals, *Petroleum and Minerals Authority Bill 1973*. The last of these was disallowed following a High Court challenge.

6   For a discussion of the Whitlam-Barnard duumvirate see Hocking, J. *Gough Whitlam: His Time* (Carlton: Melbourne University Publishing, 2012), 14-29.

7   Hocking, J. *Gough Whitlam: A Moment in History* (Carlton: Melbourne University Publishing, 2008), 45.

8   Gough Whitlam, Personal communication with the author. 18 April 2008.

CHAPTER 5

Crown Solicitor and later Crown Solicitor, and the epitome of the disinterested public servant. Fred Whitlam was a member of the Chifley Labor government's delegation to the 1946 Paris Peace conference where the crucial Paris Peace Treaties underpinning the United Nations were painstakingly negotiated. He had helped draft the 1948 Universal Declaration of Human Rights, in particular Article 18, 'Freedom of thought and religion', which reflected his own belief in the freedom to choose, espouse – and change – religion and, in the 1950s represented Australia at sessions of the United Nation's Commission on Human Rights.[9] Economist and public servant H.C. 'Nugget' Coombs, who had known and worked with both Whitlams, captured the differences, and the familial legacy, in his memorable description of Fred Whitlam as having a 'gentle, softly spoken style but as deep a commitment to social reform as his son'.[10]

Gough Whitlam recognised this intellectual and political debt to his father as more than 'filial loyalty', as encompassing also the political promise of federation and the civic aspirations of Canberra:

> It is not without significance in my own career, in my own attitude to the Public Service, to the role of the Public Service, the duties and responsibilities of the Public Service and to the role of Government, that I lived my boyhood here in Canberra as the son of a great public servant among whose colleagues were great

---

[9] in Kirby, M. 'Whitlam as internationalist' Whitlam Lecture. The Whitlam Institute. University of Western Sydney. Sydney. 25 February 2010, https://www.whitlam.org/__data/assets/pdf_file/0010/123211/SPEECH_-_WHITLAM_LECTURE_-_25_FEBRUARY_2010.pdf.

[10] Hazlehurst, C. 'Whitlam, Harry Frederick (Fred) (1884–1961)', Australian Dictionary of Biography, Australian National University, http://adb.anu.edu.au/biography/whitlam-harry-frederick-fred-12020/text21559, published first in hardcopy 2002, accessed online 21 May 2017.

public servants and that I am Australia's first Prime Minister with that particular background.[11]

In this background lies the single most important and essential element in Gough Whitlam's politics – that he was at heart an institutionalist, and in many respects a conservative one. While Whitlam is better known for his breadth of policy ideas and reformist zeal, they cannot be understood without first understanding his deep attachment to the institutions that gave them form. Like his father, Whitlam was a firm believer in the parliamentary system as enabling the electoral will of the people to be translated into peaceful action, and in what he called 'the four great institutions which provided a framework for advocacy and action: the Australian Labor Party, the Australian Parliament, the Australian Constitution and Australia's membership of the United Nations'.[12] Together those 'four great institutions' provided the critical institutional framework that would not only drive Whitlam's political ambitions and his policy vision but would also provide the means to implement them.

When Whitlam arrived in the national parliament in 1952 therefore, he understood perhaps better than anyone in that chamber, not only the difficulties but also the constitutional opportunities for a reforming government that lay dormant in the constitutional text. Despite the prevailing despondency of the ALP that its key policies could never survive the inevitable High Court challenge and disavowal, Whitlam grasped the less explored potential of section 96 for

---

11 Whitlam, E.G. 'Australian Public Administration Under a Labor Government' Sir Robert Garran Memorial Oration. Canberra. 12 November 1973. https://pmtranscripts.dpmc.gov.au/release/transcript-3070

12 Whitlam, E.G. 'The relevance of the Whitlam government today' in Hocking, J. and Lewis, C. (eds) *It's time again: Whitlam and modern labor* Circa books. Melbourne 2003: 10–32, 16.

tied grants, public enterprises and Commonwealth directed funding, as a means of indirectly expanding federal power.[13] While section 96 was the main focus of Whitlam's early cause for a reformer's constitutional optimism, it was not the only point in which he discerned opportunity where others saw only obstacles.

Whitlam's membership of the Joint Parliamentary Constitutional Review Committee in 1956–1959 alerted him further to the possibilities for effective action in sections of the Constitution that had previously been seen as irrelevant, if not antithetical, to Labor governments. He later reflected on the development of his political thinking over that time, 'It was not a question of trying to circumvent the Constitution, but to make the best use of it, not supinely to accept the limitations of powers imposed by the Constitution, but to use the powers offered by it'.[14] One such power offered by the Constitution was the remarkable section 57, 'Disagreement between the Houses', used to the full by Whitlam in the 1974 double dissolution.

When he came to office in 1972, the barriers Whitlam had identified 20 years earlier lay not only in possible High Court challenge to his government's avowedly reformist policies, but also its institutional context – specifically, the parliamentary political obstruction it confronted. The 1972 election had been for the House of Representatives only, and the government faced a hostile Senate whose members had been elected at half-Senate elections up to five years earlier – in 1967 and 1970. The years since had been a period of rapid change during

---

[13] See my discussion of this in 'Gough Whitlam and the "unapologetic principle of Equality"' in Yeatman, A. (ed) *Gough Whitlam and the Social Democratic Imagination: The Challenge for Contemporary Public Policy* 2016 http://www.whitlam.org/__data/assets/pdf_file/0015/1112262/WHIT0928_HRPL_Series_3_paper_LR4.pdf#Reclaiming%20the%20Public

[14] Whitlam, E.G. Chifley Memorial Lecture. University of Melbourne. 14 August 1975. https://pmtranscripts.dpmc.gov.au/release/transcript-3847

which the electoral mood had shifted dramatically and the two chambers were now seriously out of both electoral sync and political alignment.

The new Labor government held 26 of the 60 Senate seats, the Liberal and Country parties also held 26, the Democratic Labor Party (DLP) held 5, with 3 Independents. With the DLP splinter group vehemently opposing the 'unreconstructed' ALP, the numbers gave an easy majority support for the Opposition in the Senate. In itself there was nothing unusual about that predicament, it is in the nature of the Australian bicameral system that all governments, except those elected following a double dissolution, will have to work with a Senate elected years earlier and, in Whitlam's case, up to 5 years earlier.[15] Nor was the Whitlam government's lack of a majority in the Senate in any way unusual, governments had operated without a Senate majority for 19 of the previous 72 years since federation. What was unusual, indeed unprecedented, was the scale of obstruction that followed.

Whitlam marked the end of his first year in office with a Ministerial Statement to the House of Representatives, a lengthy documentation of his government's achievements – despite the unrelenting obstruction; 'It has been a year of progress and reform on a scale unmatched in the records of this Federation'.[16] When the leader of the Opposition, Billy Snedden, repeatedly refused leave for it to be

---

15   Elections for the two Houses had been out of sync since 1963, the Menzies government had lost its Senate majority in 1962, the Liberal-Country party governments of Holt, Gorton and McMahon had all likewise lacked a majority in the Senate, the Scullin government 1929-1932 never had a majority in the Senate, while most governments faced a hostile Senate for at least part of their term. The last government to have had a Senate majority for the entirety of its term, 1945-1949, was the Chifley government.

16   Whitlam, E.G. 'Whitlam Government: Ministerial Statement' *Hansard* HoR 13 December 1973: 4729

CHAPTER 5

incorporated in *Hansard*, Whitlam stood up and read the statement to the House – and into *Hansard*. It took two hours.[17] The government's achievements in its first year included 253 bills presented to the House, of which 203 had been passed, 13 rejected, 21 amended and 10 deferred by the Senate, 39 reports commissioned, 6 constitutional alteration Bills, 19 treaties and agreements entered into, 823 Cabinet submissions and 1675 Cabinet decisions.

It was a stark reflection of the contrast between the Labor government and its Liberal-Country party Opposition, between action and reaction, that in the first year of the Whitlam government the House of Representatives had passed more legislation than in any single year since federation, and the Senate had rejected or deferred more legislation than in any single year since federation. During the entire three-year span of the Whitlam government, the Senate would reject more bills in those three years than it had in the previous 71 years since federation put together.

By April 1974, when Snedden led his Opposition colleagues into the folly that became the 1974 double dissolution, 10 bills had been rejected by the Senate for a second time, and 6 of these could now be used by the government as the 'trigger bills' for a double dissolution under section 57. Facing pressure from the Country party, which was particularly fearful of the government's plans for electoral equity that would see an end to the pronounced rural 'gerrymander' from which it had benefited for decades, Snedden announced that the Opposition

---

17   Whitlam, E.G. 'Whitlam Government: Ministerial Statement' *Hansard* HoR 13 December 1973: 4728-4758. Whitlam began speaking at 3.27pm and finished at 5.26pm, making several requests for leave to incorporate the remaining sections of the document during that time, each of which was denied by Snedden. This statement is one of the most detailed parliamentary records of the actions taken by the Whitlam government in its first year and testament to an exceptional level of activity in the face of an equally exceptional level of obstruction.

would take the unprecedented step of delaying a vote on the government's budget bills in the Senate. The intention was simple, to force the government back to an election barely 16 months after its 1972 election victory. On this the Opposition Leader in the Senate, Reg Withers, was quite clear: he would move an amendment that the Supply bills would not be brought forward for debate until the government 'agrees to submit itself to the judgment of the people'.[18]

It was this unprecedented level of obstruction that was the essential context for Whitlam's decision to let the Constitution do as it should, and to meet the impasse of the electorally spurned Opposition parties head on by calling a double dissolution under section 57. 'You will either jump or be pushed', Withers had told the government Leader in the Senate, Lionel Murphy. And Whitlam, who recognised in this intersection of political obstruction and Constitutional foresight a rare moment of opportunity, jumped.

On 10 April 1974 Reg Withers announced in the Senate that the Opposition would move an amendment to the government's budget bills stating, for the first time in Australia's history, that the Senate would refuse to consider the government's Supply bills until the government agreed to call another election: 'the Government should not be granted funds until it agrees to submit itself to the people'. The leader of the government in the Senate, Lionel Murphy, replied that if the Opposition persisted with 'this absurd amendment' presuming to make Supply conditional on the government calling an election, Whitlam would advise the Governor-General to call a double dissolution under section 57. Murphy then moved to bring the Budget bills forward with a motion that 'the question now be put', declaring that if this motion was defeated, 'the Government will treat that as a

---

18 Withers, R. *Hansard* Senate 10 April 1974, 884.

CHAPTER 5

denial of Supply ... [and] the Prime Minister, who is conversant with the absurd proposition which has been put here, will call forthwith upon his Excellency the Governor-General and tender him certain advice'.[19] Murphy's motion was defeated and Whitlam immediately called an emergency caucus meeting and moved to proceed to the double dissolution.

In what followed it appeared that Snedden had been caught off guard. The Opposition had pushed for and anticipated an election for the House of Representatives at the same time as the half-Senate election already set for 18 May, only to recognise too late that Whitlam was prepared to take an even greater risk and dissolve the whole Senate as well. Reflecting on Snedden's terminal misjudgment the Liberal member Jim Killen later remarked, 'Nobody could say that they did not know the gun was loaded'.[20] Whitlam then spent the next two hours with the Governor-General Sir Paul Hasluck, finalising arrangements for the double dissolution. Hasluck made one proviso in accepting Whitlam's advice to activate section 57, that the Senate pass sufficient Supply at least for the period of the election. Whitlam was in no doubt, as he advised Hasluck, that the Opposition would agree to 'appropriate arrangements' once the Governor-General had accepted his advice to call the election.[21] Later that evening the Opposition did just that, passing the government's two Supply Bills and three Appropriation Bills in the Senate. A furious Murphy taunted Withers; 'You sought it; you got it and you will have to put up with it'.[22]

---

19 Murphy, L. *Hansard* Senate 10 April 1974, 931.
20 Killen, J. *Killen: Inside Australian Politics* (Port Melbourne: Mandarin. 1985), 224.
21 EG Whitlam to Hasluck, 10 April 1974, Document No. 1, in 'Simultaneous Dissolution of the Senate and the House of Representatives 11 April 1974', *Parliamentary Paper No. 257* 1975: 1-8, in 'Australian Constitution – Constitutional Crisis, 1975' NAA M4518 10 Part 1.
22 Murphy, L. *Hansard*, Senate, 10 April 1974, 931.

At a time when the fractious parliamentary relations between the major political parties, together with the reformist initiatives of the Whitlam government, were often seen as placing great strain on the Australian constitutional framework, the 1974 double dissolution provided a welcome example of constitutional practicality and prescience. No other parliamentary system has any comparable means of dealing with a legislative dispute between the Houses and, in dealing with Senate obstruction in this way, section 57 is also a clear assertion of the primacy of the House of Representatives over the Senate. As Justice Stephen noted in the first of three High Court challenges to the May 1974 double dissolution and Joint Sitting that followed, section 57 is a reassertion of the primacy of the House of Representatives and 'acknowledges that ultimately the will of the House is most likely to prevail'.[23] For section 57, as Richardson has also argued, 'operates in one direction only', it relates only to bills initiated in and passed by the House of Representatives and twice rejected or failed to pass by the Senate – and not to bills initiated in and passed by the Senate and rejected by the House; 'Thus the Constitution asserts the primacy of the House of Representatives as the "people's house" and the chamber of government'.[24] For Whitlam, both the symbolism and the substance were irresistible.

In reaching this fraught decision Whitlam had been influenced by the experience of Liberal Prime Minister Robert Menzies, whose own double dissolution election of 1951 was the sole example of a government returned with a majority in both the House of Representatives

---

23 Stephen, J. Cormack v. Cope [1974] HCA 28; 131 CLR 432 at: 468
24 Richardson, J. 'Resolving Deadlocks in the Australian Parliament' *Research Paper* No. 9 2000-1, October 2000. http://www.aph.gov.au/About_Parliament/Parliamentary_Departments/Parliamentary_Library/pubs/rp/rp0001/01RP09

CHAPTER 5

and the Senate.[25] This was not the only occasion on which Whitlam acknowledged the historical precedent set by Menzies in matters of political and constitutional initiative, as he had written to Menzies soon after coming to office; 'You would, I think, be surprised to know how much I feel indebted to your example, despite the great differences in our philosophies'.[26] Nor was the dire experience of Labor Prime Minister Jim Scullin, facing a hostile and unforgiving Senate during the worsening years of the great depression, lost on Whitlam who had arrived in Canberra as a young boy two years before Scullin took office in 1929 and had watched these events unfold with precocious fascination.[27] Scullin's predicament had fired his fierce and long-standing disdain for the pretensions of upper houses, their unrepresentative franchise and disproportionate power over popularly elected government.

As a law student Whitlam had derided the anti-democratic notion of an upper house that could counter decisions of a government formed in the House of Representatives, to temper the excesses of unchecked democracy; 'democracies do not need to be saved from themselves', he retorted.[28] For a time it seemed that even Menzies agreed, he had argued in the strongest terms in 1968 that, 'It would be a falsification of democracy if, on any matter of government policy approved by the House of Representatives ... the Senate, representing

---

25 There had been 2 previous Double Dissolutions called under section 57, in 1914 and 1951, neither of which had resulted in a Joint Sitting. At the first, Prime Minister Joseph Cook lost the election and at the second, Prime Minister Robert Menzies was returned with control of the Senate, obviating the need for a joint sitting.
26 Whitlam, E.G. *The Whitlam Government 1972-1975*, 13.
27 Hocking, J. *Gough Whitlam: A Moment in History*, 49–50.
28 Whitlam, E.G. 'A Review of the House of Review', *Blackacre: Journal of the Sydney University Law School*, February 1947, Whitlam Institute e-collection. http://www.whitlam.org/whitlam/index.php. accessed 11 June 2009.

the States and not the people, could reverse the decision'.[29] Yet just 5 years later the Liberal-Country party Opposition in the Senate would do just that, to an unprecedented degree.

Nevertheless, the 1974 double dissolution was a perilous decision, one that risked everything Whitlam had gained in 25 years of political struggle inside and outside the Labor party, to chance it all on returning to office with an improved Senate position. Even then there were two hurdles to jump – to return with sufficient numbers to pass the six trigger bills at the Joint Sitting or, at best, to gain a majority in the Senate which would obviate the need for a Joint Sitting. Whitlam conceded to Hasluck that he saw little chance of the government achieving a majority in the Senate and that he expected the government and the Opposition to return with equal Senate numbers.[30]

On the other hand, as Hasluck had counseled Whitlam in a remarkably frank assessment the previous year, the Opposition's 'general obstruction' of government legislation presented the government with an opportunity to fight an election on the theme that it had not been given 'a fair go'.[31] Whitlam agreed, and the ALP campaign centred on the slogan 'Give Gough a Go', emphasising that its program for reform had been stymied, its mandate ignored and that both should now be affirmed at the double dissolution election.

The lessons from the only two precedents for section 57 were mixed. In the first double dissolution in 1914, Prime Minister Joseph Cook's

---

29 L F Crisp, *Australian National Government*, Longman and Chesire, Melbourne. 1983, 349.
30 EG Whitlam to Hasluck, 10 April 1974, Document No. 1, in 'Simultaneous Dissolution of the Senate and the House of Representatives 11 April 1974', *Parliamentary Paper No. 257* 1975: 1-8, in 'Australian Constitution – Constitutional Crisis, 1975' NAA M4518 10 Part 1.
31 Hasluck, P. 'Mr Whitlam's outlook in June 1973' in *Copies of notes made by the Governor-General [Sir Paul Hasluck] 1969–1974*. Papers Maintained by the Governor-General [Sir Paul Hasluck] 1969–1974. NAA M1767/4

CHAPTER 5

Commonwealth Liberal government lost office to the Opposition Labor party, which was elected with a majority also in the Senate. In the 1951 election however, the Menzies government had been returned to office with a majority in both Houses. In neither instance had the double dissolution been primarily concerned with passing legislation rejected by the Senate, both Cook and Menzies had recognised this as an opportune time to call an election and neither trigger bill was seen as fundamental to their respective government's agenda. Although Menzies could subsequently have passed the trigger bill without a Joint Sitting, since his government was returned with a majority in the Senate, it was never re-presented. Cook made little of the trigger bill during the election campaign, which was overtaken by the outbreak of the 1st World War and focused on issues of security and defence.[32]

The 1974 double dissolution therefore was the first to be driven by and focused on the legislative obstruction integral to the intention of section 57, and not merely as an administrative means of calling an early election for both Houses. But the 1974 election was so much more than that. In it can be seen a number of firsts on several levels – in its process, its outcome and its consequences – which together created the precedents that still determine the use of this parliamentary dispute mechanism today.

Whitlam gave section 57 its fullest reading as an instrument of reform, as an alternative means of passing government legislation blocked by a hostile Senate. It is entirely fitting then that the 1974 double dissolution was the first to cite more than one bill as the

---

32 The 1914 trigger was a bill to abolish preferential employment for trade union members in the public service. The 1951 trigger was the Commonwealth Bank Bill which included provisions to replace the Bank's governor with a government appointed board.

basis for invoking section 57. Governor-General Hasluck accepted Whitlam's advice, armed with the written legal support of the Solicitor-General, Maurice Byers, and the Attorney-General, Lionel Murphy, that six of the ten twice-rejected bills fulfilled the requirements of section 57 and that all six could be used as trigger bills. Whitlam, through the Joint Opinion provided by Murphy and Byers, argued that the critical reference to 'any proposed law' in section 57 should be read as referring to more than just any *one* proposed law; 'section 57 of the Constitution is applicable to more than one law at each of the stages it refers to'.[33] This reading was as powerful for the government as it was devastating for the coalition which, if this interpretation proved correct, would now face the passage of several of the government's key reform bills should the ALP be returned to office.

Lost in the minutiae and drama of those few hours was another first in the 1974 election, the use of a new wording for the Governor-General's proclamation. When Hasluck issued the Proclamation dissolving both Houses of parliament the following day, there was one thing missing – 'God Save the Queen!'. Whitlam's discussion with Hasluck had included even the wording of the Proclamation and as they checked through the traditional text with its residual colonial ecclesiastical language, Whitlam crossed out the archaic invocation 'God Save the Queen!', writing in the margin: 'We'll have no more of this nonsense'.[34]

---

33 Murphy, L. and Byers, M.H. 'Constitution, Section 57: Whether applicable to more than one proposed law: Joint Opinion' 10 April 1974, Attachment E in 'Simultaneous Dissolution of the Senate and the House of Representatives 11 April 1974', *Parliamentary Paper No. 257* 1975: 30–31, in 'Australian Constitution – Constitutional Crisis, 1975' NAA M4518 10 Part 1.

34 It is this change in the wording of the Proclamation in 1974 that gives full meaning to Whitlam's furious exhortation on the steps of Parliament House on 11 November

CHAPTER 5

The return of the Whitlam government on 18 May 1974 was itself historic, as Gough Whitlam became the first Labor leader to come to office at consecutive elections. The government was returned with a slight reduction of .29% in the ALP's national first preference vote to 49.3% and with a two party preferred vote of 51.7%, down 1% from 52.7% at the 1972 election. The new seat numbers were complicated by the fact that a redistribution shortly before the election had added two new seats to the House of Representatives, increasing its number to 127 seats. So although the total number of ALP seats was reduced by just one, the government's margin was reduced from 9 to 5 seats as the coalition gained three seats in the expanded House.[35]

In the Senate the outcome was as Whitlam had anticipated, the ALP gained 3 Senate seats and was returned with 29 Senators, equal with the Coalition with the Liberal party likewise gaining 3 Senate seats and the Country party retaining five. There were 2 Independents, one less than previously. For the DLP the election had been an unqualified disaster. It lost every one of its previous 5 Senators and, having split the Labor vote and kept the ALP from office for two decades, was finished as an electoral force. That much at least of Whitlam's long parliamentary ambition had been realised.

For Liberal party leader Billy Snedden there were few positives. The threat to block supply that had precipitated the election had been an appalling miscalculation, as his colleagues were only too willing

---

1975, 'Well may we say "God Save the Queen" because nothing will save the Governor-General', after the reading by the Governor-General's official secretary Mr David Smith of the Proclamation dissolving both Houses – in which the words 'God Save the Queen' had been reinstated.

35 At the 1972 election the ALP won 67 seats, the Liberal party 38 and the Country party 20.

to pronounce. The Whitlam government had not only been returned, it had been returned with enough votes to secure the passage of the 6 trigger bills. The government now held a total number in both Houses of parliament of 95 – just one more than the absolute majority needed to pass the bills at a Joint Sitting. With the writing on the wall for Snedden, he was reduced to pleading that, 'we were not defeated, we just didn't win enough seats to form a government, but I do not believe what has occurred was in any sense a defeat'.[36]

The government then moved to the post-election stage of section 57, the Joint Sitting. The mechanism of the Joint Sitting was the institutional heart of section 57, the distinctive parliamentary means of resolving the continuing dispute between the Houses over the trigger bills. The protracted process for the passage of those bills, required them to be re-presented for a third time to first the House of Representatives and then the Senate. When the Governor-General, Sir Paul Hasluck, opened the 29th Parliament on 9 July these bills were the first items on the agenda. All six bills were again passed by the House of Representatives and all six bills were again rejected by the Opposition in the Senate, despite the government's latest election victory and despite the fact that they would now inevitably be passed at the Joint Sitting.

On 30 July the new Governor-General, Sir John Kerr, issued the Proclamation announcing that a Joint Sitting of all 187 members of parliament would be held on 6 and 7 August 1974. As the first Joint Sitting to follow a double dissolution, this would be the first time that Commonwealth legislation was passed through this alternative

---

36   'The election that changed nothing' The Whitlam Institute, Western Sydney University, online exhibition The 1974 Double Dissolution https://www.whitlam.org/gough_whitlam/jointsitting/1974_election Accessed 20 May 2017

CHAPTER 5

parliamentary means, the Joint Sitting, being in essence 'a unicameral form of legislation instead of the bicameral form'.[37] This was also the first time the parliamentary proceedings of either House had been broadcast live on television, with the entire 2 days shown on the ABC. As the only Joint Sitting ever convened every element of it was also to be agreed for the first time – its location, its procedures, its duration and even the colour of the cover of *Hansard*, had all to be determined. In the context of the bitter dispute between the House of Representatives and the Senate that had led to this point, the question of where the sitting would be held now assumed particular symbolic significance. Given Whitlam's own long-held views of upper houses, his belief in the democratic role of the House of Representatives as 'the people's House' and the Opposition's continuing Senate obstruction, the Joint Sitting was always going to be held in the House of Representatives.

In a final historical twist, the Joint Sitting was the first official function presided over by the newly appointed Governor-General, Sir John Kerr, who opened the Joint Sitting on 6 August, completing the double dissolution process begun by his predecessor Sir Paul Hasluck four months earlier. Whitlam's address to the combined Senators and Members was a rare opportunity for him to speak directly to the recalcitrant Opposition Senators, now assembled in 'the people's House', and he made full use of it. His speech was a withering denunciation of their failure to accept 'the will of the people', their arrogant expectations of power and office. Whitlam acknowledged the Joint Sitting as an 'historic and unprecedented, a sobering occasion', brought about by 'blind obstruction':

---

37 Sawer, *Federation Under Strain: Australia*, 48

> [M]omentous as the sitting is, the reasons for it are not a matter for pride. It has come about because of the repeated refusal of the Senate to pass legislation which has been approved by the House of Representatives – the people's House, the House where alone governments are made and unmade. It has come about because despite two successive election victories by the Australian Labor Party, despite the clear endorsement by the Australian people at the elections only 11 weeks ago of the Party's policies and of the specific measures now before us, the Senate and the Opposition are still resolved to obstruct the Government's program and to frustrate the will of the people. ... Let it be understood that this Joint Sitting is a last resort, a means provided by the Constitution to enable the popular will – the democratic process – ultimately to prevail over the tactics of blind obstruction.[38]

The 'blind obstruction' was not limited to the Opposition within the parliament, and four critical High Court challenges in relation to the 1974 election were taken at that time. The decisions in these cases were not only politically imperative for the Whitlam government, they also established the enduring political parameters and legal precedents governing the use of section 57 for all subsequent double dissolutions.

In the first of these cases, taken just days before the Joint Sitting was due to begin, two Opposition Senators, Liberal Senator Magnus Cormack and Country party Senator James Webster, sought an injunction to prevent the Joint Sitting from going ahead. They argued that the Governor-General's Proclamation announcing the double dissolution had been incorrect in reciting more than one bill and that the *Petroleum and Minerals Authority Bill* should not have been included as one of the 6 bills, contending that the three-month interval

---

38 Whitlam, E.G. *Hansard* House of Representatives 6 August 1974, 4.

CHAPTER 5

required under section 57 had not elapsed. The High Court heard the case urgently and, in a judgment handed down the day before the Joint Sitting was due to begin, a unanimous judgment of the Court found in the government's favour.[39] The decision also confirmed, as the government had argued, that more than one bill could be used as the basis for a double dissolution under section 57, giving that section a 'distributive' effect across any number of rejected bills.[40]

Although the Joint Sitting had been given a last minute reprieve from injunction, the fate of the six Acts subsequently passed there was less certain. Four of those Acts were later challenged in the High Court as the on-going political obstruction now continued in the legal arena. The High Court's decision in *Cormack v Cope* just prior to the Joint Sitting, had not directly addressed the question of the validity of the *Petroleum and Minerals Authority Bill*. Nevertheless a majority of the Justices had strongly suggested that the validity of individual Acts passed at the Joint Sitting could later be determined by the Court, and foreshadowed such challenges. These 'implied invitations' to pursue objections, as Sawer termed them, were soon accepted.[41]

Four conservative state governments – Victoria, Western Australia, Queensland and New South Wales – challenged the validity of the *Petroleum and Minerals Authority Act* on the grounds that the three-month interval between the first and second consideration of the bill by both Houses of Parliament required under section 57 had not elapsed. The case tested the meaning of this key phrase 'after an interval of three months' and in a 4:3 decision a narrow majority of the

---

39   *Cormack v Cope* [1974] HCA 28, (1974) 131 CLR 432
40   Richardson, 'Resolving Deadlocks'
41   Sawer, *Federation Under Strain*, 47

Court ruled that the three month interval between first and second consideration should be measured from the first rejection of the bill by the Senate to its second passage by the House of Representatives. The *Petroleum and Minerals Authority Act* was therefore ruled invalid, since the requisite three months under that interpretation had not elapsed in order for it to form one of the trigger bills.[42] In all its deliberations on this, including in the earlier *Cormack v Cope*, the High Court was careful to make clear its view that ruling one of the trigger bills invalid in this way did not invalidate the double dissolution election, the Joint Sitting or the passage of any of the other trigger bills presented there.[43]

Three state governments – the Liberal-Country party coalition state governments of Western Australia, NSW and Queensland, also joined forces to challenge the three electoral laws passed at the Joint Sitting. These were three Acts dealing with electoral matters, of which the most important was the *Senate (Representation of Territories) Act*, which introduced Senate representation for the first time for the Northern Territory and the Australian Capital Territory; and the *Commonwealth Electoral Act (No. 2)* that ended the longstanding rural gerrymander with the introduction of 'one vote one value' through equal electorates.[44] The legal effort to invalidate these key Whitlam government electoral reforms centred on the length of time between the Senate's second rejection of the trigger bills and the calling of the double dissolution – the temporal proximity of the

---

42   *Victoria v Commonwealth* [1975] HCA 39, (1975) 134 CLR 81. The Court also held that the Senate adjournment on 13 December 1973 with the bill still before it did not constitute a 'rejection or failure to pass' and so the *Petroleum and Minerals Authority Bill* had not yet 'failed to pass'.
43   See the discussion in Sawer, *Federation Under Strain* Chapter 4 'The Double Dissolutions' on this.
44   *Western Australia v Commonwealth* [1975] HCA 46, (1975) 134 CLR 201

double dissolution to the parliamentary obstruction of the bills that 'triggered' it.

In another narrow majority decision in the government's favour, handed down in October 1975, the High Court upheld the *Senate (Representation of Territories) Act*. The Court found that there was no necessary time limit within which the double dissolution had to be called following rejection of the bills, once the requirements of section 57 had been met they remained as available bases for a double dissolution.[45] Together with the previous decision in *Cormack v Cope* that more than one bill could be used as trigger bills, this decision in the *Territory Senators* case paved the way for the 'stock-piling' of several rejected bills by a government facing a hostile Senate.

In relation to the question of proximity – whether of time or substance – between Senate rejection of a bill and the double dissolution raised in both the *PMA* case and the *Territory Senators* case, High Court Justice Anthony Mason argued further than his fellow justices. Mason, in the *Territory Senators* case, found that section 57 could be used as the basis for a double dissolution, even in circumstances quite remote from the twice-rejected legislation under dispute. Specifically, Mason suggested that a double dissolution could be called for reasons *other* than passing the trigger bills: 'The power to dissolve can be exercised even in circumstances in which the Government and the House of Representatives lose their enthusiasm for the proposed law and desire a double dissolution for other reasons having no connection with the Senate's rejection of the proposed law. ... Whatever be the particular disagreement which is the occasion for a double

---

45 The only time requirement specified under section 57 is that, 'such dissolution shall not take place within 6 months before the date of expiry of the House of Representatives'.

dissolution, the ensuing election will be fought on such issues as the parties select or have thrust upon them'.[46] This view would later be of particular significance in relation to the 1975 double dissolution election, called by the newly appointed Liberal Prime Minister Malcolm Fraser, following the dismissal of the Whitlam government by the Governor-General Sir John Kerr.

Each of these cases in different and often contradictory ways traversed the key questions of the respective institutional bounds of the parliament, the judiciary and the Governor-General, and the foundational relations between these arms of government.[47] Much of the judgments, in the *PMA* case and *Cormack v Cope* in particular, gave detailed consideration to the question of the justiciability of the actions of the Governor-General – in proclaiming first the double dissolution and subsequently the Joint Sitting on the basis of all 6 trigger bills. The majority High Court view in those critical cases was that the Governor-General's actions under section 57 were justiciable, they were not binding and were open for review by the Court. Despite its carriage by the High Court, this view is controversial and by no means universal. O'Brien for instance argues that, 'it is not appropriate for the judiciary to make a judgment whether or not the proposed law or laws have met the requirements of the section'.[48]

Sawer argues rather differently, querying the imposition of judicial review over the parliamentary process set out in section 57 and noting the 'embarrassing possible consequences of exposing

---

46   Mason, J. *Western Australia v Commonwealth* [1975] HCA 46, (1975) 134 CLR 201 at 266

47   Diplock, J. 'The double dissolution and joint sitting of federal parliament' *Sydney Law Review* vol 8 no. 1 January 1977: 223–238

48   O'Brien, D.P. 'Double dissolution of federal parliament – the fifth double dissolution' *Melbourne University Law Review* vol. 14 1983: 37–52, 41 n. 17.

CHAPTER 5

gubernatorial action under s. 57 to judicial invalidation', in light of the High Court's decision in *Cormack v Cope*.[49] The action of the Governor-General Sir John Kerr in citing the six trigger bills in the proclamation announcing the Joint Sitting had been called into precisely this question, particularly strongly by the Chief Justice, Sir Garfield Barwick. Barwick referred less than respectfully to the Governor-General's proclamation as, 'purporting to convene a joint sitting' and termed it 'an excess of authority on the part of the Governor-General': 'the Governor-General has exceeded his function in specifying the business of the joint sitting and in directing that there shall be voting upon each of the specified bills, including the Petroleum and Minerals Authority Bill 1973'.[50] Kerr made no secret of the fact that he felt the embarrassment of these legal rebukes from the Chief Justice and others most keenly.[51]

What was unknown then, and would remain unknown for nearly 40 years to come, was that during the period in which these critical High Court cases were being considered, one of the sitting High Court justices was in secret discussions with the Governor-General on constitutional and legal matters, canvassing the bounds of vice-regal action and prerogative, and leading to the dismissal of the Whitlam government. It is now known that Justice Anthony Mason played a pivotal, undisclosed, role in counselling Kerr throughout 1975, as I revealed in *Gough Whitlam: His Time,* and which Mason then, for the first time, publicly confirmed. From August 1975

---

49 Sawer, *Federation Under Strain* 54
50 *Cormack v Cope* [1974] HCA 28, (1974) 131 CLR 432 at 454–458
51 Kerr, J. *Matters for Judgment*: 238-240; Kerr, J. 'Draft letter by Governor-General to Prime Minister Terminating his Commission', *Personal and Confidential Papers of Sir John Kerr: Notes and papers of the Constitutional Crisis of 1975 and the Political Events that Followed* NAA M4524 10

Mason was critically involved in Kerr's considerations as he moved towards the dismissal of the Whitlam government, while these remaining cases were still in progress, including drafting the letter of dismissal for the Governor-General.[52] Their meetings were kept hidden, secret both from Mason's fellow justices on the High Court and from the Prime Minister, Gough Whitlam, and none was announced in the Vice-Regal news. The failure to divulge such a significant interaction and the potential perception of conflict of interest during these defining High Court cases constituted at best a profound breach of institutional propriety.

Given the deeply polarised political and legal climate of that time Mason should, at the very least, have informed his fellow High Court justices of his close connection with the Governor-General and arguably should have recused himself from those cases arising from the 1974 double dissolution which bore in any way on the Governor-General's actions and powers. There was an interesting precedent of sorts here from a parallel interaction between Kerr and Mason at this same time. Mason was then a pro-chancellor of the Australian National University and in March 1975 at Kerr's request he facilitated a series of unorthodox, also secret, 'tutorials' for the Governor-General with selected members of the ANU Law School, to advise Kerr on the nature and extent of the Governor-General's powers. Having facilitated the formation of this group Mason then told Kerr that he doubted, 'whether it would be proper' for him to attend these meetings on a regular basis, since it could appear that 'we are engaged in the consideration of important questions *which may sooner or later come before the High Court for decision*'.[53]

---

52   Hocking, J. *Gough Whitlam: His Time* Chapter 10 'The Third Man' *passim*; Mason, Sir Anthony 'Statement' *The Age* 27 August 2012

53   Mason in Hocking, J. *Gough Whitlam: His Time*, 305 [my emphasis].

CHAPTER 5

Nevertheless, as the High Court heard the remaining cases stemming from the 1974 double dissolution throughout 1975, Mason was silent about his involvement with Kerr on the very matter of the Governor-General's powers, their justiciability, and indeed the fate of the Whitlam government whose double dissolution and legislation he now sat in judgment upon. The *PMA* case was heard in February 1975, the judgment announced in June and the reasons handed down on 30 September 1975. The Governor-General's Proclamation calling the Joint Sitting had been a point at issue in the case, and throughout that time Mason and Kerr were in regular communication on legal matters, the Governor-General's powers and questions of justiciability. Mason was in the majority in the decision against the government in the *PMA* Case, the only one of these Constitutional challenges which found against the government.

Arguments in the *Territory Senators* case were heard in May 1975 and the High Court's judgment was not handed down until 10 October. By the narrowest majority of four to three, the Court decided in the government's favour and four new Senate positions would now be available at the next half-Senate election. It carried immense implications for the Whitlam government's pending half-Senate election, with the additional 4 Senators to be elected for the Territories for the first time. On 15 October the Opposition, describing the Whitlam government as 'the worst government in our nation's history,' moved to block the government's budget by refusing to allow a vote on the appropriation bills then before the Senate.[54] With the budget still blocked in the Senate four weeks later, Whitlam decided to call the half-Senate election due anytime before mid-1976. On 6 November Whitlam informed the Governor-General that he would

---

54 Hocking, J. *Gough Whitlam: His Time*, 237–40.

call the half-Senate election for 13 December and that it would be announced in the House of Representatives on 11 November. The draft paperwork setting out the dates for the issuing of writs by the states was exchanged and agreed over the next few days between Government House and the Prime Minister's office.[55] Whitlam and Kerr agreed to meet at Yarralumla at 1pm on 11 November 1975 in order, Whitlam believed, to finalise the wording for the announcement of the half-Senate election that he was to make in the House that afternoon[56]. Instead, Whitlam was summarily dismissed without warning and Kerr appointed the leader of the Opposition, Malcolm Fraser, as Prime Minister.

In a tumultuous afternoon session in the House of Representatives after the dismissal Malcolm Fraser lost a motion of no confidence by 10 votes, with the same motion also calling on the Governor-General to re-commission the Whitlam government. The Governor-General refused either to see the Speaker of the House or to acknowledge the no confidence motion against Fraser, instead accepting Fraser's call to dissolve both Houses of Parliament – citing 21 twice-rejected bills as meeting the requirements of section 57. The full significance of the High Court's decision in the *Territory Senators* case can now be seen in the Governor-General's acceptance of this highly contentious use of section 57 on the basis of 21 trigger bills which Fraser's own party had twice rejected and which his newly appointed government had neither interest in nor intention of passing.

---

55 Hocking, J. The Dismissal Dossier: Everything Your Were Never Meant to Know About November 1975, Updated Edition (Carlton: Melbourne University Press. 2016), Chapter 5 'Sir John Kerr's Second Dismissal'.

56 Letter from Prime Minister E.G. Whitlam to Governor-General Sir John Kerr 11 November 1975 advising half-Senate election, in *Double Dissolution of Parliament 11 November 1975*, NAA; A1209 1975/2448, 314.

CHAPTER 5

The 1975 double dissolution was called in this entirely spurious circumstance. Justice Mason's judgment in the *Territory Senators* case is striking in this context: 'The power to dissolve can be exercised even in circumstances ... having no connection with the Senate's rejection of the proposed law'. This was an extraordinary statement. By claiming that the power to dissolve under section 57 need have 'no connection with the Senate's rejection of the proposed law', Mason had disconnected that section from its clear and stated intention – as a means of resolving a disagreement between the Houses. For section 57 is headed, 'Disagreement between the Houses', and it is perverse if not logically impossible to so fundamentally redefine it by linguistically severing it from its very essence. Colin Howard remarked on the constitutional illogicality in Kerr's 'use of the machinery of s.57 to resolve a deadlock with which it had no connection' – precisely the Mason doctrine – and queried 'whether the power which the Governor-General purported to exercise existed at all'.[57]

Section 57 describes a particular set of circumstances that evolves over several months, constructing an unusual dynamic which continues, if the government is successful, after the double dissolution election set out in its provisions. The dynamic it establishes is between a government, formed as it must be in the House of Representatives, facing repeated obstruction by the Senate and using the mechanism of a double dissolution followed by a Joint Sitting in order to resolve the disagreement *from the previous parliament*. The section is not static, it operates in stages and takes shape over time. It sets out a lengthy and complex parliamentary process that crosses

---

57 Howard, C. 'The Constitutional Crisis of 1975' *The Australian Quarterly* 48 (1) March 1976: 5–25, 22.

two parliaments and two electoral cycles. The Joint Opinion provided to Governor-General Hasluck by the Attorney-General Lionel Murphy and the Solicitor-General Maurice Byers in April 1974 highlighted this fluidity, referring to the 'various stages' of section 57: 'the double dissolution stage, the subsequent parliamentary stages [and] the convening of the joint sitting of the two Houses'.

The dynamic constructed through the provisions of section 57 read in their entirety, is a process that occurs over time. As Murphy and Byers described it; 'It is ... indisputable that the end proposed by section 57 was the resolution of a deadlock in the processes of Parliament'.[58] That process traverses both Houses, two elected parliaments and a Joint Sitting, bridged by the defining outcome of the double dissolution. Section 57 can only be understood if 'the government' referred to throughout its provisions is a reference to the same government from start to finish – from deadlock to resolution. The critical factor in the 1975 use of section 57 was that the government invoking the provision to call a double dissolution, was not the government whose bills had been twice rejected by the Senate as presumed by that same section.

Section 57 further presumes that the government retains, since all Westminster-style governments must, the confidence of the House of Representatives. In considering whether the Governor-General could exercise any discretion in calling a double dissolution under section 57, Dr H.V. Evatt, in his towering work, *The King and his Dominion Governors*, refers to this presumption of confidence

---

58   Murphy, L. and Byers, M.H. 'Constitution, Section 57: Whether applicable to more than one proposed law: Joint Opinion' 10 April 1974, Attachment E in 'Simultaneous Dissolution of the Senate and the House of Representatives 11 April 1974', *Parliamentary Paper No. 257* 1975: 31, in 'Australian Constitution – Constitutional Crisis, 1975' NAA M4518 10 Part 1.

CHAPTER 5

almost in passing, so fundamental is it to the formation of government.[59] Evatt notes the precedent established from the first double dissolution in 1914 that; 'so long as the conditions mentioned in Section 57 are complied with, the Governor-General will grant a double dissolution *to Ministers who possess the confidence of the House of Representatives*'.[60] The Governor-General should never have received the specious claim to section 57 in November 1975 from a Prime Minister, Malcolm Fraser, who lacked the confidence of the House of Representatives and who could not therefore advise him, and whose party had rejected the 21 government bills now cited as its basis.

With Kerr's decision, section 57 had been transformed from a unique constitutional means for dealing with political disagreement between the Houses and ensuring the primacy of the House of Representatives into its opposite – into a means of dissolving that House at the behest of the Senate. What a travesty. The constitutional innovation of section 57 and the rich possibilities it had afforded the Whitlam government in 1974, the first and still the only use of its full provisions, had been reduced to the level of shallow political tactic against his re-elected government barely eighteen months later.

Whitlam's decision to dissolve both Houses of Parliament in April 1974 remains the sole instance of the full use of section 57, with the passage of the six trigger bills at the Joint Sitting in August 1974 completing that process. Those six Acts remain the only legislation ever to have been passed through that exceptional unicameral legislature. In the successful resolution of the disagreement between the Houses

---

59   Evatt, H.V. *The King and His Dominion Governors* Frank Cass and Co. London. 1936
60   Evatt, H.V. in O'Brien, D.P. 'Double dissolution of federal parliament – the fifth double dissolution' *Melbourne University Law Review* vol. 14 1983: 37–52, 43 [my emphasis].

that had led to the dissolution, the role of the Governor-General, Sir Paul Hasluck, was of singular importance. It stands as a model, both for the Governor-General's relationship with the Prime Minister and for what should have happened in 1975 when Whitlam advised Kerr of the half-Senate election. It was Hasluck's constructive guidance of and communication with Whitlam that helped secure the threatened passage of Supply through the Senate prior to the May 1974 double dissolution. Whitlam had been deeply impressed by Hasluck and by his strategic acceptance of Whitlam's advice to call the double dissolution, contingent on the provision of Supply.

Whitlam was always concerned with documenting his government, its history and its record, and the historic 1974 double dissolution was no exception. In order to place its details on the parliamentary and public record, his department prepared a Parliamentary Paper setting out the 'various stages' of that process, from deadlock to Joint Sitting. It included the Joint Opinion by Murphy and Byers arguing that there could be more than one trigger bill, and Whitlam's letter to Hasluck advising the double dissolution in which he described the conditions of section 57 as 'having been established progressively over a period of time'. The Parliamentary Paper detailed this in full – from the cumulative rejection of bills in the Senate to the proclamation under section 57, from Hasluck's role in securing Supply, the double dissolution election, the continued rejection of the bills, to the Joint Sitting and the eventual resolution with the passage of the six blocked 'trigger' bills.

The Parliamentary Paper on the 1974 double dissolution and Joint Sitting was due to be tabled on 11 November 1975 when it was, ironically enough, precluded by the dismissal of the Whitlam government and by another double dissolution. A copy can be found in

CHAPTER 5

the papers of Sir John Kerr in the National Archives of Australia.[61] It remains there as an appropriately sequestered documentation of the 1974 election – an exemplar of Constitutional ingenuity, Prime Ministerial fiat, and of government by double dissolution.

Appendix I

Commonwealth Of Australia Constitution Act – Section 57

Disagreement between the Houses

If the House of Representatives passes any proposed law, and the Senate rejects or fails to pass it, or passes it with amendments to which the House of Representatives will not agree, and if after an interval of three months the House of Representatives, in the same or the next session, again passes the proposed law with or without any amendments which have been made, suggested, or agreed to by the Senate, and the Senate rejects or fails to pass it, or passes it with amendments to which the House of Representatives will not agree, the Governor-General may dissolve the Senate and the House of Representatives simultaneously. But such dissolution shall not take place within six months before the date of the expiry of the House of Representatives by effluxion of time.

If after such dissolution the House of Representatives again passes the proposed law, with or without any amendments which have been made, suggested, or agreed to by the Senate, and the Senate rejects or fails to pass it, or passes it with amendments to which the House of Representatives will not agree, the Governor-General may convene

---

61 'Simultaneous Dissolution of the Senate and the House of Representatives 11 April 1974', *Parliamentary Paper No. 257* 1975: 31, in 'Australian Constitution – Constitutional Crisis, 1975' NAA M4518 10 Part 1.

a joint sitting of the members of the Senate and of the House of Representatives.

The members present at the joint sitting may deliberate and shall vote together upon the proposed law as last proposed by the House of Representatives, and upon amendments, if any, which have been made therein by one House and not agreed to by the other, and any such amendments which are affirmed by an absolute majority of the total number of the members of the Senate and House of Representatives shall be taken to have been carried, and if the proposed law, with the amendments, if any, so carried is affirmed by an absolute majority of the total number of the members of the Senate and House of Representatives, it shall be taken to have been duly passed by both Houses of the Parliament, and shall be presented to the Governor-General for the Queen's assent.

Part II

From inspiration to implementation

Chapter 6

GOUGH WHITLAM AND THE RE-IMAGINED CITIZEN-SUBJECT OF AUSTRALIAN SOCIAL DEMOCRACY[1]

Carol Johnson

In a number of speeches, Gough Whitlam suggested that his concept of 'positive equality' sought to avoid the constitutional roadblocks encountered during the Curtin and Chifley years by bypassing much of the need for extensive government regulation (or resorts to nationalisation) and instead substituting the strategic provision of key government community services. However, this chapter suggests that Whitlam's concept of 'positive equality' in fact involved a far more substantial transformation of the Australian Labor project. Whitlam was moving beyond traditional Labor conceptions of the citizen-subject as predominantly a white, male wage-earning head of household, with female dependents receiving citizenship

---

1   My thanks to Clare Parker for her research assistance. This chapter incorporates some material produced as part of a larger ARC-funded project (DP140100168) entitled: 'Expanding equality: A historical perspective on developments and dilemmas in contemporary Australian social democracy.'

entitlements largely at second-hand. Rather, he was re-imagining the citizen-subject in a far more gender and racially inclusive way. Furthermore, it was not just that the worker was no longer predominantly perceived as being male or white. At the same time, the class subject of social democracy was also being re-envisioned via a focus on educational opportunity. In short, Whitlam was re-envisioning the Australian social democratic project.

Gough Whitlam's plans for 'positive equality' lay at the heart of his government's policy agenda. Indeed he argued that pursuing policies based on 'positive equality' could bypass some of the constitutional barriers which Curtin and Chifley had encountered in their attempts to improve the social and economic circumstances of citizens – barriers which had prevented the establishment of a national health service as well as restricting government regulatory powers over the economy.[2] Whitlam knew those constitutional barriers well given that his father, Fred Whitlam, was a former Crown Solicitor and had been both a key draftsman and legal adviser for Chifley.[3] However, Whitlam argued that 'the basic ends envisaged by Chifley could be achieved by other means'.[4] There were alternative ways of achieving key aims ranging from equality of opportunity to providing necessary services and income security for those suffering hard economic times.[5]

---

2   See further Carol Johnson, 'Gough Whitlam and Labor Tradition', in *The Whitlam Legacy*, ed. Troy Bramston (Sydney: The Federation Press, 2013), 357–365.

3   Jenny Hocking, *Gough Whitlam: A Moment in History* (Melbourne: The Miegunyah Press, Melbourne University Publishing, 2008), 97, 126.

4   E G Whitlam, 'The Constitution versus Labor', Chifley Memorial Lecture, University of Melbourne, 14 August 1975, 1, accessed 9 September 2015, http://pmtranscripts.dpmc.gov.au/release/transcript-3847; see further Johnson, 'Gough Whitlam and Labor Tradition', 357–365; Carol Johnson, 'Social Harmony and Australian Labor: The Curtin and Chifley Governments' Plans for Australian Economic Development', *Australian Journal of Politics and History* 32, no. 1 (1986): 47–49.

5   Whitlam, 'The Constitution versus Labor', 4.

CHAPTER 6

In such statements, Whitlam depicted himself very much as an heir of Curtin and Chifley, albeit over two decades on. I have argued elsewhere that there were indeed key continuities and links between Whitlam's government and the governments of Curtin and Chifley in both social policy and in attitudes towards the private sector.[6] In particular, those governments all believed in humanising and reforming rather than replacing capitalism. They believed that there were common interests between workers and many sectors of business, such as local manufacturing. However, the Curtin and Chifley and Whitlam governments also had their bêtes noires in terms of business – namely the banks in the case of the Chifley government and multinationals in the case of the Whitlam government.[7]

Nonetheless, in this chapter, I add to such previous analyses by arguing that it is also important to recognise the extent to which, while building on key aspects of the Curtin and Chifley tradition, Whitlam was also expanding Labor's concept of equality. That expansion of equality went beyond the forms of, and methods of delivery of, services that would be provided. More importantly, it involved the conception of whom the citizen-subject recipient of such services would be. In that respect, Whitlam was helping to transform and expand the conception of the citizen-subject of Australian social democracy.

Whitlam argued that his programme of 'positive equality' could achieve Curtin and Chifley's 'basic ends' without needing to change the Constitution to give governments new powers to regulate and control the economy, and without needing to resort to an attempted nationalisation when those powers weren't granted (as Chifley had in

---

6   See further Carol Johnson, *The Labor Legacy: Curtin, Chifley, Whitlam, Hawke* (Sydney: Allen & Unwin, 1989).

7   See further Johnson, *The Labor Legacy*, 16, 24–27, 43–44, 55–61.

regard to the banks).⁸ Rather, Whitlam argued that 'positive equality' could be achieved by further extending the provision of government services, beyond those conceived by his Labor predecessors. For example, a Whitlam government would set up new government service providers that would compete with the private sector, thereby forcing the private sector to improve its own performance in regard to the provision of much needed, and equitable, services.⁹

Nonetheless, Whitlam emphasised that positive equality would not involve a radical 'equality of personal income'.¹⁰ The provision of government services would be used to *complement* private provision. It was therefore assumed that the private sector would still 'play the greater part in providing employment and growth'.¹¹ Indeed, Whitlam repeatedly emphasised that the Labor government required a healthy and profitable private sector in order to provide full employment and in order to provide the revenue that would finance the government's social programme.¹²

However, although Whitlam did not adequately acknowledge this, his conception of positive equality actually went much further than using other means to achieve traditional Labor ends. It went significantly beyond Curtin and Chifley's agenda in that it extended the government's policy focus to a range of groups who had not been central to the Curtin and Chifley government's own conception of equality. Those groups ranged from women to migrant groups and

---

8   Johnson, 'Social Harmony and Australian Labor', 47–49.
9   Gough Whitlam, *The Whitlam Government, 1972–1975* (Ringwood: Viking, 1985), 215.
10   Whitlam, 'The Constitution versus Labor', 5.
11   Ibid.
12   E G Whitlam, Address to the Sydney Chamber of Commerce, Sydney, 28 February 1975, 1–6, accessed 9 September 2015, http://pmtranscripts.dpmc.gov.au/sites/default/files/original/00003632.pdf.

CHAPTER 6

Indigenous Australians and reflected the influence of new social movements in Australian politics.[13] Furthermore, Whitlam was also reconceptualising the class subject of social democracy, not only in gender and ethnic terms, but also by placing even more emphasis on equality of opportunity, particularly educational opportunity. Consequently, it will be argued in what follows that Whitlam was not just adding on extra people to Labor's agenda, he was also, at least partially, reconceiving the identity of the citizen-subject whom government policies should be designed around.

Shifting the subject of social democracy

While traditional Labor ideology had emphasised some of the common interests between labour and capital, in terms of generating employment and growth for example, there had still been a significant emphasis on ensuring that workers were employed and that their wages were adequate to support themselves and their families. Indeed that was a central part of the construction of the class subject of Australian social democracy – the male working class wage earner whose interests had to be protected in order to prevent the worst forms of economic inequality. In particular, Curtin and Chifley were determined to ensure that the terrible conditions thousands of workers endured during the Great Depression never happened again. Chifley himself could 'well remember when, by their thousands, breadwinners, ill-clad and underfed, queued at factory gates seeking work'.[14]

---

13 Verity Burgmann, *Power and Protest: Movements for Change in Australian Society* (Sydney: Allen & Unwin, 1993).
14 Ben Chifley, 'No Glittering Promises', Prime Minister's Policy Speech, broadcast 14 November 1949, in *Things Worth Fighting For, Speeches by Joseph Benedict Chifley* selected and arranged by A W Stargardt (Melbourne: Melbourne University Press, 1953), 85.

Chifley talked sympathetically of shopkeepers having to close their businesses and farmers being forced to sell their land during the Great Depression.[15] However, the citizen around whom Chifley's key economic and social policy vision was primarily shaped was the male wage earner.

> The Labour government has shaped all its financial and economic measures towards maintain full employment and it will continue to shape them so.
>
> So far as it can humanly contrive, never again will the dole queues be seen in this country. Never again will competent workmen stand idle for months and years while limitless work remains to be done. Never again will young men drift hopelessly from town to town and from State to State, searching for the jobs which, in all this wide land, did not exist for them.[16]

By contrast, Whitlam was developing his policies in a very different historical period. Whitlam began from the premise that protecting working class employment and incomes was no longer the key challenge for Labor governments (no doubt partly as a result of the Long Boom and an inherent belief that Keynesian economic policy had ironed out capitalist cycles of boom and depression). Rather the key issue was government provision of community services. In an explanation of his conception of positive equality, Whitlam explained that:

> what I call positive equality … is based on this concept: increasingly a citizen's real standard of living, the health of himself and his family, his children's opportunity for education and self-improvement, his access to employment opportunities, his ability to enjoy the nation's resources for recreation and cultural

---

15 Ibid., 84.
16 Ibid., 75.

CHAPTER 6

activity, his ability to participate in the decisions and actions of the community, are determined not so much by his income but by the accessibility of the services which the community alone can provide and ensure. The quality of life depends less on the things which individuals obtain for themselves and can purchase for themselves from their personal incomes and depends more on the things which the community provides for all its members from the combined resources of the community.[17]

It was this understanding of 'positive equality' that underlay the Whitlam government's introduction of major new social initiatives such as Medibank's government-funded provision of health services; increases in pensions and benefits and increased government provision in areas such as education, housing and urban development.[18]

However, in the process Whitlam also began to reimagine the class project and class subject of Australian social democracy. It was not just that he placed an increased emphasis on the importance of blue and white-collar workers working together to create a better society.[19] More importantly, there was no longer quite the same emphasis on a key part of a Labor government's role being to provide employment (and a fair deal between labour and capital), backed up by a safety net for the wage earner and his family if he became unemployed, or was too ill or sick to work, or died. Rather the focus became even more on providing equal opportunity and a better deal between citizens

---

17 Whitlam, 'The Constitution versus Labor', 5.
18 For an overview of key social welfare reforms, see Grant Elliott and Adam Graycar, 'Social Welfare', in *From Whitlam to Fraser: Reform and Reaction in Australian Politics*, eds Allan Patience and Brian Head (Melbourne: Oxford University Press, 1979), 88–97.
19 See E G Whitlam, Speech to the National Conference of the Australian Council of Salaried and Professional Associations, Canberra, 21 October 1974, accessed 9 September 2015, http://pmtranscripts.dpmc.gov.au/sites/default/files/original/00003423.pdf.

and *state provision* (albeit with some redistributive aspects involved via taxes and government benefits and services).

Furthermore, despite the remnants of sexist language in the previous quotation, Whitlam was beginning to extend the previously gendered conception of who should be the primary citizen-subject of services, with significant implications for what form those services should take.

Women

As I have argued previously, the key citizen-subject of Australian social democracy up to and including the Curtin and Chifley governments tended to be the male wage-earner head of household, with women receiving benefits largely at second hand via their husbands, or directly if widowed.[20] Australian Labor was not alone in privileging such conceptions. The traditional focus on the male wage earner head of household was also a central part of the European social democratic tradition.[21] The citizen-subject of Curtin and Chifley's postwar reconstruction was literally conceived of and depicted as a male wage-earning head of household in speeches and pamphlets on

---

20   See eg Carol Johnson, 'Whose Consensus? Women and the ALP', *Arena* 93, (1990): 85–104; Carol Johnson 'Incorporating Gender Equality: Tensions and Synergies in the Relationship Between Feminism and Australian Social Democracy', in *Feminism, Social Liberalism and Social Democracy in the Neo-Liberal Era*, ed. Anna Yeatman, Working Papers in the Human Rights and Public Life Program, Whitlam Institute, University of Western Sydney, No 1, June 2015, accessed 9 September 2015, http://www.whitlam.org/publications/human_rights_and_public_life. I have explored the heteronormative implications of such conceptions in Carol Johnson, 'From Morality to Equality: Labor's Sexuality Conundrum' (refereed paper presented at the Australian Political Studies Association Conference, University of Sydney, September 2014), accessed 9 September 2015, http://papers.ssrn.com/sol3/papers.cfm?abstract_id=2440135.

21   For example, as Jean Quataert, amongst others, has pointed out, "European welfare-state provisions reproduced a normative gender model that reinforced the male breadwinner and female housewife/consumer model." Jean Quataert, 'Socialisms, Feminisms, and Agency: A Long View', *Journal of Modern History* 73, no. 3 (2001): 614.

CHAPTER 6

postwar reconstruction.[22] For example, although Curtin supported women being employed to fill wartime manpower shortages, he also asserted that: 'in this country where there is no great numerical disparity between the sexes most women will ultimately be absorbed in the home ... I agree that the natural urge for motherhood, husband and home is the great motivating force in a woman's life'.[23]

By contrast with his predecessors, Whitlam deplored the fact that Labor was 'a male dominated Party in a male dominated Parliament in a male dominated society'.[24] However, he argued that it was not just parliamentary underrepresentation that needed to be addressed. Rather the very definition of the political needed to be transformed to cover the needs of women and the type of government services they required. In a statement that reflected the influence of women's movement conceptions, Whitlam argued that:

> women are insisting more and more that concerns of the home be the concerns of politics, the personal be political. Child care, family planning, housework and so on are now becoming issues for the political arena. To this extent, women are in the process of trying to re-define and to re-describe, the political.[25]

---

22 See for example the housewife and children waving their (overalled) father off to work on the front cover of J B Chifley, 'Social Security and Reconstruction', Commonwealth Government Printer, c.1941, accessed 9 September 2015, digital.slv.vic.gov.au/dtl_publish/pdf/marc/38/2499355.html; See Johnson, *The Labor Legacy*, 36–37.

23 'Why this election is vital to women', Question and Answers, John Curtin and Robert Menzies interviewed by Alice Jackson, *Australian Women's Weekly*, 14 August 1943, 10.

24 E G Whitlam, 'The Emancipation of Women', Address to the YWCA Convention, University of Queensland, Brisbane, *Australian Government Digest*, 1 July 1973 – 30 September 1973, 1152.

25 E G Whitlam, Speech at the opening of the Women and Politics Conference, Canberra, 31 August 1975, 8, accessed 9 September 2015, http://pmtranscripts.dpmc.gov.au/sites/default/files/original/00003874.pdf. For the contrast with Curtin and Chifley see Johnson, *The Labor Legacy*, 20–21, 32–33.

Consequently, Whitlam did not only seek to improve the position of women by introducing a single mothers' benefit, or by his government supporting equal pay measures in the public sphere of the economy, or encouraging women to stand for parliament, or supporting anti-discrimination measures. The Whitlam government also went on to provide government support for family planning, public service maternity leave and women's centres. He emphasised that the government wished to address the concerns of all women:

> We are concerned about the problems facing all women in Australia, be they young or old, Aboriginal or newcomers, married or unmarried, English speaking or non-English speaking ... that has prompted us to fund women's refuges, women's health centres, rape crisis counselling centres, family planning centres and multi-purpose centres where the health, welfare, educational, training, workforce, legal, recreational and childcare needs of women can be met. We have removed the sales tax from the pill and for the first time in the history of Australia have recognised that supporting mothers form one of the largest groups below the poverty line and introduced a supporting mothers' benefit.[26]

So the Whitlam government developed an impressive range of both services and benefits that were designed to attempt to meet women's needs. The citizen-subject was no longer so male-defined. In particular, the Whitlam government increased the opportunities for women to be economically independent, not just by increasing pay and job opportunities but also by providing a single mother's benefit that facilitated some women being able to leave dysfunctional relationships.[27]

---

26   Whitlam, Speech at the opening of the Women and Politics Conference, 6.
27   Anna Bligh, *Through the Wall* (Sydney: HarperCollins, 2015), 45.

CHAPTER 6

Sexuality

Admittedly, while the increasing inclusion of women potentially challenged the privileging of a male head of household as the primary citizen-subject around which government policy was designed, the Whitlam government did not go on to challenge the heteronormative assumptions that also underlay such conceptions of the heterosexual household (and citizenship) unit. A few brave Whitlam government MPs did raise early issues of gay and lesbian rights and entitlements.[28] However, as Graham Willett has noted 'it is surprising that in its three full years of power' the Whitlam government 'failed to carry through any kind of homosexual law reform'.[29] Gender issues may have begun to be tackled but key issues of sexuality remained largely off the government's policy agenda, including some heterosexual issues such as abortion law reform.[30]

Regional inequality

The focus on services that *the community* could provide also saw Whitlam putting greater emphasis than his predecessors on regional inequality, an issue that is focused on in major depth in Lyndon Megarrity's chapter in this volume.[31] Whitlam was famously concerned about the lack of basic services, including sewerage, that were not

---

28   See Johnson, 'From Morality to Equality', 3–6.
29   Graham Willett, *Living Out Loud: A History of Gay and Lesbian Activism in Australia* (Sydney: Allen & Unwin, 2000), 96.
30   See eg Ann Game and Rosemary Pringle, 'Women and Class in Australia: Feminism and the Labor Government', in *Critical Essays in Australian Politics*, ed. Graeme Duncan (Melbourne: Edward Arnold, 1978), 114. Though note that a wide range of issues were raised in The Royal Commission on Human Relationships – see Michelle Arrow's chapter in this volume – and two Labor members, David McKenzie and Tony Lamb, had unsuccessfully introduced a private members' bill to decriminalise abortion in the ACT.
31   See further Lyndon Megarrity's chapter in this volume.

being adequately provided in some outer suburbs of major cities as well as being concerned with the provision of services in regional towns and rural areas.[32] In his 1972 policy speech, Whitlam had lamented that where people lived was still having a major impact on their opportunities and quality of life.

> Increasingly, a citizen's opportunities for education and self-improvement, his access to employment opportunities, his ability to enjoy the nation's resources for recreation and culture, his ability to participate in the decisions and actions of the community are determined not by his income, not by the hours he works, but by where he lives.[33]

Whitlam's initiative in regard to establishing the Department of Urban and Regional Development (DURD) was particularly important in this regard, with DURD seeing itself as having major responsibilities in regard not just to the provision of community services but also in regard to facilitating employment opportunities in regional areas, though that often proved to be difficult given the government's lack of control over private industry investment.[34] The Australian Assistance Plan, along with the related focus on regionalisation and decentralisation, was meant to encourage community involvement.[35]

---

32 For information regarding sewers, see 'Whitlam and Western Sydney', The Whitlam Institute, accessed 25 June 2015, http://www.whitlam.org/gough_whitlam/Western_Sydney.

33 Gough Whitlam, 1972 Labor Election Policy Speech, Blacktown, NSW, 13 November 1972, accessed 9 September 2015, http://electionspeeches.moadoph.gov.au/speeches/1972-gough-whitlam.

34 Johnson, *Labor Legacy*, 67.

35 Johnson, *Labor Legacy*, 66–67; see further Melanie Oppenheimer et al's chapter in this volume.

CHAPTER 6

Education and equality of opportunity

Educational opportunity was central to Whitlam's plans for positive equality and he placed far more emphasis on education than his predecessors. The Chifley government had provided some federal government support for kindergartens and universities but, as Stuart Macintyre points out, tended to avoid secondary education (partly for its religious and states' rights implications). Education in general was not central to Curtin and Chifley's plans for postwar reconstruction, although the Commonwealth Reconstruction Training scheme did facilitate vocational training for ex-service people, including at university level.[36] By contrast, Whitlam argued that providing a high quality government-funded education was central to his idea of positive equality, which had as its underpinning 'the classic liberal idea of the career open to the talents – equality of opportunity in a vastly expanded form'.[37] Indeed, Whitlam once responded to a question regarding what he understood by 'equality' by replying: 'I want every kid to have a desk, with a lamp, and his own room to study'.[38] Education therefore played a central role in Whitlam's initial programme for government. Indeed education (rather than, for example, transforming existing class or economic structures) was conceived as the 'primary instrument' for increasing equality.

> In my policy speech last November I promised that education would be the most rapidly growing sector of public spending under a Labor Government. We see it as the primary instrument

---

[36] Stuart Macintyre, *Australia's Boldest Experiment: War and Reconstruction in the 1940s* (Sydney: New South Publishing, 2015), 146–147, 213–217.

[37] Whitlam, 'The Constitution versus Labor', 5.

[38] Cited in Graham Freudenberg, *A Certain Grandeur: Gough Whitlam in Politics* (Melbourne: Sun, 1978), 82.

for improving the quality of life of our people and promoting equality of opportunity for our children.[39]

In order to ensure that full educational opportunity was achieved, the government had to tackle inequalities in education, to ensure that there were no 'elitist, regional, sectarian or other discriminatory grounds' impacting on outcomes.[40] It was a view that saw educational disadvantage as a key factor contributing to inequality.

> We are determined that education will no longer be used as a weapon to perpetuate privilege, inequality and division. We are determined that every child who embarks on his secondary education this year shall have the same opportunity as any other child of completing that education and advancing further.[41]

Significantly, the focus on 'advancing further' implied that improving equality of opportunity might also involve substantially increasing the number of children who gained professional qualifications and left their working class origins behind.

Ethnic and racial equality

Educational inequality was also seen as playing a major role in cementing patterns of ethnic disadvantage. Whitlam acknowledged the educational and other 'deprivations and disadvantages and the handicaps of migrant children in particular in a great number of inner suburbs around Sydney and Melbourne'.[42] Consequently, educational

---

39   E G Whitlam, 'The National Government's Role in Education', Speech At The Opening Of The M B Flood Science Block of St Patrick's College, Prospect Vale, Tasmania, 18 March 1973, 1, accessed 9 September 2015, http://pmtranscripts.dpmc.gov.au/sites/default/files/original/00002853.pdf.
40   Ibid., 2.
41   Ibid.
42   E G Whitlam, *Commonwealth Parliamentary Debates*, House of Representatives, 29 November 1973, 4077.

CHAPTER 6

equality had an important role to play in creating a more equal, multicultural and multiracial society.

> There is no possibility of the children of migrants in those circumstances achieving an equal opportunity in life in their new country unless the Commonwealth provides the resources to get more teachers, particularly specially trained teachers, and better accommodation and better equipment in the schools.[43]

Whitlam's support for ethnic and racial equality already indicated a shift from conceptions of equality as largely revolving around a wage earner who was not only male but predominantly white. It built on the Chifley government's support for postwar immigration, which had seen immigration move beyond the Anglo-Celtic to incorporate other Europeans, but with the significant difference that Whitlam was proud of his role in ending the White Australia policy that the Curtin and Chifley governments had still upheld.[44] Whitlam (and his immigration minister Al Grassby) also had a much less integrationist conception of the role of migrants in Australian society than the Curtin and Chifley governments, and of former immigration minister and Whitlam's predecessor as Labor leader, Arthur Calwell.[45]

---

43   Ibid.
44   See Gough Whitlam, *The Whitlam Government, 1972–75* (Ringwood: Viking, 1985), 489–493. Although Chifley in due course supported self-government for Asian countries, see eg "We must not refuse Asia the right to self-government', in Chifley, *Things Worth Fighting For*, 372–381. Nonetheless, he had made it clear that the solution to improving the standard of living of Asian people lay in improving the economic and social conditions of life in those countries, rather than in allowing people from those countries to migrate to Australia. Chifley claimed that he did not consider whites to be superior to Asians. However, he also justified the forced repatriation of Asians who had been offered sanctuary in Australia during the war. J B Chifley, 'Report to the Nation' broadcasts, reproduced in *Digest of Decisions and Announcements and Important Speeches by the Prime Minister (the Right Hon. J.B. Chifley)*, no. 144, 15 April 1949 to 12 June 1949. National Archives of Australia: B5459, 144, speech no. 38, 14–15.
45   See Macintyre, *Australia's Boldest Experiment*.

Whitlam argued that migrants should be 'able to be integrated – not assimilated – economically and socially. We do not want everybody to be the same as everybody else, but we do want everybody to fit into the community. That is the difference between assimilation and integration'.[46] It was a very different argument from Chifley's endorsement of the White Australia policy. Chifley claimed that that policy had been instituted on economic rather than racial grounds (to avoid unscrupulous employers using cheap Asian labour to drive Australian wages down). Indeed he argued that 'one of the earliest national ideals of Australia was to establish a nation of high living standards and equal opportunity for all' and the only way to do this was to prevent the potential exploitation of cheap Asian labour – a policy he claimed was instituted 'for economic, not racial' reasons.[47] Nonetheless, despite such claims, he also argued that 'this country was, and is aware, that sooner or later, trouble and misery result when people of different races, living standards, cultures and historical backgrounds, live side by side in the same community'.[48]

Whitlam's view was diametrically opposed to that position, emphasising the importance of removing any forms of racial discrimination and ensuring racial equality:

> One of the crucial ways in which we must improve our global reputation is to apply our aspirations for equality at home to our relations with the peoples of the world as a whole. Just as we have embarked on a determined campaign to restore the

---

46 Whitlam's speech at the Opening Ceremony of the Citizenship Convention, Canberra, 18 January 1966, accessed 14 Septermber 2015, http://cem.uws.edu.au/R/IY3CF5VNQ9DR939QN3SEALEF3TYHGV3GK326IIX1LENPD5HTHT-00425?func=results&set_entry=000002&set_number=000060&base=GEN01-EGW01.
47 Chifley, 'Report to the Nation' broadcasts, speech no. 38, 14.
48 Ibid.

CHAPTER 6

Australian Aborigines to their rightful place in Australian society, so we have an obligation to remove methodically from Australia's laws and practices all racially discriminatory provisions and from international activities any hint or suggestion that we favour policies, decrees or resolutions that seek to differentiate between peoples on the basis of the colour of their skin. As an island nation of predominantly European inhabitants situated on the edge of Asia, we cannot afford the stigma of racialism.[49]

(Significantly, the Whitlam government's Racial Discrimination Act was subsequently to play a major role in the first Mabo judgement, by 'underpinning native title').[50]

As already indicated, Whitlam believed that the foundation for building a racially diverse, non-discriminatory society rested on ending discrimination against, and improving the standard of living of, Indigenous Australians.

> The Labor Government has many plans and many ambitions for the Australian people. But if there is one ambition we place above all others, if there is one achievement for which I hope we will be remembered, if there is one cause for which I hope future historians will salute us, it is this: That the Government I lead removed a stain from our national honour and gave justice and equality to the Aboriginal people.[51]

Whitlam's arguments here also marked a significant departure from the Curtin and Chifley governments on indigenous issues. The

---

49 E G Whitlam, *Commonwealth Parliamentary Debates*, House of Representatives, 24 May 1973: 2649.

50 See Tim Soutphommasane, 'The Whitlam Government and the Racial Discrimination Act,' Occasional Paper, Whitlam Legacy Series, Whitlam Institute, Western Sydney University, vol. 5 (March 2016), 7, accessed 5 May 2016, https://www.whitlam.org/__data/assets/pdf_file/0011/1044785/The_Whitlam_Government_and_the_Racial_Discriminatio_Act_Whitlam_Legacy_5.pdf

51 E G Whitlam, Speech at the Opening of a National Seminar on Aboriginal Arts, ANU, Canberra, 21 May 1973, 1, accessed 9 September 2015, http://pmtranscripts.dpmc.gov.au/sites/default/files/original/00002932.pdf.

failed 1944 fourteen powers referendum had included an extension of federal jurisdiction over Aboriginal people.[52] Nonetheless as Stuart Macintyre argues, despite H C Coombs best efforts Aboriginal Australians 'were barely noticed' in plans for post-war reconstruction.[53] Indeed, Aboriginal people were often not eligible for new social security and welfare benefits that were introduced under complex, and often contradictory, policies that restricted benefits to those Aboriginal people who showed evidence that they were 'developed', in other words that they exhibited a significant degree of assimilation.[54]

In other words, citizen identity had been conceived around a white Australian norm and values and Aboriginal Australians had to demonstrate their similarity to that norm to receive benefits. By contrast Whitlam argued that it was important that indigenous people retain their own identity as well as being fully-fledged members of Australian society.

> My Government intends to restore to the Aboriginal people of Australia the power to make their own decisions about their way of life within the Australian community. We know that most Aboriginal Australians are proud of their heritage, of their long history and of the traditions and culture which have been handed down to them. We know that most of them, in all parts of Australia, want to preserve their identity as distinctive groups within an Australian society which respects and honours that identity.[55]

---

52 Macintyre, *Australia's Boldest Experiment*, 311.
53 Ibid., 473.
54 See John Murphy, 'Conditional Inclusion: Aborigines and Welfare Rights in Australia, 1900–47', *Australian Historical Studies* 44, no. 2 (2013): 223–235.
55 Whitlam, Speech at the Opening of a National Seminar on Aboriginal Arts, 1.

CHAPTER 6

Whitlam also made it clear that his government's commitment to improving the position of Aboriginal people was based on a determination to ensure 'that the long record of injustice, repression, neglect, the record that has marked our treatment of the Aboriginal people for two centuries of white civilisation on this continent, will be brought to an end'.[56] It was definitely not just an attempt to improve Australia's reputation and image overseas given that 'We regard the Aboriginals' rights and dignity as more important than the white man's reputation'.[57] The Whitlam government's programme for tackling Indigenous disadvantage met with mixed success despite a substantial increase in funding and major advances being made in areas such as land rights, including handing back land to the Gurindgi people and introducing the first land rights bill to parliament (which failed to pass before the government was dismissed but influenced subsequent Fraser government legislation).[58] Nonetheless, despite the problems encountered, the above statements by Whitlam clearly involve a further decentering of the white citizen-subject. Furthermore, Whitlam was also decentering the construction of the worker as white and Anglo-Celtic, telling the Building Workers' Industrial Conference to remember all the government had 'done for migrants, who are such a significant proportion of your membership'.[59]

In other words, here again, Whitlam wasn't just adding on extra people and issues to Labor's agenda, he was at least partially

---

56 Ibid.
57 Ibid.
58 See the analysis by Lorna Lippman, 'The Aborigines', in *From Whitlam to Fraser: Reform and Reaction in Australian Politics*, eds Allan Patience and Brian Head (Melbourne: Oxford University Press, 1979), 172–181.
59 E G Whitlam, Speech to the Annual Conference of the Building Workers' Industrial Union, Sydney, 5 August 1974, 17, accessed 9 September 2015, http://pmtranscripts.dpmc.gov.au/sites/default/files/original/00003341.pdf.

reconceiving the identity of the citizen-subject whom Labor policies should be designed around.[60] Whitlam had therefore significantly expanded conceptions of equality beyond social democracy's traditional focus on the (white, male) working class. However, what were the implications of Whitlam's conception of 'positive equality' for the advancement of traditional working class interests via industrial relations agendas?

Industrial relations

Whitlam's aforementioned support for equal pay for women, along with his recognition that 'the majority of poor people in Australia are women, including mothers – many of them single or deserted mothers', reveals that his government was concerned to ensure adequate incomes for those constructed as disadvantaged.[61] However, as problems of stagflation, with the combination of inflation and stagnation (including high rates of unemployment), began to undermine the Long Boom and the Keynesian certainties on which his government had come into office, some of his 'positive equality' arguments were increasingly used to urge wage restraint.[62]

Whitlam had been aware of rising unemployment as an issue at the time of his 1972 policy speech – but claimed that economic planning

---

60 This was also reflected in the Whitlam government's ratification of major international human rights treaties. On the implications for human rights law in Australia, see further, Michael Kirby, 'Whitlam as Internationalist,' University of Western Sydney Whitlam Lecture, 25 February 2010, accessed 5 May 2016, https://www.whitlam.org/__data/assets/pdf_file/0010/123211/SPEECH_-_WHITLAM_LECTURE_-_25_FEBRUARY_2010.pdf.

61 E G Whitlam, Speech at the International Women's Day Reception, Melbourne, 8 March 1975, 3–4, accessed 9 September 2015, http://pmtranscripts.dpmc.gov.au/sites/default/files/original/00003643.pdf.

62 See E G Whitlam, *Commonwealth Parliamentary Debates*, House of Representatives, 12 November 1974, 3631–3632.

CHAPTER 6

in cooperation with business could tackle it by achieving growth rates of 6–7 per cent.[63] He was aware that inflation was a problem but thought that establishing a Prices Justification Tribunal would be able to tackle price rises and also lead to wage restraint and better cooperation between unions and industry given that workers would feel that it was not only employees whose income was being regulated. In Whitlam's words:

> We will exert our powers against prices. We will establish a Prices Justification Tribunal not only because inflation will be the major economic problem facing Australia over the next three years but because industrial cooperation and good-will is being undermined by the conviction among employees that the price of labour alone is subject to regulation and restraint.[64]

However, as his time in office progressed, Whitlam became increasingly concerned that wage rises were outpacing price rises by excessive amounts, thereby contributing to inflation. Whitlam argued that the fact that 'average minimum award rates have risen by 55% and average earnings by 45% over the past two years – while the cost of living, as measured by the CPI, increased by 32% in the same period', indicated that there had been a redistribution 'of the national wealth in favour of the majority'.[65] Similarly he claimed that there had been a 26% rise in real income for pensioners.[66] He therefore argued that the time had now come for employees to exercise wage restraint. Whitlam emphasised the interdependence of the government and private sector in terms of the need for adequate levels of economic

---

63   Gough Whitlam, 1972 Labor Election Policy Speech.
64   Ibid.
65   E G Whitlam, Prime Minister's Curtin Memorial Lecture, ANU, Canberra, 29 October 1975, 9, accessed 9 September 2015, http://pmtranscripts.dpmc.gov.au/sites/default/files/original/00003943.pdf.
66   Ibid., 9–10.

growth to fund the government's programmes. Consequently there was a 'need to raise profitability in the private sector', and Whitlam cited his long history of supporting such a position.[67]

Increasingly, Whitlam put forward arguments designed to reduce wage claims and counter inflation, marshalling the concept of positive equality to support wage restraint.[68]

> An increased wage alone is not going to ensure that a worker's children will receive a proper education. An increased wage will not guarantee that worker's family access to high quality medical and hospital care at a reasonable cost. An increased wage will not grant him adequate transport, roads, child-care facilities, recreation outlets and the like. It will not even necessarily guarantee him proper housing, particularly if he lives in a city with rampant inflation in land prices. The provision of adequate services and opportunities of this kind must depend on broad community action; and that means government action.[69]

Whitlam went on to argue that that was precisely why his government had been directing its public spending towards ensuring that there were schools, teachers, health services, doctors and low income housing close to where people lived, especially in those suburbs where the provision of basic services had been ignored by successive conservative governments.[70]

---

67   Whitlam, Address to the Sydney Chamber of Commerce, 1.
68   See E G Whitlam, *Commonwealth Parliamentary Debates*, House of Representatives, 12 November 1974: 3362; *Special Report on Australian Labor Party Conference, Terrigal, NSW, February 3–7 1975* (Canberra: International Public Relations Pty Ltd, 1975), 5–6.
69   E G Whitlam, Address to the Second National Convention of the Industrial Relations Society, Chevron Hotel, Surfers Paradise, 29 June 1974, 8, accessed 9 September 2015, http://pmtranscripts.dpmc.gov.au/sites/default/files/original/00003308.pdf.
70   Ibid.

CHAPTER 6

In short, as he had long argued, the key to reducing inequality lay in the provision of government services rather than in providing substantial wage increases.

> Our policies and programs have been directed towards reducing and eventually eradicating inequalities in our society while at the same time maintaining a healthy pattern of efficient economic growth. At this point I would like particularly to emphasise our efforts to create a more equal society. The achievement of equality means much more than simply providing higher wages and salaries. It means providing a range of community services to satisfy the reasonable needs of all citizens and to create reasonable opportunities for all citizens. This in turn means the creation of the best community services that the country can afford. It is no coincidence that in our first 18 months in office we have concentrated so much of our efforts in the fields of education, health and urban and regional development [71]

Whitlam's conception of positive equality then, was being increasingly used as a bargaining chip to support wage restraint in an argument that actually prefigured Hawke and Keating's Accord strategy of providing a 'social wage' in partial lieu of wage increases.[72] Ironically Hawke was President of the ACTU during the period of the Whitlam government, and Whitlam argued that one of the greatest failures of his government was its failure 'to persuade unions and their advocates before the arbitration tribunals that persons on awards were benefiting more from our upgrading of community services than they ever could from increases in their paypackets'.[73] However, Whitlam did at least argue for wage indexation to keep

---

71 Whitlam, Address to the Second National Convention of the Industrial Relations Society, 7.
72 See E G Whitlam, *Commonwealth Parliamentary Debates*, House of Representatives, 12 November 1974: 3362.
73 Whitlam, *The Whitlam Government*, 743.

pace with inflation rather than, like the Hawke and Keating governments, eventually supporting real wage cuts.[74] Curtin and Chifley had also pursued industrial harmony and had been prepared to advocate wage restraint in the process however, unlike Whitlam, they did not formulate the arguments regarding community services being provided in lieu of wage increases quite as explicitly.[75]

While many of those government and community services were highly beneficial ones that substantially improved peoples' quality of life, there was also a potential downside to such arguments. The focus increasingly shifted from the Labor Party's role being to provide employment and a better deal between labour and capital, to the focus being even more on providing equal opportunity *and a better deal between citizens and state provision*. Eventually such Labor arguments were to unintentionally fuel support for neoliberal arguments that the source of exploitation of ordinary people lay not in the labour market but in government ripping off ordinary taxpayers' money in order to support so-called elite, politically correct, special interests. The focus on education also fed into accusations of elitism. It is an argument that I have termed elsewhere, the 'state based' theory of exploitation.[76]

It was also a neoliberal and socially conservative accusation that John Howard was only too happy to exploit against Paul Keating.[77]

---

74 Whitlam, Address to the Second National Convention of the Industrial Relations Society, 14.
75 Johnson, *The Labor Legacy*, 30–35.
76 Carol Johnson, *Governing Change: From Keating to Howard*, revised ed. (Perth: Australian Scholarly Network, 2007), 180.
77 See eg John Howard, Leader of the Opposition, The Role of Government: A Modern Liberal Approach, Headland Speech, Parliament House, Canberra, June 1994, accessed 5 May 2016, http://australianpolitics.com/1995/06/06/john-howard-headland-speech-role-of-govt.html; John Howard, Leader of the Opposition, Politics and Patriotism: A Reflection on the National Identity Debate, Wednesday, 13 December 1995, Grand Hyatt Hotel, Melbourne, accessed 5 May 2016, http://australianpolitics.com/1995/12/13/national-identity-howard-headland-speech.html.

Howard explicitly stated that the seeds of this development began in the Whitlam period.

> The old left-right divide ... has been increasingly replaced by differences on environmental matters as well as on so-called socially progressive issues. This process was only just beginning when the Whitlam government came to office but has gathered pace since. In recent years it has placed a particular strain on the ALP, as it has exposed sharp divisions of opinion between its traditional blue-collar worker base, often quite socially conservative, and the new, inner-urban, tertiary-educated class that inhabits the socially progressive wing of the Labor Party.[78]

Some subsequent Labor politicians at least partially endorsed Howard's depiction of a central dilemma for Labor. For example, former Rudd government Minister Lindsay Tanner also argued that there was an increasing split between suburban voters and inner-city tertiary-educated ones:

> There is a core dilemma here which there is no solution for Labor – two fairly distinct constituencies that were comfortably in alliance from Gough Whitlam's time through to the early 90s have diverged for a range of reasons and Labor's ability to hold together those very different constituencies has just got harder and harder.[79]

Conclusion

Arguments that Labor faces a split in the so-called Whitlam coalition between working class issues and progressive social movement equality issues have now become commonplace on both the left and

---

78 John Howard, 'The Architect of our Country as We Know It', Inquirer, *Weekend Australian*, 20–21 September 2014, 18. Excerpt from his book on Menzies.
79 George Megalogenis, "Tanner Breaks his Silence: Even I would have Lost my Seat to the Greens", *Australian*, 28 April 2011, 3.

the right, as the comments cited from both Howard and Tanner above indicate. However, it is disputable how much that is due to demographic change and how much it is due to subsequent Labor governments failing to adequately defend a more inclusive Labor narrative from neoliberal attacks. Significantly, Whitlam's narrative of 'positive equality' had sought to meld together a coalition of electoral interests. It had also strongly opposed arguments that supporters of more progressive issues were elitist. For example, Whitlam did not see supporting gender or racial or ethnic equality as an issue that belonged to a tertiary-educated elite. On the contrary, he emphasised that the working class included women and migrants. Indeed, they were often among the most economically disadvantaged groups in Australian society.[80] Therefore in his view, such issues were not opposed to working class issues, they were part of them. Furthermore, in his view 'behind the pragmatism of the unions there is a deep idealism which is the ultimate source of our strength' including a belief in building 'a more just and decent society'.[81] Consequently, Whitlam saw himself as extending traditional conceptions of equality in ways that were more genuinely inclusive of all Australians and would benefit traditional Labor voters. It has been argued here that, in the process, Whitlam was not just adding on extra people, he was (at least partially) reconceiving the identity of the citizen-subject whom the policies should be designed around. Nonetheless, there were potential tensions involved in a process in which community services

---

80 E G Whitlam, Speech to the ACTU Congress, Melbourne, 18 September 1975, 23, Australian Archives (NSW) CRS M 165, folder 3, also available at http://cem.uws.edu.au; Whitlam, Speech to the Building Workers' Industrial Union, 1, 15, 17.
81 Whitlam, Speech to the ACTU Congress, 23; Whitlam, Speech to the Building Workers' Industrial Union, 1–2.

CHAPTER 6

(for diverse groups) were offered in partial lieu of wage increases and in which a focus on educational equality of opportunity encouraged people to leave the working class, via upward social mobility, rather than constructing the working class as the iconic citizen-subject of social democracy.

Furthermore, the process of inclusion and incorporation was not complete. For example, there are numerous feminist critiques that note the limitations of Whitlam's policies in respect to women, as well as their genuine advances.[82] Tensions and dilemmas remained. Indeed as Australia's economic problems worsened, it is noticeable that some projected expenditures on female-related services were among the first to be cut (such as childcare); the Whitlam government had not given sufficient concern to the impacts of tariff cuts on female dominated industries such as TCF (Textiles, Clothing, Footwear); the government's NEAT (national employment and training) scheme increasingly prioritised male unemployment instead of trying to open up opportunities for women.[83] Arguably community services primarily affecting women were also considered to be less important when trying to negotiate wage restraint with a male dominated union movement.[84] The Long Boom had given rise to conceptions that continued economic growth would fund a major expansion in the government's provision of community services. By the end of Whitlam's period in office, those certainties were being sorely tested.

---

82 Game and Pringle, 'Women and Class in Australia,' 114–115, 128; Sarah Dowse, 'The Women's Movement's Fandango with the State', in *Women, Social Welfare and the State*, ed. Bettina Cass and Cora Baldock (Sydney: Allen & Unwin, 1990), 206–210; Johnson, 'Whose Consensus', 94–96.
83 Draws on Dowse, Game and Pringle. See Johnson, 'Whose Consensus', 94–95.
84 Johnson, 'Whose Consensus', 96.

In short, older agendas regarding the relationship between (male dominated) labour and capital therefore were arguably still prioritised when it came to the economic crunch given that the economic was still conceived in fairly conventional terms. Nonetheless one should not overlook the significance of the Whitlam government's attempts to reimagine the subject of Australian social democracy in more inclusive forms that went beyond the focus on the white, indeed predominantly Anglo-Celtic, male wage-earner head of household. Both Australia and the Australian Labor Party would never quite be the same again.

Chapter 7

LABOR RECONSTRUCTS

The 1940s and the 1970s

Stuart Macintyre

The reconstruction undertaken in Australia after the Second World War and the reform program pursued by the Whitlam ministry in the early 1970s stand as bookends to a quarter-century of sustained growth. The population grew in the intervening years from under 8 million to 13 million, the workforce from 3.3 million to 5.5 million, and it was employed more fully and regularly than before or since. Such were the expectations the long boom engendered that when the unemployment rate exceeded 3 per cent for the first time in the early 1960s, the government almost lost office. The annual rate of real economic growth during the 1950s and 1960s was over 5 per cent and GDP per head doubled. Partly because of wage growth and partly as the result of income transfers, there was a significant reduction in inequality. An improvement of living standards was apparent in health and education, in readier access to better housing, a much greater range of household goods, increased leisure and a marked expansion of cultural activity.

In light of this catalogue of improvement, it might be asked why it was that Gough Whitlam came to office with such comprehensive reform program. To be sure, Labor's policy in the 1972 election was not restricted to matters of production and consumption. It encompassed a reorientation of foreign policy in the light of the Coalition's failed commitment to the Vietnam War, a recognition of the greater diversity of Australian society and a corresponding attention to gender, ethnicity and Indigenous rights – indeed, it could be argued that Labor was responding to the social changes brought about by the long boom: mass immigration, the loosening of gender roles, greater sensitivity to exclusion, discrimination and neglect. The campaign slogan 'It's Time' caught the impulse for generational change.

Even so, the program that Whitlam developed as leader of the Federal Parliamentary Labor Party from 1967 paid substantial attention to questions that had exercised his predecessors, John Curtin and Ben Chifley. How was government to ensure full employment, rising living standards and economic security? The Labor government of the 1940s sought to build and broaden the domestic economy, especially the manufacturing sector, and to reduce dependence on commodity exports that were vulnerable to seasonal conditions and sharp fluctuations in world demand. Labor in the 1970s was concerned with falling productivity, an undervalued currency, a rapid increase of speculative capital inflows and growing inflationary pressures.

At the end of the Second World War Labor had to deal with a backlog of public investment in transport, energy, communications, services and amenities. The Labor government that took office in 1972 was faced with the disparity between urban growth and a lack of physical and social infrastructure – transport, schools, hospitals, even sewerage. Labor in the 1940s began to construct a system of income support for those in need, with unemployment benefits and other payments, along with plans for free medical care, medicine

CHAPTER 7

and hospital treatment and medicine (the first two legislated but frustrated by the doctors and the High Court), leading to a successful Referendum on Social Services in 1946 that confirmed the Commonwealth's power but did not resolve the impasse with the profession. By the second half of the 1960s there was growing recognition of new patterns of deprivation, so that the Whitlam government increased welfare provision and finally established a system of universal health care.

It is commonly observed that the Whitlam government placed emphasis on the quality of life. Frank Bongiorno quotes him arguing as early as 1961 that the task was not to 'ration scarcity but plan abundance'.[1] A corollary of this was his principle that welfare in conditions of affluence was 'coming to depend less on the things which individuals obtain for themselves from their personal incomes and more on the things the community provides for all its members from their combined resources'.[2] This aspect of postwar reconstruction is less commonly noted, partly because the reconstruction was undertaken in a period of austerity, but it was integral to the planning undertaken by the Ministry of Post-War Reconstruction for the integration of work and leisure, the provision of community facilities and the promotion of community as the basis of postwar life.

Finally, the Labor government of the 1940s extended the reach of the Commonwealth and transformed the public service so that it was able to exercise a policy function that encompassed both economic

---

1   E G Whitlam, 'Socialism within the Australian Constitution', Curtin Memorial Lecture, University of Western Australia, 28 February 1961; reprinted in E G Whitlam, *Labor and the Constitution* (Melbourne: Fabian Society, 1965), 56, quoted in Frank Bongiorno, 'Origins of the Present Crisis: Fabianism, Intellectuals and the Making of the Whitlam Government', in *Its Time Again: Whitlam and Modern Labor*, eds Jenny Hocking and Colleen Lewis (Melbourne: Circa, 2003), 317.

2   Whitlam, 'Socialism within the Australian Constitution', 45.

management and social administration. Whitlam also embarked on an expansion and overhaul of the public service, and made a renewed effort to redefine federal-state relations.

We know from Jenny Hocking's biography that as a young serviceman Gough Whitlam was caught up in the allure of postwar reconstruction, and campaigned strongly for a Yes vote on the reconstruction powers the Curtin government sought by referendum in 1944.[3] Since his father, the Commonwealth Crown Solicitor H F E 'Fred' Whitlam, was so centrally involved in drafting the enabling legislation, this was hardly surprising. There were many links between that era and his own. They included H C ('Nugget') Coombs, then the Director-General of the Ministry of Post-War Reconstruction, now his economic adviser; several powerful heads of government departments in 1972, including John Bunting, Lenox Hewitt and Arthur Tange, who began their careers as junior officers in that Ministry; and Fred Wheeler, then and still the vigilant guardian of Treasury's supremacy. For that matter, Whitlam had his own troubles with Labor veterans such as Eddie Ward and Arthur Calwell, the 'terrible twins' who had made Curtin's life a misery.

The influence of postwar reconstruction extended beyond these personal links. Whitlam was able to complete his law degree in 1946 with all fees paid and a living allowance as a beneficiary of the Commonwealth Reconstruction Training Scheme. He commenced his career at the bar with briefs from the Legal Service Bureau, one of an extensive range of benefits the Commonwealth government devised for the re-establishment of those who had been on war service. Like so many other young couples, he and Margaret, with two

---

3   Jenny Hocking, *Gough Whitlam: A Moment in History* (Melbourne: Miegunyah Press, 2008), 90–103.

CHAPTER 7

young children, lived with her parents while waiting to acquire their own accommodation in a period of acute housing shortage. They took advantage of a War Service home loan to buy a block of land at Cronulla and endured the scarcity of materials and labour until they were able to move into their new home at the end of 1947. They threw themselves into voluntary organisations that were established to make good the lack of community facilities on the suburban frontier.[4]

Whitlam often made reference to the project of postwar reconstruction as an example of what an effective Labor government could achieve, though his recollection was not always accurate. Take, for example, his account of the 1944 referendum when the federal government sought to extend its wartime powers for the purpose of reconstruction. He appreciated that the proposal to secure these powers had originated with a referendum bill introduced to the Commonwealth parliament in October 1942 and that the states, fearful of its likely success, undertook at the end of that year to transfer them to the Commonwealth. He knew it was apparent by early 1943 that this undertaking would not be kept, but passed over the eighteen-month delay before the federal government proceeded to a referendum.[5]

He was wildly astray in his claim that John Curtin 'sponsored' the referendum and 'argued the case with his full logic and eloquence'.[6] On the contrary, the prime minister procrastinated for as long as he was able and spoke just twice during the lead-up to the referendum in August 1944. So far from sponsoring the increase of Commonwealth

---

4   Hocking, *Gough Whitlam: A Moment in History*, 110–120.
5   E G Whitlam, 'Dragging the Chain 1897–1997', The Second Vincent Lingiari Memorial Lecture, Northern Territory University, 14 August 1997, 3, http://cem.uws.edu.au, accessed 1 November 2015.
6   E G Whitlam, 'Socialism within the Australian Constitution', 33. He repeated this statement on several occasions over following decades.

powers, Curtin allowed Herbert Evatt to formulate them and then present government's case during the referendum campaign in the well-founded expectation that this would ensure their defeat.[7]

The Cabinet's deliberation on the terms of the referendum occasioned one of the rare disagreements between John Curtin and Ben Chifley. Evatt proposed that the government ask voters to endorse the compromise that had been reached with the states in December 1942: the Commonwealth would seek the same fourteen powers they had offered for the purposes of reconstruction and for only five years. Chifley, on the other hand, argued that since the states had failed to keep their undertaking, the compromise should be set aside and the Commonwealth should seek all the powers it deemed necessary for reconstruction and on a permanent basis.[8] Curtin took a far more conservative position. When Cabinet first considered what powers should be sought, he argued that only three – those over banking, trade and commerce, and employment – were needed.[9] It suited him to back Evatt's Cabinet submission, and for good measure endorse his Attorney-General's fateful stipulation that voters must accept all fourteen powers or none of them.

If Whitlam was mistaken in his account of the 1944 referendum, he was convinced of its lasting consequences. The Australian Labor Party suffered from a federal constitution, he said in 1957, one 'framed in such a way as to make it difficult to carry out Labor objectives and interpreted in such a way as to make it impossible to carry them out'. The Chifley government had been 'competent and

---

[7] Stuart Macintyre, *Australia's Boldest Experiment: War and Reconstruction in the 1940s* (Sydney: NewSouth, 1915), 254–270.
[8] Report by Cabinet committee and minority report by Chifley, 3 December 1943, NAA: A467, SF 44/80.
[9] Cabinet minutes, 23 November 1943, NAA: A2703, 53.

CHAPTER 7

determined to carry out the Party's policies', but because of constitutional impediments it was unable to nationalise the banks, prevented from establishing a monopoly of interstate air services, frustrated in its creation of a national health service (despite winning the 1946 Referendum on Social Services to allow it to do so), and forced to pursue its housing plans through 'a makeshift arrangement' with the states.[10]

Partly as the result of his work on the Joint Parliamentary Committee on Constitutional Review from 1956 to 1959, Whitlam came to believe that Labor was mistaken in its obsession with section 92 of the Constitution ('trade, commerce and intercourse among the States ... shall be absolutely free'), which the High Court had used to reject nationalisation – indeed that it had become an excuse for policy stagnation. His attention turned to section 96 ('the Parliament may grant financial assistance to any State on such terms and conditions as the Parliament thinks fit'), which he saw as permitting public enterprise as an alternative to nationalisation.[11] He might have added that it was the Curtin government's wresting of income tax from the states that allowed section 96 to be used to such effect. But even as he decried the negative obsession with section 92 in his 1961 address on 'Socialism within the Constitution', Whitlam maintained that the opposition to the 1944 referendum had been 'spurious and selfish', the arguments false; his hopes had been 'dashed by the outcome and from that moment I determined to do all I could to modernise the Australian Constitution'.[12]

---

10   E G Whitlam, 'The Constitution versus Labor', Chifley Memorial Lecture, University of Melbourne, 19 July 1957, in *Labor and the Constitution*, 4, 7.
11   Graham Freudenberg, 'The Art of the Matter', in *The Whitlam Legacy*, ed. Troy Bramston (Sydney: Federation Press, 2013), 45; Hocking, *Gough Whitlam: A Moment in History*, 184–186.
12   Whitlam, 'Socialism within the Australian Constitution', 37.

***

There were other invocations of postwar reconstruction as Whitlam began to formulate the policies he would follow in his own term of office. A guiding principle was the need for a comprehensive plan. As early as 1961 he stated that 'The general lines of national policy should be clearly laid down and pursued by governments in trade, transport, education, housing, health, social welfare, industrial expansion and national development'.[13]

His insistence that 'these objectives can only be achieved through national planning, both economic and physical' echoed the claims of the economists, architects and engineers, as well as urban and regional planners, health officers, demographers and educationists who had seized on reconstruction during the Second World War as a chance to make good the failures of the past. 'Planning is the organisation of the resources, human and material, of the nation for the benefit of the whole community', wrote the housing reformer Oswald Burt in his exposition of *National, Regional and Local Planning* (1944), and it would eradicate the hardship, squalor and waste caused by ignorance, selfishness and lack of foresight.[14] The experts whom Whitlam enlisted to assemble his Program made similar claims for the equity and efficiency to be gained from comprehensive national arrangements.

The planning associated with postwar reconstruction had a particular valency. While it might seem a statement of the obvious, reconstruction was a product of war. The term originated during the American Civil War to describe changes to the Confederate States that would incorporate them back into the Union, and was revived

---

13 Ibid.
14 Oswald Burt, *National, Regional and Local Planning* (Melbourne: ABC, 1944), 1.

CHAPTER 7

during the First World War for measures designed to sustain morale and justify the dreadful toll of that protracted ordeal. Here reconstruction signified not simply repatriation and rehabilitation but a commitment to create a new order that would redeem the sacrifice. As Britain's Minister for Reconstruction put it, 'Reconstruction is not so much a question of rebuilding society as it was before the war, but of moulding a better world out of the social and economic conditions which have come into being during the war'.[15]

With the Armistice that pledge fell victim to those members of the British parliament Stanley Baldwin described as 'a lot of hard-faced men who look as if they have done very well out of the war'.[16] Yet the demand for reconstruction reappeared with renewed force on the outbreak of a Second World War barely twenty years after the last one, a war that was commonly attributed to the folly of the victors in imposing their selfish interests on the Treaty of Versailles, the pusillanimity of the League of Nations in the face of international aggression, the obduracy of central bankers wedded to financial orthodoxy who allowed the world economy to collapse, and the callousness of governments that denied support to the victims of long-term unemployment.

If President Roosevelt was to overcome the isolationist suspicion of foreign entanglement and bring his country into the war, he needed to reassure his compatriots that this time there would be no such failure. Hence the declaration that was issued after he met with Winston Churchill at Newfoundland's Placentia Bay in August 1941, the Atlantic Charter, in which the two leaders proclaimed the principles

---

15 Quoted in R H Tawney, 'The Abolition of Economic Controls, 1918–1921', *Economic History Review* 13, nos 1–2 (1961): 10.

16 Quoted in John Maynard Keynes, *The Economic Consequences of the Peace* (London: Macmillan, 1920), ch. 5.

on which they based their 'hopes for a better future for the world': no aggrandisement or transfer of territories without the free consent of their inhabitants; the right of all peoples to choose their form of government; equal access by all states to the resources and trade needed for prosperity; international collaboration to secure 'improved labour standards, economic advancement and social security'; and a lasting peace in which 'all the men in all the lands may live out their lives in freedom from fear and want'.[17] While the Atlantic Charter had no legal force, it exercised a powerful influence on public expectations. In Australia the beleaguered conservative prime minister Robert Menzies hailed it as confirming that 'positively good things for men and women' must emerge from the war.[18]

Moreover, the war itself imposed planning. Resources had to be redirected from civil to military purposes with controls over trade, finance, essential industries and labour, all interlinked and requiring close coordination. Menzies was slow to appreciate the magnitude of the task, but by 1941 he had recognised its implications. 'There must be no looking back to what was in many ways an unjust society', he stated, but instead a determination to build a new way of life in which all would live 'not only free from the fear of war but free from the fear of unemployment and injustice'.[19] The demands increased at the end of 1941 when fighting spread to the Pacific and a new Labor prime minister, John Curtin, introduced sweeping new measures that 'placed the full resources of the country in men and materials at the disposal of the government'.[20] Australia was not

---

17 Douglas Brinkley and David R. Facey-Crowther (eds), *The Atlantic Charter* (New York: St Martin's Press, 1994).
18 *Commonwealth Parliamentary Debates*, vol. 168, 20 August 1941: 9.
19 *Unlimited War Effort, A National Prospectus: Two Addresses by the Prime Minister* (Canberra: Government Printer, June 1941).
20 *Digest of Decisions and Announcements*, no. 18 (4–21 February 1942), 14–23.

CHAPTER 7

alone in suspending the operation of the market and imposing direct controls, for the price mechanism was regarded as too slow and risky a method of allocating resources to where they were urgently needed, but the experience that was gained in planning and directing the war economy instilled confidence the same techniques could be bent to the purpose of reconstruction.[21] Reconstruction was thus a commitment that legitimated the demands imposed by a total war, one that required all citizens to put themselves at the service of the state and accept a draconian regimen of prohibitions, rationing and shortages.

Reconstruction planning began with the creation of a division within a new Department of Labour and National Service after the federal election of 1940, when Menzies lost his parliamentary majority and needed Curtin's cooperation. Curtin had advocated reconstruction since 1939 as a means of reconciling his party to the war, and made it the centrepiece of his election policy: 'Labor visualised postwar reconstruction to be in the nature of a new social order based upon democracy and the rights of all men and women to enjoy the fruits of honest toil'.[22] The reconstruction division initiated a number of inquiries but was understaffed and hampered by a lack of cooperation from other departments. When Curtin took office in late 1941, moreover, he put the planning on hold – for he wanted no distraction from the task of national defence – and it was only at the end of 1942, when he demanded the Labor Party accept conscription for overseas service, that he bowed to the demand for a Ministry of Post-War Reconstruction with Ben Chifley as Minister.

---

21   Alan S Milward, *War, Economy and Society 1939–1945*, (Berkeley: University of California Press, 1977), ch. 4.
22   'Labour Election Policy', *Argus*, 29 August 1940.

Over the following 30 months that Ministry expanded in size and scope as reconstruction took on an irresistible momentum. Its ambitious plans encountered criticism: you could hardly move in official circles, complained an Opposition backbencher when the new department began, 'without tripping over 'professors, economists and other-cap-and gown gentlemen' who 'would not be able to run a hot-pie stall successfully'. 'It is a department of blueprints', he said later, 'of doctrinaire professors with an outlook sometimes Utopian and always idealistic, and nearly always divorced from the realities of life'. The Institute of Public Affairs warned during the 1944 Referendum on Post-War Reconstruction and Democratic Rights that a Yes vote would bring 'planning by politicians and professors, bungling bureaucracy, red tape and 'forms for everything'.[23] Menzies exploited such sentiments in his opposition to the fourteen powers, but he could hardly deny the need for reconstruction, a project he had initiated and one that had acquired such compelling legitimacy.

There is a marked contrast between this powerful momentum and the genesis of Whitlam's reform program. We know from Jenny Hocking's biography of the way he worked as a backbencher, using the parliamentary library and questions on notice to acquire information across a range of subjects; and the series of public lectures delivered from 1957 document the development of his thought about how the Commonwealth government could be used to greater effect. As deputy leader of the Parliamentary Labor Party from 1960, he had the services of John Menadue as private secretary; when he became leader in 1967 Race Mathews took over this post and extended the

---

23 *Commonwealth Parliamentary Debates*, vol. 173, 3 February 1943: 245; vol. 182, 15 May 1945: 1729; IPA leaflet, *Powers for This*, 1944, in the papers of L F Crisp, NLA, MS 5243/11/16.

CHAPTER 7

network of policy advisers. Colleagues to whom he assigned shadow portfolios contributed to policy development, as did the Party's policy committees, and the results were systematically incorporated into the Party platform.[24]

This long gestation of the Program, as Whitlam called it, culminated in the policy speech at the 1972 election, which contained no fewer than 140 undertakings. It was the culmination of a systematic process of development that allowed for modification: Whitlam initially proposed a universal health service but was persuaded of the advantages of an insurance system by Dick Scotton and John Deeble. Yet there was never any doubt as to its comprehensive design – as Hocking puts it, 'No portfolio was left untouched by Whitlam: he had ideas across every policy and from every imaginable source'. All of them were guided by his 'insights', the central axioms recorded on cards that he carried in his jacket pocket, and his exposition of their underlying principles.[25]

He was contesting a number of Labor shibboleths, and was also arguing for an expansion of the public sector at a time when the breakdown of the Bretton Woods financial system and the demands of organised labour were straining economic stability in the OECD countries. Postwar reconstruction was an international endeavour and one that inaugurated a new era of managed welfare capitalism in which governments were expected to intervene in markets and correct their outcomes in the interests of citizens. Whitlam took office as the long boom came to an end and the reconciliation of capitalism with democracy was breaking down.

---

24   Hocking, *Gough Whitlam: A Moment in History*, chs 8–11.
25   Ibid., 284.

Postwar reconstruction had the advantage that it was prepared by government, using the full resources of the public service. Whitlam was in opposition and depended on the voluntary effort of his network of policy advisers. Some were academics, some had experience of public administration, but the preparation of such detailed proposals at a remove from government presented a challenge to the powerful heads of major Commonwealth departments. Nor did the attachment of some of these advisers to the staff of the new prime minister and other ministerial offices ease the tension. Curtin and Chifley were shrewd administrators who knew how to make the public service work for them; Whitlam did not enjoy such support.

***

While Whitlam began implementing the Program at breakneck speed, reconstruction began slowly. If Curtin's reluctance to allow discussion of the postwar order to distract attention from the war effort was overcome by his need to secure the Labor Party's acceptance of conscription, he remained determined to restrict its scope. From the outset he gave repeated undertakings that his government would not use its wartime powers to introduce socialism. Nor was he anxious to extend those powers beyond the war, even though it was clear that many of them would be needed during the long and difficult conversion of the war economy back to peacetime conditions. In keeping with his procrastination, Curtin entrusted the Ministry of Post-War Reconstruction to his Treasurer and closest ally, Ben Chifley, in the expectation that Chifley would keep it on a tight rein. A frugal, cautious product of the labour movement and imbued with its values, Chifley began with a deliberately circumscribed statement

CHAPTER 7

of its objectives: full employment, rising standards of living, a modest welfare safety net. He resisted those who urged an immediate publicity campaign, and insisted the government had no interest in 'starry-eyed dreams'.[26]

But Chifley entered into a fruitful partnership with Coombs, his Director-General, and drew on the enthusiasms of policy intellectuals who shared Coombs' view that this was a unique opportunity to break with the past. Together the two men hit on the method that would guide the Ministry: the use of commissions of inquiry to gather evidence, conduct research and produce detailed reports. Whitlam would also use commissions but these ones went further: they travelled the country to hold hearings, encouraged popular participation and mobilised support. From its initial work on rural reconstruction, secondary industry, housing and public works, the Ministry moved into regional development, town planning, community facilities, education, immigration, Aboriginal welfare and substantial reform in Papua New Guinea. Chifley did not accept all of Coombs' proposals, and Treasury (to which he allocated the design of social welfare and health policy) became an increasingly obstructive brake on the work of Ministry – though Coombs had considerable success in contesting its primacy in economic policy. But Chifley played a crucial role in translating the ambitious plans of the reconstructionists into the idiom of Labor ideology and using them to extend its policy repertoire.

Compare this with the breakneck speed with which Whitlam began implementing his reform program upon winning office. It was not just the 40 decisions taken by the duumvirate even before the full ministry was established and the euphoria that surrounded this series

---

26 Broadcast, 15 May 1943, NAA: A448, 33.

of announcements. There were the appointments he made to his office, the unprecedented influence they would wield and the suspicion they aroused among senior public servants.

While Whitlam was on leave from the Air Force for the birth of his first child in early 1944, he and his father attended the summer school of the Australian Institute of Political Science in Canberra. The subject was Postwar Reconstruction, and Evatt and Menzies gave two of the addresses, but the other three speakers were Coombs, Douglas Copland and Lloyd Ross, all public servants in the wartime administration. Coombs gave a measured account of the economic objectives of reconstruction, the problems that were likely to arise after the war and the need for government to maintain controls; but he did not hide his eager anticipation that 'we have the opportunity to move consciously and intelligently towards a new economic and social system'.[27] Copland, the Prices Commissioner, was more outspoken: he said there could be no going back to an uncontrolled economy of free enterprise that brought unemployment, inequality and deprivation, and he argued (or, more accurately, his assistant Dick Downing did in preparing the address for publication) that banking, insurance, coal, transport and other strategic industries should be turned into public utilities.[28] Ross was the most evangelical in his pronouncement of obsequies for the old order.

These were public servants of a new kind, recruited as a result of the war and in order to meet the new demands it imposed on government. Copland had previously advised the Commonwealth on economic policy but from 1939 he had a key administrative post, price

---

27   H C Coombs, 'The Economic Aftermath of War', in *Post-War Reconstruction in Australia*, ed. D A S Campbell (Sydney: Australasian Publishing Company, 1944), 99.
28   D B Copland, 'The Change-over to Peace', in *Post-War Reconstruction*, 121–182.

CHAPTER 7

regulation, and performed it with very little ministerial oversight. Coombs was recruited from the Commonwealth Bank to serve as an economic consultant to the Treasury, which at that time was largely restricted to the collection of revenue and oversight of public expenditure. In 1941 he became director of the Rationing Commission, another of the wartime agencies that had to devise its procedures from scratch. Lloyd Ross was a union official (who had only recently left the Communist Party); but he was also a university graduate and former teacher for the Workers' Educational Association, and was appointed (probably at the behest of Curtin) to direct public relations for the Ministry of Post-War Reconstruction.

Ross and Coombs played a prominent role in the 1944 referendum. The government's strategy was to conduct an extended educational campaign to explain the additional powers and then a short, intensive electoral campaign after the referendum was called to persuade voters of their necessity. The Department of Information worked out the educational campaign in conjunction with the departments of the Attorney-General and Post-War Reconstruction, but Coombs and Ross were dissatisfied with the material provided by Information. They had their own department produce an extensive range of publications (including 600,000 copies of a pamphlet, *You and the Referendum*); created a network of discussion groups and provided them with speakers and materials and speakers; and obtained a special appropriation to fund a press, radio and cinema campaign. Their appearance at the summer school of the Institute of Political Science – months before the referendum legislation was even introduced to parliament – was only one of a program of public engagements that occupied the two men throughout 1944. Other officers of the Ministry appeared frequently on radio programs.

As this educational campaign gained momentum, it was hardly surprising that Menzies asked if the government still regarded Dr Coombs and Dr Ross as public servants – and Chifley's statement that the Director-General's view did not necessarily represent those of the government was tacit acknowledgement that the conventional separation of public servants from matters of public controversy was suspended.[29] They were not alone in their advocacy; Sir Robert Garran, the former head of Fred Whitlam's department, urged the expansion of powers, as did Kenneth Bailey, a future Solicitor-General who at this time was working as a consultant to the Attorney-General. But the senior officials of Post-War Reconstruction were by far the most outspoken; Coombs went so far as to engage in public debate with the head of the employers' federation. When an Opposition member asked for an explanation of the 'almost continuous broadcasts' by officers of the Department of Post-War Construction, Menzies interjected: 'It ought to be called the Post-War Propaganda Department. That is all it does.'[30]

Coombs was aware he was 'rousing considerable hostility' by 'talking in public' on such a contentious subject, though he judged it 'a risk which must be taken'.[31] The hostility was not restricted to business leaders and members of the Opposition. Arthur Calwell, the Minister for Information, chastised Coombs for exceeding his authority and another minister complained to the Party conference of the 'bright boys' who seemed to have such licence. Labor parliamentarians singled the Department of Post-War Reconstruction out

---

29 'Post-War Reconstruction', *West Australian*, 19 April 1944; 'Not Answered, Says Mr Menzies', *Argus*, 19 June 1955.
30 *Commonwealth Parliamentary Debates*, vol. 179, 21 July 1944: 362.
31 Coombs to Allen Edwards, 16 May 1944, NAA: M448, 40; see Tim Rowse, *Nugget Coombs: A Reforming Life* (Cambridge: Cambridge University Press, 2002), 331–337.

CHAPTER 7

for censure in the recriminations that followed the referendum defeat, and there was lengthy discussion of a motion from backbenchers 'That Caucus assume responsibility for Post-War planning'.[32]

Curtin's tribulations at the hands of the Caucus are well known. Before taking office he was attacked for collaborating with Menzies in the war effort and he endured stormy party meetings while prime minister; there were occasions when critics reduced him to tears. Yet Curtin was a skillful manager of Caucus and even his displays of emotion were employed to advantage. He lost no Caucus vote of major significance and his last ruling from the chair was that the motion for a Caucus committee to coordinate postwar planning was lost.[33] He had to manage rebellious ministers such as Evatt, Arthur Calwell and Eddie Ward, each one of whom caused him grief. Caucus gave him a ministry of nineteen members, many of limited ability, and it was for this reason that he assigned wide-ranging powers to the extra-parliamentary heads of commissions and directorates who dealt with crucial tasks: price control, rationing, the production of munitions and allocation of the workforce. He made the more restricted War Cabinet an effective inner ministry and relied heavily on Chifley to oversee the war economy, but remained in close contact with his colleagues and used ministerial and interdepartmental committees to coordinate their activity.

The imperturbable Chifley was less troubled by party discord. He faced a challenge in both Caucus and Cabinet over the decision

---

32 Arthur Calwell to Coombs, 31 March 1944, NAA: A9816, 1943/759, PART 3; Richard Keane quoted by Ross Gollan, 'ALP Conference Issues', *Sydney Morning Herald*, 13 December 1943; Patrick Weller (ed.), *Caucus Minutes, 1901–1949*, vol. 3 (Melbourne: MUP, 1975), 336.

33 Weller (ed.), *Caucus Minutes, 1901–1949*, 357; see Graeme Freudenberg, 'Victory to Defeat: 1941–49', in *True Believers: The Story of the Federal Parliamentary Labor Party*, eds John Faulkner and Stuart Macintyre, (Sydney: Allen & Unwin, 2001), 81–82.

to join the International Monetary Fund, but on this and all major matters his authority prevailed. Indeed, the reverence he commanded probably did him a disservice. Holding both the prime ministership and the Treasury, and often acting as Minister for External Affairs during Evatt's lengthy overseas absences, he suffered from overwork and increasing obstinacy. He badly needed colleagues who could share the load and put an alternative view – the impetuous decision in 1947 to nationalise the banks is a conspicuous example. But while the dwindling fortunes of his government caused increasing muttering in the party room, there was no questioning of his leadership.

* * *

It was otherwise with Whitlam's tenure of office. The expectations aroused by his ambitious plans were heightened by the elation of an election victory that terminated 23 years of Coalition rule. With some seats still in doubt and therefore delaying the Caucus meeting to determine the ministry, it was perhaps understandable that he made an immediate start with the interim administration of himself and his deputy, Lance Barnard. Each of the 40 decisions announced in this first fortnight was in line with the undertakings given in his policy speech, but the consequences were damaging. As Graham Freudenberg observes, 'The flurry of decisions seemed to follow no discernible order of priorities', for the measures were determined by what could be done by executive decision without parliamentary sanction.[34] The ease with which such decisions were announced disguised the problems of securing other policies that depended on

---

34 Graham Freudenberg, *A Certain Grandeur: Gough Whitlam in Politics* (Melbourne: Macmillan, 1977), 248.

CHAPTER 7

enactment by a parliament in which the government lacked control of the Senate. Moreover, such a display of personal ascendancy was bound to lead to difficulties with ambitious ministers. As one of them recalled, 'some of us … immediately started looking for ways to protect ourselves from what Gough or Lance might do'.[35]

Whitlam's extensive plans for expanding the role of the national government were not matched by consideration of how its new responsibilities were to be administered. On the eve of the election he relied on Peter Wilenski, who would become his principal private secretary, to devise a structure that expanded the number of departments to 37. Then on leave at the Australian National University to undertake research on the machinery of government, Wilenski had been a member of the public service since 1967 and warned Whitlam it was likely to resist his reforms; but the prime minister, schooled in the ethos of his father of determined public service neutrality, immediately confirmed the tenure of the heads of major departments.[36]

His colleagues, lacking any experience of ministerial office, had to establish working relations with officials accustomed to serving the Coalition. To help them do so, ministers relied heavily on their own personal staff but these intermediaries inflamed a mutual suspicion. Whitlam, who had 23 advisers, said their purpose was 'to de-politicise the public service so that the persons who are responsible for carrying out political decisions will be known to be appointed by a minister at his whim and disposable at his whim. The public service, of course will be less political if there are such

---

35 Gordon Bryant, quoted in James Walter, *The Leader: A Political Biography of Gough Whitlam* (Brisbane: University of Queensland Press, 1980), 39.
36 C J Lloyd and G S Reid, *Out of the Wilderness: The Return of Labor* (Melbourne: Cassell Australia, 1974), 62–69.

personal advisers'.[37] That claim was weakened when he subsequently appointed two members of his staff – Wilenski and Jim Spigelman – as well as a former private secretary – John Menadue – as heads of departments. There were precedents for such appointments: Evatt had selected a junior member of External Affairs, John Burton, as his private secretary and in 1947 made him secretary of the Department; but this was only the instance of preferment during the Curtin and Chifley administrations and the resentment it caused should have been heeded.

The breakdown of trust between the government and the 'mandarins', the highly influential long-standing secretaries of key departments – would prove disastrous. Chifley had commanded the absolute loyalty of Treasury but Whitlam's first two Treasurers, Frank Crean and Jim Cairns, were both ineffective. From the outset Treasury was excluded from key economic decisions and after Cabinet overturned its 1974 Budget, this powerful department effectively went on strike, refusing to brief the press, offering the government no alternative course of action and systematically providing the Opposition with damaging information.[38] Whitlam had by this time abandoned his earlier confidence in the political neutrality of the public service, but while he replaced the head of Prime Minister and Cabinet, the Treasury secretary resisted all efforts (including a threat to charge him with a breach of the Public Service Act) to move him.

There was a similar irresolution in Whitlam's dealings with his ministers. He was not helped by the Caucus decision in December 1972 that all 27 members of the ministry would sit in the Cabinet.

---

37 Quoted in Lloyd and Reid, *Out of the Wilderness*, 266.
38 Greg Whitwell, *The Treasury Line* (Sydney: Allen & Unwin, 1986), 15–16, 213–217; Freudenberg, *A Certain Grandeur*, 281–282, 307–308.

CHAPTER 7

Implementation of the Program imposed an impossible load of Cabinet business and although many submissions incorporated the relevant passage of Whitlam's election policy, there were frequent disputes over responsibility for their implementation. Ministers were required to circulate submissions to their colleagues, but there was no reciprocal requirement to give notice of objections, so those initiating the proposal were often rolled in Cabinet because they were unprepared for the criticisms of rivals. Standing committees of the Cabinet were created to give preliminary consideration to submissions, but their meetings meant that the full Cabinet began late in the afternoon, when arguments were often repeated. It was not until 1975 that Whitlam established an Expenditure Review Committee of Cabinet and required all comments on submissions to be submitted in advance.[39]

With most ministers fighting on behalf of their fiefdoms, there was little chance to consider the government's overall operation. And with no determination of priorities, the absence of any process of coordination prevented orderly decision-making – it was telling that Whitlam turned to his economic consultant, Coombs, for a review of government expenditure commitments in 1973. James Walter has suggested that Whitlam was 'a man with a vision but without a design'. It was not that he lacked knowledge in the extensive range of subjects contained in the Program, but rather the absence of an understanding of how they were to be accommodated into a coherent whole. Walter quotes Coombs' observation that Whitlam lacked 'a sense of systems – things being linked together in ways that make it impossible to change one part without changing the lot'. Coombs

---

39 Gough Whitlam, *The Whitlam Government 1972–1975* (Ringwood: Penguin Books, 1985), 690.

thought Whitlam had 'a lawyer's attitude' that the passage of a law would suffice. No one could have made that observation about Coombs' own design of postwar reconstruction.[40]

The prime minister's attempt to expedite business by restricting the length of Cabinet submissions to four pages and imposing a speaking limit of five minutes on any minister did not curb the more vehement; on the contrary, Clyde Cameron accused him of censorship.[41] Moreover, this was a Cabinet that refused to be bound by collective decision-making, so that ministers who were rebuffed took their case to the Caucus, and trumpeted their arguments to the media. Such leaking of proceedings was by no means new – Evatt had regularly beaten a path from the Cabinet room to the Canberra residences of press correspondents – but became habitual with this government.

The Cabinet reached its nadir with the consideration of the Budget in July 1974. Whitlam was by then persuaded of the need to rein in expenditure, but neither he nor his hapless Treasurer, Frank Crean, were able to convince their colleagues to accept the cuts. After this rebuff the prime minister was noticeably more truculent in his subsequent chairing of Cabinet meetings, and decided to replace some key ministers. Yet here again he was an uncomfortable executioner. He wanted Jim Cairns to take over as Treasurer but could not persuade him to do so until the end of 1974. He decided that Clyde Cameron must go but had great difficulty in saying so directly. Even the dispatch of Xavier Connor, inevitable as a result of the loans scandal, caused him great discomfort. Curtin was prone to self-doubt but

---

40   Walter, *The Leader*, 32–33.
41   Bill Hayden, *Hayden: An Autobiography* (Sydney: Angus and Robertson, 1996), 216–217, Troy Bramston, 'The Cabinet', in *The Whitlam Legacy*, ed. Troy Bramston, (Sydney: Federation Press, 2013), 102.

CHAPTER 7

no one doubted his preparedness to wield the knife, not after Eddie Ward was summarily transferred from Labour and National Service in 1943 to take charge of Transport and Territories with the prime minister's pointed observation that 'the Japs have got the territories and the Army's got the transport'.[42] Whitlam was temperamentally unfitted to 'be the bastard'. Prone to explosions of anger, he shrank from personal confrontation and took recourse in an overbearing style of personal denigration, with the result that each demotion became yet another political crisis.[43]

As the ministry fell into disarray, so did the Caucus. At the outset Whitlam decided not to chair the meetings of the parliamentary party. If his performance in opposition managing its discussion of his contentious overhaul of the Party policy had been subject to criticism, the consequences of a confrontation between Caucus and the prime minister would be far more damaging. He professed confidence in a harmonious relationship: 'Is Caucus going to embarrass a successful, positive Government? They are proud of it. They are part of it'[44] Policy committees, with whom ministers discussed their legislative proposals, facilitated this participation. But as the government's stocks fell, Caucus became more restless. It delivered a strong rebuff to the prime minister following the 1974 election by electing Cairns as deputy leader in place of Whitlam's close supporter, Lance Barnard, and went further than the Cabinet in watering down the Budget in that year. Whitlam himself asked Caucus to overturn

---

42 As recalled by his press secretary, D K Rodgers, interviewed by Mel Pratt, 29 April 1971, NLA TRC 121/14.
43 Race Mathews, 'Whitlam Re-Visited: A Personal Memoir', in *Whitlam Re-Visited: Policy Development, Policies and Outcomes*, eds Hugh Emy, Owen Hughes and Race Mathews (Sydney: Pluto Press, 1993), 9.
44 Interview with Mike Willesee, 4 June 1973, in Lloyd and Reid, *Out of the Wilderness*, 107.

a Cabinet decision to increase parliamentary salaries.[45] He enjoyed greater support as the government entered its final phase, but by then the damage was done.

*　*　*

Perhaps the most striking difference between the two periods of Labor government was the duration of one and the brevity of the other. It was by no means clear when Curtin became prime minister late in 1941 that his party would remain in office until the last month of the decade. He depended initially on the votes of two independent members of the House of Representatives who had switched their support from the Coalition, but won an overwhelming election victory in 1943, one that gave Labor control of both houses and effectively destroyed the United Australia Party. Chifley fought the following election in 1946 on reconstruction, and was returned with a smaller but still decisive majority. Whitlam began with an electoral triumph, the Opposition parties in disarray, and reckoned that he had eight years as prime minister and at least three terms for a Labor government.[46] He called a double dissolution eighteen months later, and won it narrowly, but that only intensified the Opposition's obstruction.

How might we explain these contrasting outcomes? Public opinion turned quickly against the Whitlam government, perhaps because so much was expected of it. In all State and Territory elections from 1973, with the exception of South Australia, Labor was unsuccessful;

---

45 Paul Kelly, 'Caucus Under Whitlam: 1967–75', in *True Believers*, eds Faulkner and Macintyre, 114.
46 Freudenberg, *A Certain Grandeur*, 405.

CHAPTER 7

its vote in by-elections fell dramatically. The press quickly became hostile. Rupert Murdoch had given substantial assistance to Labor in the 1972 election, with cash as well as coverage, but the relationship turned frosty when Whitlam rebuffed his attempts to be appointed High Commissioner in London. (By remarkable coincidence, Evatt had dangled that same post before Keith Murdoch in an inducement to win his support.)[47] But the press proprietors in the 1940s were no friends of Labor. 'Murdoch is a bastard', Curtin told the press gallery on the eve of the 1943 election, and Frank Packer was so confident Labor would be turned out that he arranged a dinner at a Sydney hotel to celebrate the Coalition victory.

When Whitlam looked back on the abrupt termination of his government, he saw the dismissal of his government by the Governor-General as the product of an unceasing effort by conservatives to deny its legitimacy.[48] The same theme runs through Graham Freudenberg's account of Whitlam's three years as prime minister, tempered by awareness of mistakes and misjudgements under conditions of acute stress. Whitlam believed that he had an electoral mandate to implement his Program in its entirety, a claim that members of the Opposition rejected from the outset; thus Freudenberg quotes Reg Withers, the Leader of the Opposition in the Senate, insisting in March 1973 on that chamber's right to protect 'the national interest' from 'the temporary electoral insanity' that had created a Labor majority in the House of Representatives.[49]

---

47 John Menadue, *Things You Learn Along the Way* (Melbourne: David Lovell Publishing, 1999), 107–116; Eric Walsh, 'Whitlam and the Media', in *The Whitlam Legacy*, ed. Bramston, 153–155; C E Sayers, typescript biography of Keith Murdoch, 584, NLA MS 2823/11.
48 Whitlam, *The Whitlam Government 1972–1975*, 734.
49 Freudenberg, *A Certain Grandeur*, 266.

The contest between the two chambers would extend from legislative measures to the provision of supply and create the circumstances of the dismissal. Well before that final crisis, the contest strained the conventions of Australia's federal Constitution as a Liberal and a National premier refused to follow the established practice of filling a Senate vacancy with a nominee of the same political party. The breakdown of propriety began, however, with Whitlam's audacious attempt in March 1974 to secure a majority in the Senate by enticing Vince Gair to defect from the Democratic Labor Party with appointment as Ambassador to Ireland. It was a botched expedient (as the Queensland premier issued writs for the half-Senate election before the additional vacancy was created) that gave credence to the Opposition's allegations of malpractice and emboldened it to threaten to reject the government's appropriation bill.

The wartime parliament was by no means free of such chicanery. When the Labor government secured the legislation to authorise a referendum in March 1944, it lacked a majority in the Senate (the Labor senators elected in 1943 did not take their seats until the middle of the year) and won the vote by bringing a disaffected member of the Opposition to Canberra by car. A government senator who had been lured from an earlier division to Opposition safekeeping with a bottle of whisky was this time escorted, still noticeably unsteady on his feet, by two sturdy Labor colleagues.[50] As Chifley observed, politics was a 'hard game' with two sets of rules, 'Marquis of Queensbury's and Rafferty's. I like Marquis of Queensbury's when I am fighting, but I also learned to fight

---

50   'Referendum Bill Passed by Senate', Canberra Times, 24 March 1944; Don Whitington, *Ring the Bells: A Dictionary of Australian Federal Politics* (Melbourne: Georgian House, 1956), 6.

CHAPTER 7

Rafferty's'.[51] A government did not lose its legitimacy by resorting to Rafferty's rules – so long as it was proficient in them.

In the 1940s Labor thus had the opportunity to implement much of its policy, with lasting effects. That opportunity was denied in the 1970s, despite the Whitlam government's substantial legislative record, so that the dismissal cut short a number of measures. It was followed by the erratic performance of the Fraser government, winding back many of the reforms, maintaining some, unable to find a solution to stagflation, reliant politically on exploiting Whitlam's discredited authority and impugning the record of his government. Such was the success of postwar reconstruction that its benefits came to be assumed. Such was the fate of the Whitlam experiment that the Hawke government repudiated it.

Labor's turn to neoliberalism during the 1980s sacrificed a number of Whitlam's hallmark measures, among them his abolition of university fees. The former prime minister was loath to criticise his successors, though he broke his silence as John Dawkins prepared to change the Party's policy in 1988 to allow the introduction of the Higher Education Contribution Scheme. 'It's a terrible idea', he declared.[52] Contrary to the widespread belief that Robert Menzies opened access to Australian universities, it was the Curtin government that began federal financial support of tertiary education and the Chifley government that introduced the first Commonwealth scholarships. Education was only one of the areas in which the Whitlam government completed the unfinished business of Curtin and Chifley.

---

51   Victor Courtney, *All I May Tell: A Journalist's Story* (Sydney: Shakespeare Head Press, 1956), 176.
52   Kate Legge, 'Hawke To Sell Out Students for Gold?', Melbourne *Herald*, 15 May 1988.

Chapter 8

FURNISHING THE PRIME MINISTERIAL MIND

Whitlam and the national capital

Nicholas Brown

From the age of eleven in 1928, until enrolling at the University of Sydney aged 18, Gough Whitlam walked (his family always walked) the landscape of Canberra as both a potential city and an actual practice of government. His father, H F E (Fred) Whitlam, had come from Sydney in 1927 on his appointment as Assistant Crown Solicitor, becoming Crown Solicitor in 1936. Joined by his wife, son and daughter the following year, Fred Whitlam became a prominent figure in a small, select community as his family made their home in the sparsely settled but already imprinted curlicues of the capital's better suburb. When the Whitlams arrived the population of the Federal Capital Territory was edging towards 6 000. It would exceed 8 000 by the end of the decade, as a rising tide of Commonwealth public servants followed the formal transfer of parliament from Melbourne and began marking out their own hierarchies among, or above, those building the city.

CHAPTER 8

In 1977 Graham Freudenberg observed that Gough Whitlam's early experience of Canberra 'furnished' the future prime minister's mind.[1] Whitlam himself considered his childhood in Canberra one of the major influences on his political development.[2] As he later reflected: 'whatever one thought of the place – bleak, remote, embryonic as it was in those days – one shared the excitement of seeing a city grow, literally watching a new city being planned and made'.[3] How comfortably the diverse elements of that influence sat with his later national leadership is worth closer attention. To some, such as Patrick Troy – who contributed much to shaping the Whitlam government's urban and regional development agenda from a base in the capital's Australian National University and then as deputy secretary of the department created to address those issues – the prime minister never entirely escaped 'a childlike faith in the integrity and neutrality of the bureaucracy'.[4] Others, like journalist Mungo MacCallum, recall the enthusiasm of the 'sans-culottes of Canberra' who rallied from 1969 to push forward the many fronts of change, their ranks including writers and commentators yearning to capture the all-important 'feel' of the city under Gough.[5] Others, at the time, charted the failures inherent within the impatience the new ministry brought with it into the capital's corridors, or in the obstructions they faced there.[6] How should we understand the relationship between the

---

1 Graham Freudenberg, *A Certain Grandeur* (Ringwood: Penguin, 1987), 66–67.
2 Jenny Hocking, *Whitlam: A Moment in History* (Melbourne: MUP, 2014), 48 *passim*.
3 Quoted in C J Lloyd and Patrick N Troy, *Innovation and Reaction: The Life and Death of the Federal Department of Urban and Regional Development* (Sydney: Allen and Unwin, 1981), 13.
4 Patrick Troy, interviewed by James Walter, 30 July 1977, transcript in Walter Papers, NLA MS 7846, Box 6, 8.
5 Mungo MacCallum, *The Whitlam Mob* (Melbourne: Black Inc, 2014), 2
6 F A Mediansky and J A Nockles, 'The Prime Minister's Bureaucracy', *Public Administration* 34, no. 3 (1975): 211–212.

Whitlam government, and what it aspired to, and Canberra, and all that it was taken to represent?

The Whitlam family had been part of a first-wave investment in what government from Canberra might comprise. Another wave came with the demands of war in the 1940s, and a surge of political ambition to take that wartime reformist conscience more firmly into the powers of state intervention. Whitlam senior spanned both those first infusions, the search for a distinctive identity for national government and then the frustrations that came with the constitutional hurdles to expanding that role. Another more gradual infusion came under the Menzies government into the 1960s, consolidating that power but far too cautiously for Whitlam junior, elected to the Commonwealth parliament in 1952. And then came the opportunities promised by Labor's election twenty years later.

The professional consolidation of the public service through the postwar decades, and certainly of the central agencies increasingly based in Canberra, had been based on its role in *managing* the affairs of state, of 'keeping the gates' and the balances through the competing demands of growth and prosperity. With Labor in 1972 came a different ethos of ministers *using* the bureaucracy – if possible – to force the pace in the 'creation and implementation' of policy in the name of 'positive equality', or of erecting instead another layer of enquiry or advice if necessary.[7] At the time, it was anticipated that the transition between these phases would be far from smooth: the restless ranks of Labor – charged with an agenda for change – were expected to confront officials invested in habits of patronage and control developed with a government in power since 1949. Their leader, however,

---

7   Bruce Juddery, *At the Centre: The Australian Bureaucracy in the 1970s* (Melbourne: Cheshire, 1974), 21; Mediansky and Nockles, 'The Prime Minister's Bureaucracy', 210.

CHAPTER 8

proved disinclined to act quickly on those enthusiasms, remaining a 'defender of the bureaucratic faith' even as colleagues pushed for an overhaul of personnel and systems they found obstructionist.[8] More than any other prime minister, and to a significant degree due to this personal association, Gough Whitlam drew much inspiration from the image and reality of the national capital. Equally, his government challenged the traditions, interests and capacities of its defining agencies and actors. Canberra, then, can provide its own perspective on the trajectory of 'Whitlamism' – that momentum for reform – and the Whitlam government, as it wrestled with the realities of office.

The 'crash through or crash' ethos that is often taken to define the 'Whitlam experiment' needs to take account of its ambivalence in relation to the role of Canberra. Federal instrumentalities, at once vital to what was to be achieved, were also regarded with suspicion as guardians of the past, and would become the sites of some of the most scarring controversies in political and policy practice. Conventions mattered during the Whitlam years, both as the trip-wires encountered in hasty reform but also in conditioning the relationships that had, if possible, to be maintained for the sake of order. 'As the son of a distinguished federal public servant', Weller and Smith argue, Whitlam 'valued the traditions of the service' and was slow to see the obstacles those traditions, or the defenders of them, posed to his goals.[9] Peter Wilenski, a central participant in those processes

---

8   James Walter, *The Leader: A Political Biography of Gough Whitlam* (St Lucia: QUP, 1980), 57.

9   Patrick Weller and R F I Smith, 'Inside the Inquiry: The Problems of Organising a Public Service Review' in *Reforming Australian Government: The Coombs Report and Beyond*, ed. Cameron Hazlehurst and John Nethercote (Canberra: ANU Press, 1977), 7–8, 10.

as Whitlam's private secretary, observed in 1973 that the official resources of the capital had proved 'quick to respond to the new policies of the government', but 'much slower in embracing the administrative changes necessary to carry them out'.[10] This was not a matter of simple intransigence. Canberra, as itself an 'experiment' in its planning, community and politics, was a microcosm of the challenges the government faced in addressing the political and social pressures that fed into and would define the Whitlam years. The city would prove to be a vital actor, as much as the stage, for that drama.

Canberra, of course, was not just the public service. Nor were all Commonwealth public servants in Canberra. But the synergies between the city and its defining caste had thickened through the 1960s, providing both a receptive and a resistant context for the new government. Receptive as a fresh generation of university-educated recruits began coming straight to the capital, seeking more than clerical duties, happy to adopt the city's ambitions and intrigue, and acquiring a competitive solidarity in the business of policy that stood in contrast to the resentments bred of lesser opportunities in State branch offices.[11] By the early 1970s Canberra seemed a rich seam of 'gold' to those interested in a remarkably self-defining, self-contained network of policy and politics.[12] In the lead-up to the 1972 election, Wilensky planned the administrative arrangements that would be required to support the government, and the sweep of those changes is familiar enough. First

---

10 *Sydney Morning Herald*, 13 April 1974.
11 Patrick Weller, *Australia's Mandarins: The Frank and the Fearless* (Sydney: Allen and Unwin, 2001), 54–60; P H Bailey, 'The Political Factor in Administrative Change', *Public Administration* 35, no. 1, (1976): 77; L F Crisp, 'Politics and the Australian Public Service', *Public Administration* 31, no. 4 (1972): 308.
12 David Butler, *The Canberra Model* (London: Macmillan, 1973), 4–6.

CHAPTER 8

came the creation of sixteen new Commonwealth departments and the abolition of six, and soon the establishment of 96 committees, commissions of inquiry and task forces. None of these measures – Whitlam assured at the time – would challenge the 'traditional role of the public service': they were instead to provide 'for a meeting of minds'.[13] They energised the ranks of career-minded officers with unprecedented opportunities and mobility. But resistance developed as territory was tested, and as the capital's distinctive culture adapted to such a pace of change.

From the start, Canberra had been envisaged as nurturing a distinct culture of government, just as it would come to be defined by it. The first arrivals in the 1920s were advised by those coaxing them to come that they were engaged in 'the world's biggest experiment in the systematisation of the happiness of humanity', and should behave accordingly.[14] Baptist turned Presbyterian, Whitlam senior exemplified the non-conformist, self-improving Protestant strata who disproportionately staffed Canberra's first offices, drawn by the prospect that a job in government might recognise merit and reward good works at a time when the activities of the state were acquiring higher standing. Catholics also became a relatively large group in the new city: jobs in the public service, their teachers and priests advised, might enable them to edge aside establishment bigotry, or at least compete more equally with it. Canberra thus became a distinctive experiment in careers open to talent, recognising aspirations while also seeking to rise above the mediocrity of officers too exposed to the enthusiasms of politicians, or denied (as Frederic Eggleston lamented, drawing on his experience in Victoria) inducements to develop 'the type of

---

13 Walter, *The Leader*, 56–57
14 *Canberra Community News*, 14 October 1924.

judgement or mental training which is necessary for the conduct of such huge concerns' as the modern state required.[15]

Fred Whitlam was a tireless, if tactful, advocate for this cause. He was invited to give the inaugural Garran Memorial Oration in 1959, as tribute to his mentor – Sir Robert Garran, the Commonwealth's first public servant as secretary of the Attorney-General's Department, and an early transferee to Canberra – and to his own role in crafting a higher meaning for 'public administration'. By then he felt it was at last safe to risk the proposition that the term 'bureaucracy' no longer evoked the 'continental nuisance' Thomas Carlyle had dismissed. The term, Whitlam said with some pride, recognised instead 'a public consciousness that more and more government power is concentrated in the public service'.[16]

Inevitably, such perspectives extended beyond the office. Whitlam junior noted the extent to which his father's expertise was sought in a wide range of less formal 'legal aid' advice the growing and not always settled community might seek from a sympathetic lawyer.[17] On those walks with his father, and in conservations with colleagues and politicians met along the way, Fred evoked what would be built where, eventually, and what purposes the new premises of government would serve. Fred is recalled by H C Coombs, himself a vital figure in the 1940s fusion of expertise, and in the 'experiments' of 1972–75, as 'a quiet, gentle man', but a significant presence. His wife, Martha, was more formidable in her own engagement with the fusion of family and community life that mattered in early

---

15   F W Eggleston, *State Socialism in Victoria* (London: King, 1932), 143–144.
16   H F E. Whitlam, *Sir Robert Garran and Leadership in Public Service* (Canberra: RIPA, 1959), 5.
17   Cameron Hazlehurst, 'Whitlam, Henry Frederick Ernest (1884–1961)', *Australian Dictionary of Biography, Vol. 16* (Melbourne: MUP, 2002), 541.

CHAPTER 8

Canberra.[18] The first, and so far the only, prime minister to have had such an association with the city, Gough Whitlam spoke fulsomely of the model the national capital provided for the program his government would bring to Australia, and with a personality shaped by his time there. He would recall, for example, the contrast between the solid provision of education in Canberra's one public high school – where he seemed precociously intelligent – and the shallower elitist gloss of the new Anglican grammar school to which he transferred at the age of fifteen.[19] The planned and cultivated suburban growth of Canberra through the late 1950s and 1960s might have been a sharp contrast to the paucity of provision in the south-western Sydney electorate Whitlam represented from 1952, but he had at least seen what planning could do.

None of this was forgotten. As James Walter has observed, 'Whitlam ... always deployed information as a personal resource', and perhaps this early exposure to the fashioning of roles in a protean landscape influenced this trait.[20] Equally, Whitlam's 1972 policy speech returned at several points to the theme that in Canberra, as a territory under Commonwealth control, the government 'could not avoid responsibility' for acting on issues of need, opportunity or aspiration. Why should that imperative not apply across the nation? Whitlam concluded that speech: 'We shall need the help and seek the help of the best Australians. We shall rely, of course, on Australia's great public service; but we shall welcome advice and co-operation from beyond

---

18 James Walter, 'Achievement and Shortfall in the Narcissistic Leader' in *The Leader: Psychological Essays*, eds Charles Strozier and Daniel Offer, (New York: Springer, 1985), 248–249.
19 Jenny Hocking, *Gough Whitlam: A Moment in History* (Melbourne: Miegunyah Press, 2008), 42, 55.
20 Walter, *The Leader*, 57.

the confines of Canberra'. Those linkages, that balancing, and what seemed even at the time to be the 'dangerous dichotomy' suggested between 'the confines of Canberra' and the nation at large, anticipated much of his government's course.[21]

Canberra, clearly, has never been a representative Australian community – that was precisely Whitlam's point. But it was, in a phrase echoed by Whitlam and several of his ministers before and after their election, a 'laboratory' in which the enlightened exercise of government could be tested, and then applied elsewhere. There were many dimensions to this process, often with a paradox at their core. Since being stripped of their franchise in 1909 with the creation of the Federal ('Australian' after 1938) Capital Territory, the capital's residents had wrestled with wanting the vote but also with the likely burden of shouldering the responsibilities for running a city carrying the privileges (and costs) of the national capital. Once in office, Whitlam boosted representation for Canberra in the creation in 1974 of a second House of Representatives seat and two Senate seats (first contested in 1975) for the ACT, and in moving from a partially appointed to a fully elected Legislative Assembly. But while the former initiatives brought a sequence of significant politicians (from both parties) into government, Whitlam showed little desire to give Canberrans full self-government: the place still had value as a controlled experiment. After 1972 an expanding range of government departments and statutory bodies gained an interest in aspects of that experiment the capital could be, with the effect that – as the Department of the Interior observed in 1973 – 'there is probably no place in Australia where individual viewpoints can secure such

---

21 Mediansky and Nockles, 'The Prime Minister's Bureaucracy', 211.

a wide hearing'.[22] But the proliferation of 'viewpoints', and expectations of government to represent them outside formal political processes, created tensions of their own. In a useful formulation, Graham Little made a distinction between the Whitlam 'program', developing through the 1960s and essentially constitutional, parliamentary, institutional and rationalist in its terms, and a more volatile social and institutional restlessness developing around the cusp of the government's election.[23] Canberra would prove a microcosm for these elements, and the friction between them. The capital was not the creation of the Whitlam government's principles in the way that a 'growth-centre' such as Albury-Wodonga was.[24] Nor did it become the heartland for an image (however romanticised) of the government's achievements in social transformation that Mark Peel discovered in the outer suburbs of Sydney or Melbourne.[25] But it was deeply implicated in the rise and fall of the government, and offers its own angle on the Whitlam experiment.

There are two core aspects of this role. First, there are the elements of the 'laboratory' from which Whitlam drew inspiration, including the extent to which Canberra contributed disproportionately to the drafting of 'the program' itself. And Canberra's well-educated, aspirational population certainly demonstrated the 'Whitlamism' Little noted. Second, there is the role of senior, central ranks of the 'great public service' as they grappled with that 'program' – a task only

---

22   David and Trevor Kanaley, 'The ACT Dilemma: Self-Government and Realpolitik', *Australian Quarterly* 46, no.4 (1974): 98.
23   Graham Little, 'Whitlam, Whitlamism and the Whitlam Years' in *The Whitlam Phenomenon*, Australian Fabian Society, (Ringwood: Penguin, 1986), 63.
24   Bruce Pennay, *The Experiment: Imagining the Albury-Wodonga National Growth Centre* (Albury: Albury-Wodonga Corporation, 2013), 6–10.
25   Mark Peel, *The Lowest Rung: Voices of Australian Poverty* (Melbourne: CUP, 2003), 55.

heightened by the unfamiliarity of Labor policies and structures after decades of conservative government. Fred Whitlam's sense, in 1959, of increasing acceptance that 'more government power is concentrated in the public service' was to play out for his son in unexpected ways.

Beginning with the 'laboratory', Canberra's community had developed significantly through the 1960s, largely reflecting the consolidation of the departmental transfers initiated by the Menzies government to encourage more 'direct and continuous contact' between ministers and departments, and closer attention to the latter's advice on complex policy.[26] If those transfers could do little to correct for the disconnect between ministers based in Parliament House offices and their departments – one distinct legacy of the capital's early development – it did at least consolidate the more coordinated identity for national government already noted. At the start of the sixties Canberra's population was planned to grow annually by 10–12 per cent, reaching 100 000 by the early 1970s. That process had distinct impacts on the city's demography. It was relatively younger, more affluent and better educated than the rest of Australia, and best defined – demographers advised – as 'a population of families'.[27] There were impacts, too, on its political culture. Attuned to policy if lacking self-government, Canberra's citizens acquired their own activism. Again, passages of Whitlam's 1972 policy speech map neatly over the national capital:

> increasingly, a citizen's real standard of living, the health of himself and his family, his children's opportunities for education

---

26 A W Martin, *Robert Menzies: A Life, Vol. 2* (Melbourne: MUP, 1999), 270.
27 W D Borrie, H W Arndt and G Rudduck, *Canberra; The Next Decade* (Canberra: Sociological Society, 1962), 8.

CHAPTER 8

> and self-improvement, his access to employment opportunities, ... his ability to participate in the decisions and actions of the community, are determined not by his income ... but by where he lives.

Canberrans were already adept in working with these principles. In several instances, their activism had wider influence; in many, it was representative of the emphases that shaped the Whitlam 'program'; in some, it demonstrated features of the 'cultural politics' that, as Little suggests, both enabled the 'program' and were caught up in its frustration.

The form of the city itself embodied the ethic of citizenship Whitlam described. By 1970 Canberra represented what Hugh Stretton declared to be a 'quiet revolution' in Australian urban planning. With enlightened technocracy, the all-powerful National Capital Development Commission (NCDC – established in 1957 to shape the growing city and community) was well-embarked on its y-plan model, adapting state of the art American traffic engineering to create a city of town centres as hubs around which suburbs developed as 'neighbourhood units' satisfying a series of criteria. Children should be able to walk safely from home to school in less than half an hour; schools and local amenities would be provided for all 'units' of around 4000 people; population densities within those units would recognise the overwhelming preference for detached family housing, offering social mix within a homogeneity of design reflecting both efficiency in construction and modern trends in domesticity; and units were organised around town centres in which government offices provided the core for both employment and services, enabling minimal journeys to work. Within this framework, by the late 1960s the Commission was seeking to become more consultative, given its tendency to a rather autocratic practice of 'finger-tip control'. It never quite achieved that balance, but its success in planning was such that ALP policy began to reflect on the significance of the ACT as an area in which to trial initiatives in urban planning and public participation in community affairs.

Stretton's enthusiasm for Canberra arose from a fellowship at the Australian National University in the late 1960s, at a time when the university's Research School of Social Sciences – drawing on an unmatched capacity in the Australian system to support such work – was consolidating an interdisciplinary engagement with urbanism. Since 1966 the School's Urban Research Unit had focused on the strains evident in Australian cities as a result of postwar growth which far outpaced the provision of infrastructure or the coordination of policy. Whitlam's 'program' was already attuned to these issues, but they gained focus once the Unit's Patrick Troy began to consult with Whitlam's private secretary, Race Mathews, particularly with regard to questions of spatial planning and the financial and constitutional powers required by the Commonwealth to effectively deal with the 'austerity and inconvenience' Whitlam despaired of in Australian suburbia.[28] An engineer and town planner by training, Troy, like Stretton, was among the experts making connections with the shadow ministry Whitlam assembled. The model for such contacts might have been – as Whitlam allowed – the revival of Fabian thinking in Melbourne in the 1960s, as synthesised by Matthews and building a momentum that healed 'the estrangement of the party mainstream from

---

28 See Margaret Bowman and Michelle Grattan, *Reformers: Shaping Australian Society from the 60s to the 80s* (Melbourne: Collins, 1989), 45–48; Lloyd and Troy, *Innovation and Reaction*, 17.

CHAPTER 8

intellectual influences'.[29] But Canberra began to exert a distinct kind of gravitational pull over much of that work.

That pull reflected the kind of society planning had already produced. The city, for example, had fostered an environmentalism defined by the particular proximities of a planned suburban form, a diverse human and natural landscape conditioned by concepts of amenity and recreation, and an aesthetically and scientifically literate constituency. In 1966 the foundation of the Australian Conservation Foundation (ACF) owed much to associations between Australian National University (ANU) and CSIRO scientists, and to related networks of interest and influence in the capital.[30] By 1970 the community mobilisation of the Society for Social Responsibility in Science, founded in Canberra by Peter Ellyard, drew on a more questioning model of ecological awareness which soon spread beyond the city. Ellyard's recruitment as chief of staff to Whitlam's Minister for the Environment, Moss Cass, focused his energies on national issues of environmental protection which in turn proved divisive for the ACF and testing for those seeking to manoeuvre between the wider political, specific policy and mounting social movement dimensions of those debates.[31] The poet, Judith Wright, was one of them. By 1974 she found herself consumed by 'the thousands of clubs and societies which Canberra abounds in, all of which want a nice cheap speaker' while taking any opportunities to advance causes through fleeting access to government the city

---

29 Graham Freudneberg, 'The Program' in *The Whitlam Phenomenon*, Australian Fabian Society (Ringwood: Penguin/McPhee-Gribble), 137–138; Race Mathews, interviewed by James Walter, 3 January 1983, Walter Papers, Box 6, transcript, 2.

30 Drew Hutton and Libby Connors, *A History of the Australian Environment Movement* (Cambridge: CUP, 1999), 107.

31 Ibid., 134–135.

offered.³² That skilled, articulate community rallied through the early 1970s to prevent the erection of a telecommunications tower over a bush-land reserve in the centre of the capital, but ultimately failed in the face of official obstructionism and political indifference bitterly chronicled by the leader of the campaign, retired ANU historian W K Hancock. The issues, as J M Powell has judged, might have lacked the national prominence of 'media-fuelled controversies over the Blue Mountains, Victoria's Little Desert ... [or] Lake Pedder' – perhaps in part because of the nation's 'customary resentment' for the capital itself. But, Powell adds, the campaign was a 'turning point' in its own way, testing in close proximity 'the relationships between government, bureaucracy and academia', stinging the 'status and conscience' of each, and signalling that future activism might well take a more radical form.³³

Questions of expectation and mobilisation in Canberra's 'laboratory' were also tensions of opportunity and identity. As Peter Beilharz has argued, Whitlam's positive equality rested on a number of normative assumptions (gendered, individualised, meritocratic) that were tested in the transition from the political aspirations of the 1960s to the practice of government.³⁴ The former was evident in the campaign of group of ANU based academics, extending to local networks in the law and journalism, to push for the decriminalisation of male homosexual acts. Again, the context was distinctive to Canberra: lacking

---

32 Judith Wright to Jack Blight, 22 May 1974, in *With Love and Fury: Selected Letters of Judith Wright*, eds Patricia Clarke and Meredith McKinney (Canberra: National Library of Australia, 2006), 258.

33 J M Powell, '"Signposts to Tracks": Hancock and Environmental History' in *Keith Hancock: The Legacies of an Historian*, ed. D A Low, (Melbourne: MUP, 2001), 224–225.

34 Peter Beilharz, *Transforming Labor: Labor Tradition and the Labor Decade in Australia* (Cambridge: CUP, 1994), 81–97.

CHAPTER 8

self-government, the Australian Capital Territory had no capacity to generate its own laws but plenty to push for change. By the late 1960s – as on environmental issues – it did host groups identifying with (so it seemed in retrospect) the 'last phase' of liberal reform politics, and keen to make a difference short of confrontation. In 1969 one such group mounted, as Graham Willett notes, if not the first then 'the most public attempt' to raise awareness of homosexual law reform.[35]

The prompt for their engagement was a report by the Law Council of Australia, following a review of the criminal code for all territories, including the ACT, with the prospect that the exercise might serve as an 'experiment' for national application. The Council's recommendations, and the Commonwealth's acceptance of them, declined to deal with several areas of 'controversy', including homosexuality. In response, the Homosexual Law Reform Society of the ACT was formed in a public meeting in July 1969 and soon gained national attention through coverage by major newspapers. It also attracted political support – including from Whitlam, but most prominently from Cass and Bill Hayden – if not the backing of the wider party. Yet translating this momentum into a crowded and already contentious legislative program after 1972 was, as Willett shows, another matter. In October 1973 former Liberal prime minister, John Gorton, gained House of Representative's support in a free vote for a private members bill to remove 'homosexual acts between consenting adults in private' from the criminal code, and by 1974 the ACT Legislative Assembly – still with only advisory powers – was supporting such reform. Decriminalisation ultimately came to the

---

[35] Graham Willett, '"We Blew Our Trumpets and ... ": The ACT Homosexual Law Reform Society' in *Out Here: Gay and Lesbian Perspectives VI*, eds Yocik Smaal and Graham Willett, (Clayton: Monash University Publishing, 2011), 9.

ACT in 1976, if second only to South Australia and albeit with a higher age of consent for homosexual activity.[36] And issues of liberal principle still had to be lived out in suburban 'population of families'. In the early 1970s Canberra's branch of the Campaign Against Moral Persecution conceded the limits of building the solidarity of an open social movement among those who were reluctant to 'come out' in a one-industry town.[37]

The women's movement dealt with comparable challenges, but with a surer purchase on the rising political agenda. Founded in Melbourne in 1972, the Women's Electoral Lobby soon had an active Canberra branch that hosted the WEL's first national conference in 1973 and became the centre for representations to government on issues such as divorce, abortion law reform and paid maternity leave. While other branches would question whether the Canberra group's focus on 'insider' lobbying was consistent with 'grass roots democratic structures', its influence was valued as was its role in capturing the politicians featuring on WEL's 'form guide' of electoral approval, which surveyed and ranked them in terms of their support for such issues.[38] Canberra already had a depth of local feminism – not surprisingly when gendered divisions in marriage, childcare and employment were so conspicuously entrenched in its affluent suburbia and planning principles. Susan Ryan, later a Senator representing the ACT, also recalls the stimulation of Canberra's relative 'cosmopolitanism' through the 1960s, particularly among the 'new' Labor Party members growing 'mad for Whitlam' and making

---

36   Willett, "'We Blew Our Trumpets'", 16.
37   *Camp Ink*, May 1972: 8.
38   Marian Sawer, *Making Women Count: A History of the Women's Electoral Lobby in Australia* (Sydney: UNSW Press, 2008), 8–9, 22, 33, 37, 40, 94.

CHAPTER 8

the meetings of the local ALP an 'explosive' vanguard for changes in the party more generally.[39] This fusion in itself was productive, and reflected wider trends. Chris Monnox's history of ACT Labor highlights the 'enduring fissure' emerging through the Vietnam years in particular between old-guard, local Labor stalwarts, such as the ANU's professor of political science, Fin Crisp, who sought to stamp out the 'infantile leftists' with white-collar jobs and 'lifestyle' issues.[40] Forced to a controversial preselection tussle in 1968, ACT Labor was well into Whitlamism.

Canberra's branches went from being 123rd in terms of federal enrolments in 1961 to 39th by 1967, and became a national model both in terms of the participation of women and – once free by 1973 of NSW control – in adopting a constitution giving members unprecedented representation and influence in party forums. Pressure for reform of policy on child care, abortion, rape in marriage and opposition to uranium mining emerged forcefully from these discussions, and the creation of a second parliamentary seat for the ACT in 1974 increased this voice: it was won for Labor by Ken Fry, a farmer turned public servant and later ANU graduate who embodied not the polarisation of 'blue' and 'white' collars but the transitions between them. In 1973 Elizabeth Reid, a founding member of WEL and a tutor in philosophy at the ANU, was appointed to Whitlam's prime ministerial staff as Australia's first adviser on women and children.

Reid has reflected on the strains of compromise between 'reform from within or revolution from without' she experienced in that

---

39   Susan Ryan, *Catching the Waves* (Sydney: Harper Collins, 1999), 75, 128.
40   Chris Monnox, *ACT Labor 1929–2009: A Short History* (Canberra: Ginninderra Press, 2013), 45, 67.

position until her resignation in October 1975.[41] Such disillusionment, however, should be framed by tensions within the goals sought as well as in the processes encountered. In the area of secondary education, for example, Canberra produced another prominent 'experiment' which reflected the mix of institutional and cultural politics of the time. From 1966 a parent-initiated campaign gained traction and expert backing for an 'imaginative and experimental' approach to education, which would reflect the social and cultural character of their community more effectively than derivative and under-resourced models imposed on ACT schools from New South Wales. Don Anderson, head of the ANU's recently-established Educational Research Unit, undertook an innovative survey of students that probed the ways in which their educations failed to connect with their experience or capture their aspirations.[42] These findings, too, reflected the investments being made in a model of reform attuned to aspirations as well as need.

Components of a proposed alternative model, centring on the development of a secondary college system, included greater recognition of the 'professionalism' of teachers by giving them control over curriculum, and the creation of school councils that would facilitate parent and community contributions to the setting of school priorities. The goals here were clear, but so was a sense of the problems to be addressed in the particular context of the capital. Most ACT students stayed until their final year of high school, an affluent community enhancing the value they attached to education but also exerting on them a 'greater pressure to succeed' that came with its

---

41 'The Life of Elizabeth', interview recorded 5 August 2005, accessed 12 December 2015, at http://.abc.net.au/stateline/act/content/2005/s1432182.htm.

42 Clifford Burnett, 'How the ACT Schools Authority Came Into Being', *Australian Education Review* 10 (1978): 13–17.

CHAPTER 8

own costs. The 'discernibly hierarchical' nature of a public service town and the relatively high proportion of married women in paid work were also found to be adding to a mounting pressure of expectations among Canberra's youth. If alienation were to be avoided, they needed an education more attuned to the development of a sense of individual responsibility and choice. Critics derided the 'privileges' the capital once again assumed in arguing for such a model, but this vanguard of 'post-industrial society' was increasingly troubled by the demands students felt to conform to the narratives of career, status and security driving their parents.[43]

The Commonwealth responded positively to this campaign, assuming responsibility for education in the territory in 1968 and presenting these initiatives as possible models for national reform. In July 1972 Malcolm Fraser, as Liberal Minister of Education, announced that a statutory authority would control Canberra's government schools from 1974. After its election in December, Labor accelerated this process. An Interim Schools Authority for the ACT was among the first initiatives of the incoming government, reflecting the broader prominence of education in Whitlam's program. The Authority's first report in May 1973 encouraged 'experimentation' in education and 'confident self-initiated learning'.[44] Based in Canberra – although concerned not to be seen as seeking to 'centralise' power – the Authority did not claim a lineage from the ACT model, but equally when the first of the ACT's secondary colleges opened in 1974 they were seen as the outcome of a process judged 'one of the most dramatic and important [Australian] experiments

---

43 *An Independent Education Authority for the ACT* (Canberra: ANU, 1967), 5–7, 14; *Secondary Education for Canberra* (Canberra: AGPS, 1973), 10, 12–15, 21–24.
44 Interim Committee for the Australian Schools Commission, *Schools in Australia* (Canberra: AGPS, 1973),14–15.

in educational administration'. If the Canberra initiative captured the trend of the times, it should be noted that the problem it sought to address as well as the solutions identified adapted awkwardly to the times, particularly as issues of youth alienation began to encompass steep increases in youth unemployment, again with a pronounced spike in the ACT. Points of conflict also emerged as school boards clashed with teachers and their unions over the selection of staff, and a resistance to interference in industrial rights overtook a recognition of professionalism. Participatory systems left processes of decision making uncertain as a new administration sought its feet.[45]

In each of these areas Canberra presented if not a microcosm of the tensions between the Whitlam program and Whitlamism – between a policy agenda and the accumulating political pressures surrounding it – then at least a forcing house for elements of each. The social composition of the city was part of this mix, and was replicated (if in more balanced ways) across the nation in the interests carefully targeted by the 'It's Time' campaign. Some elements were more distinct to the city, but significant for that. The alignment of academic expertise with the development of Whitlam's program, heightened in Canberra by the particular resources of the ANU, was one of these. Established in 1946 with research-only Schools, the ANU had a foundational remit and span of fields reflecting its origins in postwar 'nation building', drawing on an even earlier concept, in the case of Sir Robert Garran's advocacy, for a university that would 'afford inspiration and guidance to the national Government, Parliament and Public Service'.[46] The

---

45 Barry Price, 'Planning a New School System', *Canberra Historical Journal*, March (2004): 23–34; Grant Harman, 'The New ACT School System' *Australian Education Review* 10 (1978): 89; and Hedley Beare, 'Developments and Major Issues', *Australian Education Review* 10 (1978): 75.
46 Robert Garran, 'A National University', *Prometheus*, 1945: 3.

CHAPTER 8

1950s and 1960s had not favoured that view: one of those centrally involved in shaping the university of the 1940s, H C Coombs, lamented the diversion of the ANU from its potential as a 'powerhouse of social reconstruction'.[47] The obstacles to that contribution were not peculiar to the ANU, but they had there a distinct form and influence. As charted by Stuart Macintyre in the case of the social sciences, another 'Canberra paradox' had taken hold through the 1960s, as a university so dependent on Commonwealth funding, and whose professors had major roles on bodies funding research agendas for the nation, played safe in upholding essentially 'self-referential ... standards' and avoiding controversy.[48] Patrick Troy was not the only ANU researcher to respond to the 'less formal sort of search and deliver mechanism for ideas' Race Mathews began to develop in the late 1960s, to garner such expertise, nor to respond to opportunities for more formal association with the Whitlam government once it was elected.[49]

Another was Fred Gruen, a professor of economics at the ANU, who became in 1973 a special consultant to the Department of Prime Minister and Cabinet. Gruen recalled the 'liberating influence' of Labor's courting of expertise after the pervasive 'anti-intellectualism' of decades in which governments rejected 'outside' advice. As Gruen adds, many responding to this invitation had no prior commitment to Labor, but a desire to contribute to practical policy.[50] Determining whether the support of academics for the Whitlam government – which was especially open and noted by

---

47 Tim Rowse, *Nugget Coombs: A Reforming Life* (Cambridge: CUP, 2005), 318, 371.
48 Stuart Macintyre, *The Poor Relation: A History of the Social Sciences in Australia* (Melbourne: MUP, 2010), 109–110, 147, 150–151.
49 Race Mathews, interviewed by James Walter, 3 January 1982, transcript in Walter Papers, Box 6, transcript, 8.
50 Fred Gruen, *Australian Economics 1967–1977* (Adelaide: University of Adelaide, 1978), 7–8.

the 1974 election campaign – was a matter of party alignment, class affiliation or professional interest is a tricky matter. But the distinctions may not matter. What is striking is that the affiliation was not always easy. As Walter observes, the informalities of the networks Matthews assembled up to 1972 had to adapt to the formalities of processes in government, and this transition could seem to leave the prime minister 'playing in the middle' of information flows he could not control.[51] And if the Whitlam years saw – Macintyre judges – an 'unprecedented enlargement of government activity' in supporting research, that alignment was open to sudden reappraisal once political fortunes changed after 1975.[52] Gruen has reflected on the challenges Whitlam's corps of advisers faced in implementing ambitious but still 'unresolved' policies, especially as volatile economic and political circumstances chipped away at their fundamentally Keynesian paradigm of state intervention. In 1978 he noted wryly that the ANU had become one of the leading centres for the 'new orthodoxy' of libertarian economics, although that turn was most pronounced among those in engaged in undergraduate teaching, producing students whose paths would feed the later rise of a more market-based view of the world. Those in research positions began refashioning a more pragmatic nexus between social and economic policy that would find a measure of recognition in the return of Labor in 1983.[53] Both institutional and disciplinary settings had clearly changed.

All of these influences circled around the central focus in Canberra during the Whitlam years: the 'great public service'. By the end of

---

51   Walter, *The Leader*, 57.
52   Macintyre, *Poor Relation*, 175–176, 216–217.
53   Gruen, *Australian Economics*, 8.

CHAPTER 8

the 1960s that entity was ever more closely associated with the capital, symbolically and physically. Logistical bottlenecks had brought a temporary halt to the transfer program in 1966, following the move of the Department of Social Services; it resumed in 1968 with Supply. Transfers to Canberra might have again been postponed in 1973–74 and 1974–75, to be replaced by movement (no more welcome) to new government units located in the growth centres Whitlam had identified as spurs to decentralisation. But the capital still surged with new agencies, acronyms, programs and commitments. The public service itself was rebadged 'Australian' rather than 'Commonwealth' in 1973, and its officers no longer required to pledge allegiance to the Crown. But for all that, the inherent ambivalence of the Whitlam project in relation to the bureaucracy remained – and has endured as a standard theme in most accounts of the government. As noted, conflict had been anticipated if Labor gained power, and Canberra observers kept a vigil for the first signs of trouble. Those in the party and beyond expecting heads to roll were initially disappointed. Sir Frederick Wheeler, for example, as Secretary of the Treasury, seemed to the weekly *Canberra Survey* in early 1973 to have secured 'the resurgence of Treasury' for a government keen to reassess the costs of old-style protectionism.[54] It would soon prove not policy that was the problem so much as processes.

The first wave of appointments of advisers to ministerial staffs generated resentment from departments used to unmediated influence on ministers, deepening the 'distaste' with which senior officials were said to regard their new charges. This view was compounded by the announcement that the salary differentials for heads

---

54   *Canberra Survey*, 26 January 1973.

of departments, which once marked the hierarchy and rivalry between them, was going. All would have the same pay, in part to make it possible to move them around a more integrated Canberra network – a prospect which did little to abate entrenched territoriality.[55] If the prime minister had been at first reluctant to interfere with the bureaucracy, practices began to have that effect anyway.[56] As Patrick Weller records, over Whitlam's three years 'the majority of department secretaries were shifted', some left without a position when departments were abolished, some were sent overseas.[57] The convention that the public service had a 'virtual monopoly … on the formulation and coordination of policy' collapsed, and by April 1973 an entrenched 'anti-mandarin' sentiment in Labor Caucus was requiring active management by the prime minister for the sake of stability. The *Canberra Times*' Bruce Juddery gained prominence in reporting what was going on inside departments, instigating a genre that spread to other newspapers. 'Too few public servants realise', he advised, 'that the new administration is willing to risk a few failures, if that is the price for rapid success'.[58] This was not how business had been done in Canberra up to this point.

Coupled to those changes, however, was a determination that the public service should provide its own laboratory for improving the conditions of the Australian workforce. A 35 hour week, four weeks annual leave, equal pay for women and maternity and paternity leave were among the precedents it set 1973. Some commentators decried

---

55 *Canberra Survey*, 2 February 1973.
56 Michael Sexton, *The Great Crash: The Short Life and Sudden Death of the Whitlam Government* (Melbourne: Scribe, 2005), 299.
57 Patrick Weller, *Australia's Mandarins: The Frank and Fearless* (Sydney: Allen and Unwin, 2001), 25–26.
58 Colin Hughes, 'Australian Political Chronicle: The Commonwealth', *Australian Journal of Politics and History* 19, no. 2 (1973): 244.

CHAPTER 8

these provisions as rash and inflationary, and questioned whether the privileged should also be the first beneficiaries of reform.[59] Others, however, argued that there was little point in increasing the policy demands to be made of the bureaucracy, of creating new departments in response to new agenda, even of improving the conditions within departments, if there was no corresponding review of the structures and assumptions guiding the ways in which work was done. The public service, it was argued, would need to model the cultural change required not just in policy but practice.[60]

In June 1974, after extensive discussion across government, the Royal Commission on Australian Government Administration was established as a (perhaps belated) recognition of the scale of the challenges the government faced. Chaired by H C. Coombs, its terms of reference were broad, covering relations between departments and ministers, program evaluation, coordination and centralisation of policy and the management of personnel. It was, arguably, a relatively late addition to a series of such inquiries – such as the 1968 Fulton Committee in the United Kingdom – into the challenges public administrators faced in addressing the demands of specialisation, professionalisation and the pressure of new systems, technologies and expectations. Coombs' approach to such questions was distinctly of its time. The Commission gave priority to issues of participation and adaptability: the public service must be defined more as the manager of services to communities rather than an adviser to ministers on what services should be provided; it should take as guide in such provision the priority of efficiency in face-to-face delivery and an ethos of

---

59 Hughes, 'Australian Political Chronicle', *Australian Journal of Politics and History* 19, no. 3 (1973): 403.
60 P H Bailey, 'The Political Factor in Administrative Change', *Public Administration* 35, no. 1 (1976): 79.

social participation; and – fundamentally – it needed to become less a 'self-contained elite group exercising influence in the interests of the status quo' and more engaged with offering 'stimulation and innovation'.[61]

With these emphases, 'Canberra' was a distinct problem for the commissioners. They appreciated the 'lively and consistent' interest their hearings generated in the city (not matched elsewhere), but this in itself underscored a realisation that Canberra was a world unto itself. Running through their report was the refrain that 'one can justifiably talk of "two services"': a 'Canberra' service, with markedly high levels of education, mobility, engagement, remuneration and recognition, and the 'non-Canberra' elements, who largely existed for those in the centre in an essentially indistinct, under-resourced, unappreciated 'regional' space.[62] Despite the inevitable trend towards centralisation in a modern bureaucracy, Coombs' report reflected at length on the 'isolation' of the capital:

> The concentration in Canberra of the central sources of authority, the separation of the point of decision from that of first or personal contact, the concentration of lines of responsibility and accountability exclusively towards ministers rather than also towards the public, and organisational weaknesses encouraging an apparent unresponsiveness among officials in contact with members of the community, all contribute to this dichotomy and to the inwardlooking character of the administration, especially in its most senior levels. The strong preference for promotion from within, despite modifications in recent years, which exists within key departments and with the administration as a

---

61 'Summary of Major Themes' in *Reforming Australian Government: The Coombs Report and Beyond*, ed. Cameron Hazlehurst and John Nethercote (Canberra: ANU Press, 1977), 177–181.
62 *Report of the Commission on Australian Government Administration* (Canberra: AGPS, 1976), 148.

CHAPTER 8

whole, undoubtedly strengthens this cultural and intellectual inbreeding.[63]

The judgement was hard, but still seemed to some critics not to go far enough. The report amply demonstrated what Peter Bailey, one of its commissioners, described as the 'diminishing capacity' of ministers to direct administrative practice and the 'breakdown between actual practice and outworn theory'. But how to change entrenched attitudes?[64] There was, for example, the concern of one experienced public servant that recommendations relating to open advertisements for jobs in Canberra tended only to accentuate the insularity of the capital as the place to be, rather than encouraging recognition of the experience 'non-Canberra' officers had to offer in transfers.[65] There was also – political scientists added – an insufficient sense of the history that had produced the problem in the first place, given the role the Canberra bureaucracy had once been allocated as being above and better than the states. Coombs' report was not delivered until 1976, by which time questions of accountability in government were beginning to assume a different tone under the austerities of the Fraser government.

Yet even as Coombs took evidence, tensions in Canberra intensified. Savvy correspondents such as McCallum, writing for *Nation Review*, predicted that 'the inertia or sheer bastardry ... of the public service would continue as it has for so many years – except that this

---

63   Ibid., 23
64   Peter Bailey, 'A Challenge to Change' in *Reforming Australian Government: The Coombs Report and Beyond*, ed. Cameron Hazlehurst and John Nethercote (Canberra: ANU Press, 1977), 29.
65   K L Jennings, 'The Coombs Inquiry: Reactions of a Former Commonwealth Public Servant', *Public Administration* 35, no.4 (1976): 341.

time it doesn't have the tacit approval of the government'.[66] By March 1975 Whitlam was showing his impatience with criticisms of his government's centralism and 'bloated bureaucracy'. 'Bureaucracies of course are always bloated', he sarcastically parried, and 'unfeeling'.[67] But strains, and confusions of role, were undeniable. The Coombs report took particular aim at the control Treasury sought to exercise over finance and economic policy, narrowing the possibilities for reform. That identification became emblematic of the breakdown in relations between 'the great public service' and the government.

Sir Frederick Wheeler, recalled as 'a master of guerrilla warfare in the bureaucracy', morphed steadily from the touchstone of continuity in impartial administration to – according to his critics – exemplify the 'relentless dedication to minutiae of government procedures' that frustrated the Whitlam program.[68] As Chairman of the Public Service Board through the 1960s, Wheeler had been instrumental in tactically engineering the reform of the service towards a more progressive, independent, professional and merit-based institution: the status of a public service career rose greatly under his stewardship. He had also, as Ian Hancock shows, exercised considerable influence over the 'style' that defined those at its most senior levels.[69] Appointed to Treasury in 1971, he took it as his task to ensure that whatever 'risks' the Whitlam government might take on assuming office did not violate the 'due process' fundamental to good government.

---

66   *Nation Review*, 10 April 1974.
67   E G Whitlam, 'People and Power – Community Participation in Government', *Australian Quarterly* 47, no. 2 (1975): 37.
68   Sexton, *The Great Crash*, 65.
69   Ian Hancock, 'Sir Frederick Wheeler: Public Servant' in *The Seven Dwarfs and the Age of the Mandarins*, ed. Samuel Furphy (Canberra: ANU Press, 2015), 196.

CHAPTER 8

Around Whitlam, as Wheeler later reflected, there had clustered an 'ebullient community ... in which groups claim the right to push and act on the basis of self-interest, often using whatever power is to hand'.[70] That 'community' perhaps extended to the new infusions into the public service itself, who appeared to him not to respect their vocation. Treasury clashed with some of the boldest architects of the Whitlam program, especially in the new Department of Urban and Regional Development, which argued it needed resources ranging from higher salary scales to greater executive responsibility if it was to achieve goals that were set beyond the usual parameters of a Commonwealth department.[71] All such pressures, Wheeler judged, needed careful watching. In late 1974 his attention to propriety brought him into open conflict with the prime minister over the 'loans affair' and, again in mid-1975, the fund raising activities of his minister, Jim Cairns. By then, Whitlam's distrust of Wheeler led to his open admission that he wanted him gone from the Treasury, and the Public Service Board concede that a range of fundamental principles in bureaucratic practice were in need of urgent review and repair.[72] In these tests of wills, discretion and loyalties, the conventions that defined core business in the capital were coming under unprecedented strain. Revealingly, one of Wheeler's bitterest responses arose from the 'local smell' he detected among peers who did not abide by the sense of propriety among themselves he had long cultivated: in December 1974 he confided 'I've never seen a worse example of a lack of trust and lack

---

70 F H Wheeler, 'The Professional Career Public Service', *Australian Journal of Public Administration* 39, no. 2 (1980): 179.
71 Lloyd and Troy, *Innovation and Reaction*, 74.
72 Public Service Board, *Annual Report*: 7–8, 1975.

of confidence and lack of openness between civil service colleagues in Canberra'.[73]

Such erosion of relationships *within* the 'great public service', and not only in its relationship to government, was striking, and awaits a full account. That account is likely to add another dimension to our understanding of the strains internal to the Whitlam project as well as the obstacles placed in its way. Canberra put many of those strains into sharp focus. It was equally to be profoundly changed by them. Becoming NCDC Commissioner in 1974, Tony Powell noted that the organisation's staff had doubled in recent years, in large part because Canberra functioned as being a 'practical expression of the ideology of the Whitlam government'. Powell brought in a new breed of management consultants to reign in ideals for the capital, given clear signs of a 'levelling out' in development, and a marked 'falling-off' in private sector investment. The causes included the mounting signs of economic uncertainty, and a questioning of the capacity of the government to continue driving the growth of the city. They were coupled, however, to new ideas of what government itself should look it.[74] Among the early acts of the Fraser government, after its election in December 1975, was to pre-empt the findings of the Coombs Report by tasking Sir Henry Bland to report on 'Commonwealth activities that might be curtailed or terminated without significant effect on administration'. Bland was one of those permanent heads who had eschewed transfer to the capital – he distrusted its insularity. The staff ceilings that were imposed on the public service over coming years had a particular impact on Canberra, where commentators

---

73 J. Selby, note for file, 20 December 1974, NAA A571, 1974/96, Part 3: my thanks to Ian Hancock for this reference.
74 Tony Powell, interviewed by Margaret Park, 19 October 2005, NLA TRC 5532, 8.

CHAPTER 8

began observing a 'serious decline' in morale and 'uncertainties to a degree unimaginable a few years ago'.[75] Through the Fraser years the reality and symbolism of Canberra changed in decisive ways. In 1976 Tony Staley, as Minister for the Capital Territory, urged Canberra's 'normalisation' – the end of its privileges: more diversification, less planning, 'more grime' – as he put it – along with 'more crime and pollution'.[76] Whether that process resolved the insularity that worried Coombs is debatable: public service accountability would come to be defined in ways he hadn't anticipated. The city that furnished one prime ministerial mind generated little affection or spurred little imagination among Whitlam's successors. That the next incarnation of the capital was to be in terms of hosting 'economic rationalism' marks the scale of its transformation not simply as site of political change, but as an historical agent in it.

---

75 Administrative Chronicle, *Australian Journal of Public Administration* 35, no 4 (1976): 348–349.
76 Phillip Grundy, Bill Oakes, Lynne Reeder and Roger Wettenhall, *Reluctant Democrats* (Canberra: FCP, 1996), 89.

Chapter 9

WHITLAM'S TRANSFORMATION OF THE PRIME MINISTERIAL OFFICE, ITS PRECURSORS AND ALL THAT FOLLOWED

James Walter

There have been two varieties of development that have influenced the transformation of the prime ministerial office in Australia, the way we understand it, and its capacity to drive policy processes. The first is incremental change; the second is significant innovation by a particular administration or leader that adds to executive capacities. Incremental change can be briefly registered: here the focus will be on significant innovation. It is argued that there were three innovative historical moments, all of them within 'the short twentieth century', and the third of which – initiated by the Whitlam government – capitalised on and brought to fruition the potentials of earlier innovation. These three were Stanley Bruce's resort to and early institutionalisation of expert advice; John Curtin and Ben Chifley's augmentation and recalibration of the public service

CHAPTER 9

and of executive capacity during war and postwar reconstruction; and Gough Whitlam's transformation of the prime ministerial office itself. The Whitlam reforms drew on those earlier innovations – particularly the spirit of Curtin's and Chifley's ambitions for a postwar new social order.

After each such moment, a new administrative regime becomes routinized, and there is a return to incremental refinement and elaboration. But there has been no further such innovation since the Whitlam period: the functioning of the prime ministerial office as we understand it now has been essentially a product of that reform moment. Arguably, every successor prime minister has benefitted from the opportunities for policy ambition and executive intervention afforded by Whitlam's transformation of the prime ministerial office. It is a foundational event in understanding what has happened since 1975, especially the achievement of substantial economic reform in which the prime ministerial office (PMO) played a significant part between the 1980s and 2001. What, then, have been the benefits, the costs and the unintended consequences of that transformation? And does the relative absence of subsequent reform indicate that under Whitlam the inherent potential of the office was finally realised? Or does it instead signify a loss of political imagination as we have watched a series of recent prime ministers flounder in the role, each trapped within an unaccountable inner circle? What is suggested here is that Whitlam augmented the resources of the core executive by introducing private office staff with the intention of expanding options, establishing that ideas were contestable and fostering robust policy debate. At its best, this was what later occurred in periods of productive reform. The unintended consequence was that this initiative could also allow leaders to withdraw into a closed inner-circle of loyalists who hindered adequate reality testing, preventing optimum decisions being reached.

The incremental strand

In the first decade after Federation, prime ministers had only two sources of support – a private secretary, and a small administrative cohort initially within External Affairs and then after 1911, in the newly created Prime Minister's Department (PMD).[1] The PMD, oriented at first simply to organising the prime minister's affairs and correspondence, can be regarded as an incremental development. The first secretaries of PMD, Malcolm Shepherd and Percy Deane, began in the federal public service as private secretaries to the early prime ministers: indeed, Shepherd's ambition was said to have been influential in Andrew Fisher's decision to establish the department. While the duties of PMD initially were modest, with World War I its role (and staffing) expanded. One initiative Billy Hughes took during Word War I was his appointment of a press secretary, Lloyd Dumas (of the *Argus*), who assisted him in the 1916 conscription campaign, and accompanied him to the Imperial Conference of 1918, where he was responsible for the published statements and press releases attributed to Hughes. In 1918, Hughes carried this innovation further, inviting a prominent journalist, Bertie Cook, to establish the first federal press bureau in the PMD.[2] Scullin apart, subsequent prime ministers followed Hughes' initiative in appointing press secretaries, some of them with notable influence: Cecil Edwards

---

1   Patrick Weller, Joanne Scott and Bronwyn Stevens, *From Postbox to Powerhouse: A Centenary History of the Department of Prime Minister and Cabinet* (Sydney: Allen & Unwin, 2011), 5–7.
2   James Walter, *The Ministers' Minders: Personal Advisers in National Government*, (Melbourne: Oxford University Press, 1986), 41.

CHAPTER 9

with Stanley Bruce (later his biographer); Irvine Douglas and Dick Dawson with Joe Lyons (and later with Robert Menzies); and – the most effective of them all – Don Rodgers with John Curtin and Ben Chifley.[3] Attention to managing publicity and public relations had become part of the leadership repertoire. But press secretaries, too, often served as political antennae and sounding boards: there were no specifically political appointees in the prime minister's office until 1973.

During and after World War I, PMD became the instrument for Billy Hughes impulsive, wide-ranging and all-encompassing ambitions, 'a maelstrom' according the then Governor-General, Sir Ronald Munro Ferguson, 'into which business from all departments is sucked and continues to swirl round and round, seldom getting back again into ordinary channels, where presumably it might be carried further'.[4] The department's responsibilities became increasingly miscellaneous, driven by Hughes' pet projects, the acquisition of functions that had no obvious home, and the propensity of those initial secretaries, Shepherd and Deane not to differentiate between departmental and party political issues.

Stanley Bruce determined to set this to rights: he did not trust Deane (who had been close to Hughes), and he stripped back the department's functions to a more ordered, limited core while re-allocating roles amongst other federal departments: PMD was, he said, 'really a clearing house'. According to the *Argus*, it had 'developed into a departmental octopus and it was impossible for any administrator to keep in close touch with all its multifarious branches'.[5]

---

3   Ibid., 42.
4   Quoted in Weller, Scott and Stevens, *From Postbox to Powerhouse*, 13.
5   Ibid, 8–21; quotations cited on 20, 21.

Bruce finally removed Deane by appointing him to the Department of Home Affairs in 1928. Subsequent departmental secretaries between 1929 and 1949, John McLaren, John Starling and Frank Strahan, were far more conventional products of the public service of their day. They had joined the service on leaving school and worked their way up through the ranks. Following Bruce's expectations, they would consolidate the administrative role of the department.

Despite the fact that PMD became larger, with responsibility for co-ordinating a number of outlier agencies, with the exception of Scullin (who sought its policy input), prime ministers following Bruce would regard it largely as a postbox and mechanism to deal with protocol[6] – until a transformation envisaged by Nugget Coombs in the Department of Post-War Reconstruction and instituted by Allen Brown in late 1949 took effect. Despite its origins in Ben Chifley's 'official family' that transformation would principally benefit Robert Menzies. A much enhanced PMD would play its role in the successes of the Menzies government but would also become acclimatised to his approach. It is telling that the chapter devoted to senior Commonwealth officials in departmental secretary (1959–1966) John Bunting's affectionate memoir is titled 'The boys'.[7] Menzies grew so accustomed to the senior officers in PMD that they in turn became a sort of official family to him. In consequence, the PM's personal office remained attenuated, with a private secretary seconded from PMD, a personal secretary, a press secretary, some typists/stenographers and two Cabinet room attendants.[8] There were no political appointees

---

6   Ibid., 25–29.
7   Sir John Bunting, *R.G. Menzies: A Portrait* (Sydney: Allen & Unwin, 1988).
8   Sir William Heseltine, 'I did but see him passing by'. *The Second Menzies Lecture* (University of London: Sir Robert Menzies Centre for Australian Studies, 1989), 2–3.

CHAPTER 9

(though Menzies consulted closely with his politically attuned press secretaries such as Hugh Dash and Tony Eggleton).

Innovations

Stanley Bruce was the catalyst for an innovation that expanded the range of the prime minister: the outreach to expert advisers. Conscious of the limitations of a bureaucracy staffed by those who had entered the service on leaving school and achieved promotion through seniority, and seeking knowledge not available to him through those channels, he pioneered the incorporation of the 'new liberal' intelligentsia into policy deliberation. It was Bruce's interest during the 1920s in 'scientific' business methods that precipitated his introduction of economic inquiries, commissions and bureaus of economic research staffed by economists, establishing the liaison between political power and the nascent economics profession.[9] Subsequently, the Tariff Report of 1929, issuing from an inquiry whose members included a stockbroker, E C Dyason, academic economists D B Copland and L F Giblin, government economist J B Brigden and Commonwealth statistician C H Wickens, established what would become the norm for membership of such inquiries later in the century.[10] It was a practice that would last, and these figures would reappear. As the next war approached, they were again mobilised to advise Robert Menzies, and later John Curtin and Ben Chifley.

World War II not only brought the national bureaucratic machine to fruition, but provided the platform for support that would become

---

9   William Coleman, Selwyn Cornish and A J Hagger, *Giblin's Platoon: The Trials and Triumphs of the Economist in Australian Public Life* (Canberra: ANU E Press, 2006), 59.

10 Stephen Alomes, 'Intellectuals as Publicists 1920s to 1940s,' in *Intellectual Movements and Australian Society*, eds B Head and J Walter , (Melbourne: Oxford University Press, Melbourne, 1988), 78.

taken-for-granted by postwar prime ministers. It was a product not only of an expanded public service, but also the determined mobilisation by Curtin and Chifley of the cognoscenti.[11] An appreciation of the demands of war management (and its command economy) and the realisation that the promise of a new order in the future would compensate for the sacrifices of the present impelled their establishment of new agencies and wide-ranging recruitment of those whose knowledge was essential to these purposes. Experienced technical and business leaders not usually associated with Labor joined; 'every economist of note ... [was] seconded to work in the various departments and agencies that directed the war effort';[12] key agency figures were given direct access to Curtin and Chifley and there was a proliferation of 'brains trusts' in the Department of Post-War Reconstruction (PWR).[13]

The augmentation in the range and quality of advice saw Curtin and Chifley the best resourced and supported prime ministers since Federation. Many of the personnel recruited in these novel circumstances would go on to play a significant part in the postwar Australian Public Service (APS). At a more personal level, since Curtin had relied on Frederick Shedden (Secretary of the War Cabinet) and Chifley utilized his Treasury officials for advice, these developments saw no immediate augmentation of the PMD, though it had, since late in Joseph Lyons' term (1931–1939) had a more direct

---

11   Sol Encel, *Equality and Authority: A Study of Class, Status and Power in Australia* (Melbourne: Cheshire, 1970), 66; Stuart Macintyre, *Australia's Boldest Experiment: War and Reconstruction in the 1940s* (Sydney: NewSouth, 2015).

12   Stuart Macintyre, *The Poor Relation* (Melbourne: Melbourne University Press, 2010), 32.

13   H C Coombs, *Trial Balance: Issues of My Working Life* (Melbourne: Sun Books, 1983), 1–75; Macintyre, *Australia's Boldest Experiment*, passim.; Tim Rowse, *Nugget Coombs: A Reforming Life* (Melbourne: Cambridge University Press, 2002), 154–165.

CHAPTER 9

relation with Cabinet (PMD secretary, Strahan, by then having taken over the Cabinet records). But the networks that had been established around Curtin and Chifley provided a template for a more general mode of distributed leadership that could be a platform for future prime ministers. It was this that Coombs argued for in urging that the accumulated expertise of the economic policy unit of PWR be transferred to PMD in 1949, and that, steered by Brown, would shape the department that supported Menzies when he took office later that year.

The Whitlam transformation

Gough Whitlam's record as leader of the ALP between 1967 and 1972 stands as one of the most outstanding instances of opposition parliamentary leadership in the twentieth century.[14] Through argument, provocation and intervention he transformed the Labor Party; through effective performance in the house he not only challenged government but also came to dominate policy debate; and through initiative and persistent pursuit of policy relevant knowledge he rewrote the party's platform and created a program for government.[15] He did none of these things alone, but was the catalyst and driver for them all. It was in pursuit of policy relevant knowledge that the foundations for change of the prime ministerial office (PMO) itself once he assumed power can be seen.

---

14 His only peers in their capacity as party leaders to transform their party and bring it back into contention from dire circumstances, are John Curtin (ALP) between 1935 and 1941, and Robert Menzies (Liberal Party) between 1943 and 1949.

15 See Graham Freudenberg, *A Certain Grandeur: Gough Whitlam in Politics* (Sydney: Macmillan, 1977), chapters 5–15; Jenny Hocking, *Gough Whitlam: A Moment in History* (Melbourne: The Miegunyah Press, 2008), chapters 11–14; James Walter, *The Leader: A Political Biography of Gough Whitlam* (Brisbane: University of Queensland Press, 1980), 29–36.

Whitlam had some grounds for his claim to be the 'author' of nearly all of the program he brought to government in 1972. He was much influenced by the spirit of social reform promoted by Curtin and Chifley in the 1940s, and his conviction that the limits they had finally encountered must be overcome. The development of comprehensive detail as he pursued the ideas for contemporary reform had initially been his alone, a product of observation, constant enquiry, his own research, and above all his extraordinary use of parliamentary questions to draw from government itself and the Commonwealth bureaucracy the information needed for what became 'the Program'. His forte was in developing grand schemes from irksome details, and he would later assert that 'the party platform is studded with things I was the first to suggest'.[16] But as the demands of party leadership grew, he would rely more and more on others, and key staff would orchestrate the advice and expertise of specialists in areas of policy interest.

The first of these was John Menadue, his secretary between 1960 and 1967, who gives a good account of the development of networks of outside advice integral to policy development.[17] Menadue was succeeded by Race Mathews. As Graham Freudenberg confirmed:

> In the development of policy prior to 1972, the input of the staff was enormous, particularly in the case of Race Mathews, and before Race, Menadue. Specifics of the health insurance, or medibank scheme ... were worked up very much by Race Mathews. He also contributed greatly to the specifics of the urban program. But the drive came from Whitlam.[18]

---

16 Quoted in Walter, *The Leader*, 31.
17 John Menadue, *Things You Learn Along the Way*, (Melbourne: David Lovell, 1999), 63–67.
18 Graham Freudenberg, quoted in Walter, *The Leader*, 32.

CHAPTER 9

Pat Troy, called in to consult on urban planning, remarked that one generally worked through Mathews as the intermediary: 'You have to be aware of the importance of men like Race ... who did the groundwork and built up the contacts needed to facilitate Whitlam's ideas'.[19] Staffers and advisers alike were drawn to Whitlam because it was where the action was: one spoke of it as like being 'near a huge generator of power', and Mathews recalled it as 'probably the most useful five years I'll ever spend'.[20]

One of those drawn, like the others, into Whitlam's orbit because it was a means of attaching his own ambitions to a larger cause, was Peter Wilenski: 'I was very conscious of this idea of a great reform government ... and I thought he was the sort of fellow who would lead a great reform government, and I was quite happy to be associated with [that]'.[21] Wilenski, then a public servant on temporary leave at ANU, was approached first by one of Whitlam's advisers, Dick Hall: 'Whitlam didn't really choose me. In general, his own staff choose their own staff ... his staff were chosen by their predecessors'.[22] Hall instigated a meeting six months before the 1972 election, in which Whitlam asked Wilenski for papers on three things: a reorganisation of the public service; a draft administrative arrangements order for the new ministry, and the organisation of the prime minister's personal staff. Wilenski undertook to prepare these on the condition that they would be delivered only if Whitlam won government. When he did, Wilenski became his initial principal private secretary, and started the roll-out of these plans: the focus here is on those that related to PMO.[23]

---

19 Pat Troy, quoted, ibid., 32.
20 J. Walter, interview with Race Mathews, 3 January, 1982.
21 J. Walter, interview with Peter Wilenski, 20 July, 1977.
22 Ibid.
23 See Jenny Hocking, *Gough Whitlam: His Time* (Melbourne: The Miegunyah Press, 2012), 34–37.

The elaboration of the PMO was part of a more general augmentation of ministerial personal staff. This was later complemented by the initiation of inquiries and outsourcing to consultants.[24] The objective was to retain the broad advisory networks developed in opposition by the Whitlam team. The careers of many of those in senior APS positions originated in the initiatives of Curtin, Chifley and Coombs, and Whitlam emphasised the link by appointing Coombs his personal adviser on economics and the arts (and later, in 1974, as Chair of a Royal Commission on Australian Government Administration). Even so, it was suspected that those who had become Menzies' 'boys'[25] were now habituated to the Coalition's world view, and would not readily adapt to Whitlam's ambitious reform agenda. The intention was that the APS would remain a key source for policy advice, but that advice would now be contestable. The initial plan was that the PMO would manage government priorities, coordination across portfolios and differentiation of political demands from policy objectives. Within a year, however, it was evident that the PMO was too small to handle such a complex brief.[26] It was decided instead to strengthen the policy and coordination capacities of the Department of Prime Minister and Cabinet (PM&C).[27] Arguably PMO influence declined thereafter. Wilenski himself rated it only a 'modest' success

---

24 Michael Howard, 'A Growth Industry? Use of Consultants Reported by Commonwealth Departments 1974–1994,' *Canberra Bulletin of Public Administration* 80 (1996): 62–74.
25 On Menzies' 'boys', see Bunting, *Menzies: A Portrait*, chapter 6.
26 Peter Wilenski, 'Ministers, Public Servants and Public Policy,' *Australian Quarterly* 51, no. 2 (1979): 37–38.
27 The title of the Prime Minister's Department (PMD) had been changed when John Gorton (then Liberal Prime Minister) first split off the Cabinet Office from PMD in 1968, and then again when Gorton's successor, William McMahon re-united those elements in the newly titled Department of Prime Minister and Cabinet (PM&C) in 1971.

CHAPTER 9

relative to initial aspirations. A study commissioned by the Royal Commission on Australian Government Administration concluded: 'The work done by ministerial advisers varies considerably, but their part in the policy process has been essentially limited and confined.'[28]

There are four reasons, however, to question that conclusion. First, it was undeniable that from that point on prime ministers were better resourced in the information game than their colleagues, and hence had increased capacity, if they chose, to control their Cabinet and the government. Second, it provided a means by which a politically engaged group with strong network ties could be drawn into the parliamentary political process. As one commentator remarked,

> when I walked into Parliament House earlier this year [1973], I would have known half the personal staffs who had already arrived through nothing more conspiratorial than a left-liberal history in the local Labor Party, the Sydney and NSW Fabian Societies, the anti-Vietnam movement ... It was as though part of a whole generation had marched through Kings' Hall and filtered through to the various ministers' offices.[29]

These networks allowed advisers to reach out into the party, academia, the media and the community in a way never open to the APS, and this outreach activity was to remain an important potential of the private office under future prime ministers. Third, these network activists were immediately to hand in a way that traditional public servants could not match, and soon the effect was noticed. At the very least, the public service was gingered up, forced to argue for and justify its case in an unprecedented way, its inner working opened up to scrutiny and challenge. As early as 1974 it was evident

---

28 R F I Smith, 'Ministerial Advisers: The Experience of the Whitlam Government,' *Australian Journal of Public Administration* 36 (1977): 157–158.
29 John Edwards, quoted in Walter, *The Ministers' Minders*, 54.

that Treasury sensed the erosion of its influence over economic decision-making:

> Treasury's up to the minute submissions have had to meet the view of ministerial advisers who ... have been overwhelmingly hostile witnesses. There is a feeling within the Treasury that the balance has been rather lop-sided: that ministerial advisers get to make comments to ministers entering cabinet, but that the Treasury does not get anything like a fair chance to reply.[30]

Being the agent at the principal's side was no small advantage; thus, as Clyde Cameron, one of Whitlam's ministers remarked:

> at the prime ministerial level ... staffers regard themselves as being more powerful than ministers or private members of parliament. Indeed, they almost invariably do have more influence with their prime minister than do the ministers ... in all cases, the staff can, and do, influence a minister's relations with his peers and senior public servants. This is crucial in the case of the prime minister.[31]

Fourth, even if initial degrees of PMO influence were debatable at the time, it would become clear over the next 40 years that the reforms under Whitlam were the catalyst for a remarkable elevation of the role of the PMO within the core executive.

Building on the Whitlam initiative

Malcolm Fraser, Liberal Party leader from March 1975, also developed an advisory group while in opposition, the nucleus of which he would carry into government at the end of that year. While initially he accepted the advice of PM&C that ministerial staff should be cut back, the PMO itself was not reduced from the level it had reached

---

30 Robert Haupt, 'Treasury Opts Out', *Australian Financial Review*, 27 August 1974.
31 Correspondence with the author, quoted in Walter, *The Ministers' Minders*, 57.

CHAPTER 9

under Whitlam. As the only minister to retain an extensive staff, he enjoyed an even greater measure of policy dominance over his colleagues than had Whitlam. It was a resource that suited Fraser's intensely task oriented, controlling administrative style.[32] Nonetheless, the office was initially set up in a conventional manner: at first there was no attempt to make the office a policy dynamo as had been attempted under Whitlam. Fraser worked closely with PM&C on policy and coordination. Indeed, in 1978, following a less than successful attempt (urged by the Liberal Party secretariat) to make the PMO more politically attuned that led to administrative deficiencies, a career public servant was appointed to the position of chief executive: bureaucratic dominance was briefly restored.

It was not to last. Dissatisfied with the lack of political support provided by his office during the 1980 election campaign, Fraser turned again to the staff that had helped him win power. David Kemp, an academic who had served Fraser as a senior adviser in 1975–76 was brought back to head the office. Key staff were paid on a consultancy basis, with the intention that bringing their salary to near equivalence with permanent heads would signal their importance and status. The Director of the PMO was now the apex of the whole ministerial staff structure, the point of direction and coordination. By 1981, Fraser's PMO exceeded that of Whitlam numerically (23 compared with 21 in 1974) and its senior officers were paid substantially more.[33] The PMO was a body of senior status and impressive credentials. It had been accepted that any advice entailed certain values and assumptions, that the values of the APS might not complement those of the government, and that it was necessary to have a capacity

---

32 Patrick Weller, *Malcolm Fraser: PM*, (Melbourne: Penguin, 1989).
33 See Walter, *The Ministers' Minders*, 83–84.

for evaluation shared by those who shared the government's aims and philosophy. The intention was not to compete with the APS in developing policy, but to bring technical competence and political sensitivity to bear on what was being proposed, thus ensuring that policy development was harnessed to the government's purposes. It was a refinement of what Whitlam and Wilenski had aimed at, and now with the resources to make a difference. It was a decided extension to the prime minister's directive and controlling capacities.

The Hawke ALP government elected in 1983 introduced measures to reduce the ad hoc approach to ministerial staffing that had prevailed when Whitlam's initiative was first introduced, and to bring a level of formality to the processes adopted by Fraser. It sought to avoid 'cronyism' and to ensure candidates of calibre were appointed, and in opposition had commissioned a consultancy report on the appropriate roles of ministerial staff, which was circulated to shadow ministers. It was made clear that *all* staff appointments would be subject to Hawke's approval, and that ministerial autonomy on staffing would be circumscribed, with the PM reserving the right to terminate appointments. In government, Hawke instituted a Ministerial Staff Advisory panel to vet appointments (1983), involving advice from some of those who had first worked on the Whitlam initiative (including Peter Wilenski and Terry Moran). In 1984, legislation to regulate the basis on which staff were employed and to provide protection for public servants working in ministerial offices, the Members of Parliament (Staff) Act (MOPS), was passed. These processes had their flaws,[34] but they did much to defuse the sort of criticisms that had been levelled at Whitlam and at Fraser. In effect they placed

---

34   Ibid., 91–93.

the prime minister (and hence the PMO) at the end of the line as arbiter, reinforcing the centrality of the PMO in the relationship between the executive and the bureaucracy.

The actions of the Fraser and Hawke governments constituted a fine-tuning of the staffing innovation initiated by the Whitlam government. They enhanced the potential of ministerial staff to influence policy, and introduced a level of due process to their appointment and allocation. Above all, by making the PMO the apex of the system, they gave successor prime ministers an enhanced potential to dominate executive deliberation and the direction of policy travel. To date, there have been no further process innovations. Instead, what has happened in the following decades has depended primarily on the preferences and personal style of prime ministers and those they have appointed to the PMO.

Costs and benefits

At the time of writing, there has been considerable emphasis placed on the dysfunction said to be inherent in the way that ministerial staff, and the PMO in particular, have operated under successive governments. Between 2010 and 2015, three prime ministers, Kevin Rudd, Julia Gillard and Tony Abbott, were deposed by their colleagues, and in each case it was said that a PMO inattentive to reality testing and given to over reach played a part in their demise.[35] Even earlier, it had been shown that while John Howard used the PMO

---

35 On Rudd and Gillard and the PMO, see R A W Rhodes and Anne Tiernan, *Lessons in Governing: A Profile of the Prime Ministers' Chiefs of Staff* (Melbourne: Melbourne University Press, 2014), 204–206; on Abbott's demise and his PMO, there was copious commentary at the time – see eg Paul Sheehan, 'The Sacking of Tony Abbott was Personal. It was also about the Removal of Peta Credlin', *Sydney Morning Herald*, 15 September, 2015.

cleverly to reinforce his dominance,[36] there had been startling instances of executive over reach and perverse misinformation.[37] The unintended consequences of Whitlam's innovation, then, have recently been starkly evident. Less attention, however, has been given to the way in which reform of the PMO initiated in the 1970s and 1980s was integral to what some now celebrate as the heroic reform era characterised as 'the Australian moment'.[38] Here both costs and benefits are reviewed.

The augmentation of ministerial staff and the enhanced capacity of the PMO was criticised from the first, but initially concern was most apparent at senior levels of the APS. And arguably as confidence in the way these entities could work together grew in the 1980s and 1990s, that concern lessened (see further below). It was, rather, in the early 2000s that criticism flourished anew, driven by specific incidents and a concern that reform in this domain had gone too far. There appeared a series of comprehensively documented cases where, evidently as a result of pressure to deliver what a minister or the government demanded, staff exceeded their authority or breached ethical and professional standards.[39] These cases demonstrated the ability of staff to intervene in departmental processes; to drive, sieve, and skew advice; to deny transparency and to insist on what the minister wanted as opposed to the public interest or the integrity of the policy process. Contemporaneous inquiries found that the

---

36 Paul Kelly, *Re-thinking Australian Governance: The Howard Legacy*, The Cunningham Lecture (Canberra: ASSA, 2005).
37 See eg Patrick Weller, *Don't Tell the Prime Minister*, (Melbourne: Scribe, 2002).
38 George Megalogenis, *The Australian Moment* (Melbourne: Viking/Penguin, 2012); Paul Kelly, *The March of Patriots* (Melbourne: Melbourne University Press, 2009).
39 D Marr and M Wilkinson, *Dark Victory* (Sydney: Allen & Unwin, 2003); Anne Tiernan, *Power Without Responsibility* (Sydney: UNSW Press, 2007), chapters 7–9; Weller, *Don't Tell the Prime Minister*.

MOPS Act was inadequate as a guideline for governance and that there were significant weaknesses in the management framework for ministerial staff.[40] There was a manifest failure of accountability. Successive governments argued that confidentiality concerning the interaction between staff and a minister was essential to maintaining trust: if questions about private office operations were to be raised they should be directed to the responsible minister. Yet in a series of controversial cases ministers defended themselves from criticism by claiming that advisers did not pass on crucial information and so denied responsibility for 'mistakes' while refusing to allow their staffers to be questioned by parliament.[41]

It had become clear that the intention that such staff would on the one hand relieve APS officers of having to deal with politically sensitive matters, while also providing alternative evaluation of policy options, had been subverted by fact that many were themselves political activists with their own ambitions. Given the precarious nature of their employment, with no induction, performance management or professional development, the co-dependent nature of the relationship between ministers and their staff encouraged competition and partisan zealotry. Progress depended on an ability to protect and advance the interests of one's minister. It was a situation conducive to extremes of court politics, where bureaucratic routine, professional expectations and the public interest could easily be subordinated to the imperatives of loyalty to the boss and of competing for his or her favour.[42] Thus, as

---

[40] Senate Finance and Public Administration References Committee (F & PA), *Staff Employed under the Members of Parliament (Staff) Act*, October 2003; Michael Keating, 'In the Wake of "A Certain Maritime Incident": Ministerial Advisers, Departments and Accountability', *Australian Journal of Public Administration* 62, no. 3 (2003): 92–97.

[41] Ibid., 92.

[42] James Walter, 'Elite Decision Processes and the Perception of Global Imperatives: The Renaissance of Court Politics,' International Society for Political Psychology

Pat Weller forcefully argued, ministerial staff became 'the "junk-yard attack dogs" of the political system: the hard men and the hit men. They are politically dispensable ... [and] will take the bullet for their minister and protect them from political fallout'.[43]

Such debates were vigorously pursued well before the even more contentious criticism of the PMO surrounding the extraordinary events related to the failings of Rudd, Gillard and Abbott. Now the deficiencies of ministerial staff management were played out at the apex of the system and in the public arena as never before. In each instance, the combination of personal style and the way that influenced the choice of and relations with personal staff was conspicuous. Rudd's interventionist wish to have a hand in every issue, disdain for his colleagues, increasing distance from his APS advisers and penchant for relying on the advice of the clever but politically inexperienced young men with whom he surrounded himself left him exposed when policy challenges increased and his colleagues turned against him. Loyalists had mismanaged and protected him from the coming backlash. Gillard, more inclined to be consultative, and with a considerable administrative gift, was nonetheless driven back into an inner circle because in a now divided party she was unsure whom she could trust. She was also a fixer, given to making deals involving only a few trusted lieutenants and a handful of players: this led to serial misjudgements that plagued her government. Abbott was said to be over-reliant on Peta Credlin, his chief of staff: tellingly he characterised her as the fiercest 'political warrior' he knew. A political warrior, however, was hardly the best choice for refining policy objectives and identifying the expert, APS and stakeholder networks that could

---

Conference, San Francisco, 10 July, 2010.
43   Weller, *Don't Tell the Prime Minister*, 72.

CHAPTER 9

support their development and implementation. Instead, Abbott's PMO exhibited the most intense and insular court politics dynamic, emphasising loyalty over all other values and practising harsh and intrusive micro-management. Finally, paralleling the failure of Rudd's PMO, it was argued that Credlin's 'most damaging role was in keeping Mr Abbott in a small and distorting political ecosystem which lulled him into thinking he was safe and even widely applauded'.[44]

It must be acknowledged then that the costs of the private office staffing systems developed since the mid-1970s can be significant; that amongst other potentials, the PMO can be a dysfunctional element within the core executive. The calls for a more robust management framework have issued not only from independent analysts but also from the parliament itself from 2002 on: they should no longer be ignored. It should also be accepted as suggested earlier, that these have been unintended consequences.[45] The founding intentions of Whitlam and Wilenski, and the practices of Fraser, Hawke, Keating and Howard (in the early part of his reign), were not solely partisan but primarily oriented to enhancing policy effectiveness, and indeed can be seen to have done so. The PMO and ministerial staff reforms of the Whitlam period were decisively to influence the policy revolution of the 1980s and 1990s.

---

44 Malcolm Farr, 'Peta Credlin's Most Damaging Role was Creating Distorted View that Tony Abbott was Safe', news.com.au, 16 September 2015, at http://www.news.com.au/finance/work/peta-credlins-most-damaging-role-was-creating-distorted-view-that-tony-abbott-was-safe/story-fn5tas5k-1227528486625, accessed 13 October 2015.

45 F & PA, *Staff Employed under the Members of Parliament (Staff) Act;* Ian Holland, *Accountability of Ministerial Staff?* Research Paper no. 19, 2001–2 (Canberra: Department of the Parliamentary Library, 2002); Anne Tiernan and Patrick Weller, *Ministerial Staff: A Need for Transparency and Accountability?* Submission to the Senate Finance and Public Administration References Committee Inquiry into Staff Employed under the *Members of Parliament (Staff) Act*; *Report of the Senate Select Committee on a Certain Maritime Incident,* October 2002.

Initial gains were small: as Wilenski observed, compared with its aspirations, the Whitlam PMO was only a modest success. Fraser quickly realised the capacity of the platform Whitlam had introduced to enhance executive direction and control, and later, with Kemp, made the office a more significant policy resource, but his remaining time in office was too limited fully to exercise its potential. Only with the lengthier tenures of Hawke, Keating and Howard was its promise realised in what became 'the longest decade'.[46]

The Hawke government adopted much the same PMO staffing structure as had finally been arrived at under Fraser, but with salaries related to specific job designations. Status was still signalled by maintaining equivalence in the remuneration of senior officers with the lower ranges of APS permanent heads: there was to be no amelioration of the gains achieved by Whitlam and Fraser. There was a greater degree of functional rationalisation of tasks, and legislation was introduced providing a capacity for ministers to appoint consultants in addition to their staff establishment. The mix of private office advisers and consultants working in tandem with departments proved a notable feature of policy development thereafter.[47] The partisan element still had an important place – the centrality of political operatives Peter Barron and Bob Hogg in the early Hawke years, or like successors under Keating, was undoubted. But significantly, during the Hawke and Keating governments, the chiefs of staff in the PMO were all people with extensive public service experience: Hawke wanted those who knew how the system worked. It was a principle also adopted by Keating.

---

46 George Megalogenis, *The Longest Decade* (Melbourne: Scribe, 2006).
47 See, for instance, the cases analysed in Meredith Edwards, with Cosmo Howard and Robin Miller, *Social Policy, Public Policy: From Problem to Practice* (Sydney: Allen & Unwin, 2001).

CHAPTER 9

It was the skilled facilitation of these knowledgeable bureaucratic insiders, such as Graham Evans, Sandy Hollway, Dennis Richardson, Geoff Walsh and Don Russell that allowed for cooperative policy operations involving PMO staffers, consultants and APS officers. Hawke, it was said, 'assumed those around him – ministers, staff, public servants – were his allies, his supporters and, even, his friends'.[48] Hawke showed a considerable talent for distributed leadership, working closely with Keating (at least for the first eight years), setting targets, then letting his ministers, his staff and APS officials get on with their jobs.[49] Keating also developed close relations with key staffers and public servants. The mistrust between the PMO and the APS of the Whitlam era, and the somewhat critical edge maintained by Fraser, had gone. There was a relatively clear demarcation of political and policy roles. Staffers took their responsibility for good policy outcomes seriously and worked closely with their bureaucratic counterparts. It was expected that, while PMO advisers might put a political overlay on what had been generated by the APS, if there was a difference of view, this was made clear to the PM: 'it led to a relationship of ... [a] sort of professional enjoyment between two people interested in policy [in that] the contact was virtually daily. And I'm sure both the policy outcomes and the political outcomes were better for it'.[50]

The pattern was temporarily disrupted when John Howard took office in 1996. In dramatic contrast to Whitlam's insistence that

---

48   Stephen Mills, *The Hawke Years* (Melbourne: Viking/Penguin 1993), 161.
49   James Walter and Paul 't Hart, 'Distributed Leadership and Policy Success: Understanding Political Dyads,' *Australian Political Studies Association Conference*, (Sydney, 21 July, 2014) at http://papers.ssrn.com/sol3/papers.cfm?abstract_id=2469597 accessed 15 October, 2015.
50   Sandy Hollway, chief of staff to Bob Hawke, 1988–90; interview with the author.

leading mandarins remain, his L-NCP Coalition famously signalled its reservations about the APS by dismissing six departmental heads on assuming office. Howard brought in an outside appointee, Max Moore-Wilton to head PM&C. His PMO was dominated by political appointees, with a chief of staff who lacked bureaucratic experience and had some initial difficulty in engaging with the Canberra policy community.[51] Howard's office struggled, and his first term was widely regarded as rocky.[52] Eventually, however, the tide turned. One factor was the appointment of Arthur Sinodinos, certainly a partisan loyalist, but also an experienced public servant, to head the PMO in 1997. He brought to bear political understanding, appreciation of the prime minister's objectives and bureaucratic experience in achieving order in the PMO and facilitating the networks necessary for policy development. In conjunction, a partisan Cabinet Policy Unit was established, which relieved the PMO of responsibility for long-term planning and freed it to concentrate on day to day and tactical imperatives.[53] But significant, too, was Howard's leadership style: the development of authority and increasing discipline in Cabinet; an emphasis on explaining every policy initiative and relating it to the 'Liberal' narrative; a dogged commitment to his objectives, but a politically astute ability to draw back, regroup and seek alternative options when impediments loomed; and yet a degree of courage in tackling big issues – gun control legislation and the introduction of the GST, for example. These were the capacities that

---

51 Rhodes and Tiernan, *Lessons in Governing*, 59–60.
52 Anne Tiernan, 'Advising Howard: Interpreting Changes in Advisory and Support Structures for the Prime Minister of Australia,' *Australian Journal of Political Science* 41, no. 3 (2006): 309–324.
53 Rhodes and Tiernan, *Lessons in Governing*, 61–63.

CHAPTER 9

allowed the reform momentum to be sustained, at least until about 2001 (I return to this point below).

In their increasingly celebratory accounts of the policy journey between the mid-1980s and about 2001, Paul Kelly and George Megalogenis provide an incidental account of the successes of prime ministerial government and the significance of the PMO in those achievements.[54] Neither adequately traces the origins of these developments in the Whitlam reforms, and their concentration is on the economic thread, but their stories are replete with references to the importance of PMO staffers, individuals who were there only because of the office structures introduced in 1972–73. John Rose and Cliff Walsh in Fraser's office, Ross Garnaut early in the Hawke period, Don Russell with Keating and Arthur Sinodinos with Howard, to name only a few. A clearer sense of the mix, of the integral relations between ministers, prime ministers, ministerial and PMO advisers, consultants, academics and APS officers can be found in Cabinet diaries (such as those of Neal Blewett and Gareth Evans), insider PMO accounts (notably that of Don Watson), close reading of prime ministerial memoirs, Meredith Edwards' detailed policy case studies and the recent analysis of chief of staff roles in the PMO by Rod Rhodes and Anne Tiernan.[55] All of these testify to the importance of

---

[54] Paul Kelly, *The End of Certainty: The Story of the 1980s* (Sydney: Allen & Unwin, 1992); Kelly, *March of the Patriots*; Megalogenis, *The Longest Decade*; Megalogenis, *The Australian Moment*.

[55] Neal Blewett, *A Cabinet Diary* (Adelaide: Wakefield Press, 1999); Gareth Evans, *Inside the Hawke-Keating Government: A Cabinet Diary* (Melbourne: Melbourne University Press, 2014); Don Watson, *Recollections of a Bleeding Heart: A Portrait of Paul Keating PM* (Sydney: Knopf, 2002); Malcolm Fraser and Margaret Simons, *Malcolm Fraser: The Political Memoirs* (Melbourne: Meigunyah Press, 2010); Bob Hawke, *The Hawke Memoirs* (Melbourne: William Heinemann, 1994); John Howard, *Lazarus Rising: A Personal and Political Autobiography* (Sydney: HarperCollins, 2010); Edwards et al. *Social Policy, Public Policy*; Rhodes and Tiernan, *Lessons in Governing*.

the Whitlam/Wilenski transformation of ministerial staff structures, and of the PMO in particular, in understanding subsequent reform.

Conclusion

From one perspective, the policy record between the 1980s and the early 2000s was a vindication of the staffing reforms first devised by Wilenski, at Whitlam's behest. That transformation revitalised elements of earlier innovations, such Stanley Bruce's pioneering utilisation of 'experts' in inquiries and quasi-consultancy modes and Curtin and Chifley's recalibration of the public service and of executive capacity in an exercise of distributed leadership aimed at social reform. It broke with a pattern of path dependency that had developed postwar, in which government had grown accustomed to relying on the public service: a pattern deemed inadequate to the challenges Whitlam sought to address. In consequence established patterns of executive-public service relations were unsettled, reinvigorating processes of policy deliberation and development. It was also cognisant of international debates about contestable policy advice. The opportunity for policy reform enjoyed by Whitlam's successors, then, depended on the more complex policy dynamic generated by these initiatives.

So what went wrong around 2001? As indicated earlier, the inherent flaws in the ministerial staffing system with the PMO at its apex, introduced under Whitlam and refined under Fraser, had been there from the first. An enhanced capacity for direction and control was not matched by systematic constraints or, above all, by transparent scrutiny and accountability. Arguably, the potential for adverse potential had been held in check because there had been a balance between the

CHAPTER 9

partisan element and bureaucratic realism (with the inherent APS concern for a professional ethic) promoting cooperative endeavour and induced by forms of distributed leadership, bureaucratic insiders at the heart of the PMO, mutual trust and what was, from the mid-1980s on, effectively a bipartisan reform project.

Leadership that, instead of asserting personal centrality and absolute control, acknowledges distributed capacities and orchestrates and enables the diverse others who, together, can address the complex demands of modern government seems to capitalise effectively on Whitlam's staffing model. It is a catalyst for activating the networks that must balance the inherently political, the inevitably bureaucratic and the essential knowledge resources demanded for policy success. If the incipient threat to that balance was first signalled by Howard's incursions against APS executives and elevation of a partisan PMO in 1996, 'the triumph of the political'[56] and the dangers of personalised rather than network leadership did not fully emerge until later.

Paul Kelly signalled the danger of Coalition hubris following the 2001 election, and places the death of the reform project – and the subsequent series of botched policies – around 2003.[57] By then bipartisan commitment had failed. With increasing electoral ascendancy and ever greater authority, Howard began to resort to a command and control style of rule, relying on a loyalist insider group that exhibited the failings of court politics. It no longer observed the reality checks that had once been a strength: witness, for instance,

---

56   Rhodes and Tiernan, *Lessons in Governing*, 59–68.
57   Kelly, *March of the Patriots*, 613–627; Paul Kelly, 'How to Design and Deliver Reform that Makes a Real Difference: What Recent History has Taught Us as a Nation,' in *Delivering Policy Reform: Anchoring Significant Reforms in Turbulent Times*, eds E A Lindquist, S Vincent and J Wanna, (Canberra: ANU E Press, 2011): 43–51.

the 'children overboard' affair, the failure to attend to evidence in Howard's commitment to the Iraq intervention, and the debacle of his WorkChoices policy.[58]

If, with Howard, hubris may have been what David Owen suggests can be an acquired syndrome (generated by long tenure and the incremental accretion of power),[59] with Rudd it seemed present from the start, born of his conviction of being the cleverest man in the room. Gillard did not share such delusions, and her regard for the public service and administrative process enabled a record of legislative achievement against the odds, but her inclinations as a fixer, with a proclivity for making deals in which few outside her office were engaged, also led to damaging policy misjudgements. Abbott's reliance on an authoritarian, micro-managing PMO and inability to break out of 'a small and distorting political ecosystem' showed that a leader can be entrapped, instead of being enabled, by such an institution.

The PMO that has developed from Whitlam's transformation can clearly be an enormous asset for a gifted leader. It was an integral element in the development of what came to be, as Megalogenis characterised it, 'Australia's moment'. But the high costs incurred when it fails indicate that we cannot rely solely on the fortuitous conjunction of this institution with the right sort of leader – a leader

---

58 Weller, *Don't Tell the Prime Minister*; James Walter, 'Why Prime Ministers Go Too Far: The Case of John Howard,' in *Australian Security After 9/11: New and Old Agendas*, eds D McDougall and P Shearman, (Aldershot: Ashgate, 2006), 189–206; James Walter, 'Is There a Command Culture in Politics: The Australian Case,' in *Public Leadership: Perspectives and Practices*, eds P 't Hart and J Uhr, (Canberra: ANU E Press, 2008), 189–202.

59 David Owen and Jonathan Davidson, 'Hubris Syndrome: An Acquired Personality Disorder? A Study of US Presidents and UK Prime Ministers over the last 100 years,' *Brain*, 132 (2009):1396–1406.

CHAPTER 9

given to trusting all parties essential to policy development and using the PMO to coordinate them in a common cause. The reform challenge now is to ensure that the appropriate checks and balances ensuring professional ethics, transparency, and accountability are grafted onto Whitlam's innovation.

Chapter 10

IT'S TIME

Spectrum's market research, modern campaigning,
and Whitlam's mandate

Murray Goot

Hindsight is a wonderful thing. Looking back on the 1972 election, historians are inclined to see Labor's victory as inevitable, narrow though that victory was. The Coalition had been in office for 23 years, it was defensive and divided, and it was led by a man who was little more than a laughing stock. Labor, by contrast, had got its act together, especially in Victoria and New South Wales, it had crafted a modern program and it was led by a man who towered over his Liberal Party rival – politically as much as he did literally. Capping it all was the 'It's Time' campaign, as memorable as it was unstoppable.

It was not only in hindsight that a Labor victory was taken for granted. 'By late 1971', Rod Tiffen remarks, 'Whitlam already felt sure he would win the next election'.[1] By Gough Whitlam's own account he already felt sure some months earlier. Told that Henry Kissinger, President Nixon's National Security Adviser, had visited

---

The author is grateful to Nathalie Apouchtine, Cam Binger, Josh Holloway, and Chris Monnox for research assistance and to Jenny Hocking for her comments and suggestions. The research was supported by the Australian Research Council Grant DP0987839.

1   Rodney Tiffen, *Rupert Murdoch: A Reassessment* (Sydney: NewSouth, 2014), 108.

CHAPTER 10

China at the same time that he had been there in early July, and that a visit by Nixon would follow, an ecstatic Whitlam was said to have announced: 'Kissinger has just won the next election for me'.[2] Prime Minister McMahon had derided Whitlam's visit undertaken at a time when neither Australia nor the United States recognised the People's Republic. The Chinese Premier, McMahon insisted, had 'played' Whitlam 'as a fisherman plays a trout.'[3] Unfortunately for McMahon, he had not been forewarned about the Americans' own initiative. Others date the 'inevitability' of a Labor victory even earlier. In a note written in April 1971, Paul Hasluck, formerly Minister for External Affairs, now the Governor-General, predicted that by 'the end of 1972' McMahon 'will have exposed enough of his [own] shortcomings … as to be certain of defeat'.[4] Others date the 'certainty' to the 1969 election that had brought Labor to within four seats of winning power. '[T]here was no time after October 1969', says Graham Freudenberg, Whitlam's press secretary and speech writer, 'that we were not utterly convinced of victory next time'.[5]

If the Whitlam camp was sure, Labor's advertising agency was not. Sometime after the October 1970 Senate election – which saw Labor's vote slump to 42.2 per cent from 45 per cent at the corresponding election in 1967 and 47 per cent at the election for the

---

2   Quoted in George Munster, *A Paper Prince* (Ringwood: Viking, 1985), 96. For the sequence of events, see Graham Freudenberg, 'Introduction', in *Gough Whitlam's Mission to China, 1971* (Sydney: Whitlam Institute, University of Western Sydney, 2013), 4–5.

3   Billy Griffiths, *The China Breakthrough: Whitlam in the Middle Kingdom, 1971* (Clayton: Monash University Publishing, 2012), 53.

4   Paul Hasluck, *The Chance of Politics*, ed. Nicholas Hasluck (Melbourne: Text, 1997), 194.

5   Graham Freudenberg, 'The 1969 and 1972 Election Campaigns', in *It's Time Again: Whitlam and Modern Labor*, eds. Jenny Hocking and Colleen Lewis (Armadale: Circa, 2003), 69. See also Laurie Oakes, *Whitlam PM: A Biography* (Sydney: Angus and Robertson, 1973), 190.

House of Representatives in 1969, the Coalition vote fall to 38.2 per cent from 42.8 per cent in 1967 and 43.3 per cent in 1969, while the Democratic Labor Party increased its vote to 11.1 per cent (9.8 per cent in 1967; 6.0 per cent in 1969), the Australia Party won 2.9 per cent of the vote (0.9 per cent in 1969), and other minor parties and Independents 5.6 per cent (up from 2.4 per cent in 1967 and 2.7 per cent in 1969)[6] – Sim Rubensohn, the head of Hansen-Rubensohn-McCann-Erickson (H.R. McCann) the firm responsible for Labor's 1970 advertising campaign, asked himself whether 'the product' [the Labor Party] was 'attractive'. The 'answer at the moment', he said, 'is doubtful'.[7]

Whether H.R. McCann would be re-hired by Labor for the next campaign was far from settled. A number of people close to Whitlam wanted Rubensohn dumped. An alternative emerged when Peter Shenstone and Wayne Young, the principals of Spectrum International Marketing Services, a Sydney-based market research firm, were introduced to Whitlam's staff by Tony Whitlam, the leader's son. Shenstone and Young told Whitlam's office that they had 'two talented friends' working for H.R. McCann: Paul Jones, who had worked on Liberal Party campaigns in Queensland; and Mike Shirley, a graphics expert. Dick Hall, one of Whitlam's private secretaries, met the two and suggested they 'lobby within the agency for the ALP account'. That way they, not just Rubensohn, would be responsible for the campaign. 'The move succeeded'.[8]

---

[6] Colin A. Hughes, *A Handbook of Australian Government and Politics 1965–1974* (Canberra: Australian National University Press, 1977), 84–91.

[7] Hansen-Rubensohn-McCann-Erickson, 'Report for the Australian Labor Party on the Senate Election Campaign and Proposal for a Two-Year Plan to Achieve Maximum Success in the 1972 Election', [c. December 1970], 20; author's collection.

[8] Laurie Oakes and David Solomon, *The Making of an Australian Prime Minister* (Melbourne: Cheshire Publishing, 1973), 94.

CHAPTER 10

Spectrum's initial work for the Party – more accurately, for Whitlam's office – was based on focus groups. Since the technique had not been used in Australian politics before Spectrum felt the need to describe what a focus group was: a 'discussion group compris[ing] 6 to 8 respondents, led by an experienced moderator who guides the topics of conversation without stifling free trains of thought'.[9] In August 1971, Spectrum reported to Whitlam on a 'pilot study' of voters attitudes. Based on seven focus groups, variously constituted, the report warned that 'if present conditions prevail and an election is held in November this year' – at the time, talk of a 1971 election abounded – 'the A.L.P. will have little chance of winning'. Apart from there being '[n]ot one person in any [focus] group' who 'expressed with any confidence [sic] a belief that the A.L.P. could win the next election', there was 'no one' who knew 'what the A.L.P. stands for'.[10] As late as August 1972, Shenstone and Young would report that of the eight seats 'most likely to swing' in New South Wales only three (Cook, Evans and Phillip) seemed 'definite winners' with three others (Mitchell, Parramatta and Macarthur) 'still pretty much touch and go' and two more (Gwydir and Hume) apparently 'lost unless something drastic is done quickly'.[11] New South Wales was important: most of the Coalition's most marginal seats were there.[12] This report, its last, was based not on focus groups but on sample

---

9 Spectrum International Marketing Services, 'Political Parties, Leaders & Issues: A Pilot Study of Voters Conducted for The Australian Labor Party', 11 August 1971, 3–4; Whitlam Institute.
10 Ibid., 6, 69, 71. For the Prime Minister's apparent desire to go to an early election, see R F I Smith, 'Political Review', *Australian Quarterly* 43, no. 3 (1971): 87.
11 Spectrum International Marketing Services, 'N.S.W. Political Study, August 1972, for Australian Labor Party', 29 August 1972, Summary, 7; Whitlam Institute.
12 Malcolm Mackerras, *Australian General Elections* (Sydney: Angus and Robertson, 1972), 40, 188.

surveys – a method made familiar in previous elections not only through the published findings of the Gallup Poll but also, for those granted access to them, by the surveys conducted for the Party since 1961 by Marplan a subsidiary of H.R. McCann.[13]

Not a single Gallup Poll in 1971 pointed to a Labor victory. Indeed, in August 1971 the Gallup Poll and the first of the Australian Nationwide Opinion Polls (ANOP) pointed to the Coalition being returned with an increased majority. Only Irving Saulwick's Australian Sales Research Bureau poll suggested that Labor might be headed for a comfortable victory; but its sampling was confined to Sydney and Melbourne.[14] In August 1972, as Spectrum was voicing doubts about Labor's gaining more than three seats in New South Wales of the four it needed nationally, its campaign director in Western Australian, Joe Chamberlain, was warning the National Campaign Committee (NCC) that Labor could lose seats in the West.[15] Losses anywhere else would make Labor's task that much more difficult.

The (market research) program

In late May 1971, after their initial introduction, Wayne Young wrote to Mick Young with 'some preliminary ideas' for him to consider. His letter included seven 'Objectives', among them:

> To test ALP *policy planks* to decide what slant is most acceptable to the majority, and what slant could be emphasised in individual electorates to influence the swinging voter.

---

13 See Murray Goot, 'Labor's 1943 Landslide: Political Market Research, Evatt, and the Public Opinion Polls', *Labour History* 107 (2014): 153–154.

14 Malcolm Mackerras, 'Can Labor Win in 1972?' *Sunday Australian*, 21 November 1971, 12.

15 'Minutes of the National Campaign Committee', 10 August 1972, ALP-Federal 72 Election RH9/Z/F12, Bob Hawke Collection, University of South Australia.

CHAPTER 10

To turn up new issues important to voters, and determine how to present those issues to the people in persuasive terms.

For each issue, to study whether it affects voters rationally or emotionally.

To study the image of the ALP, and of the leaders, Gough Whitlam, and to recommend which aspects of each should be played up or down.

An accompanying list of 'proposed methods', included:

A pilot study consisting of group discussions to define the ALP's problems and reveal opportunities ...

Study of potential swinging seats ... to determine which issues would have most influence ... and how they should be presented.

Study of attitudes towards parties and their leaders. This will produce recommendations on what aspects of the images of the ALP and Gough Whitlam should be played up or down.[16]

Surveys

The proposal also envisaged the commissioning of a large-scale survey 'on the needs and attitudes of Australians' funded by contributions from 'major institutions'.[17] This didn't happen. Instead, from July 1971 to July 1972, Spectrum undertook a series of sample surveys, mostly in selected seats, in New South Wales and South Australia.

The Sydney survey

The first survey was timed to coincide with Whitlam's visit to China at the head of a Labor Party delegation, at the beginning of July

---

16   W L Young to M Young, 28 May 1971, 1–3, emphasis in the original; author's collection.
17   Ibid., 4.

1971. Between the first week of July, when the delegation was in China, and mid-July on the weekend following the delegation's departure from China, Spectrum conducted interviews in Sydney with 280 respondents, two-thirds of them men – an undisclosed number of 'blue-collar' workers in the first week, 'middle and upper management' and 'professionals' in the second.

China

Even before his declaration that Kissinger had 'won the next election' for him, those close to Whitlam hoped his visit would generate an electoral pay-off. The results of the survey suggested it hadn't. Most respondents did not agree that it was 'a good thing the Opposition [was] taking the initiative on this issue' and most respondents did not agree that the trip 'show[ed] Whitlam to be a potentially good Prime Minister'. 'Too many white collars and blue collars say[ing] "no"', the report commented, 'could be (a) the "opposition" image (b) a personal image problem'.[18] If, as a result of the China visit, Whitlam's 'political image' had 'been made over',[19] he had come to be 'accepted',[20] or 'a transformation of public opinion' had been 'set in train',[21] there was little evidence of it here. Perhaps, it needed time.

---

18   Another 1000 interviews were being conducted in Sydney and Melbourne, according to the preliminary report. However, the results have not been located; Spectrum, 'Top Line Results: A.L.P. Survey' n.d.; Whitlam Institute.

19   Griffiths, *The China Breakthrough*, 59. See also Neal Blewett, 'Labor 1968–72: Planning for Victory', in *Labor to Power: Australia's 1972 Election*, ed. Henry Mayer (Sydney: Angus & Robertson, 1973), 8.

20   Mick Young, 'The Build Up to 1972', in *The Whitlam Phenomenon* (Ringwood: McPhee Gribble and Penguin Books, 1986), 104.

21   Stephen FitzGerald, *Comrade Ambassador: Whitlam's Bejing Envoy* (Carlton: Melbourne University Press, 2015), 90. See also view that 'The China incident reinforced in the minds of the Australian electorate the image of an Opposition more in touch with the realities of foreign policy than the government'; Peter Sekuless, 'Sir William McMahon', *Australian Prime Ministers*, revised edition, ed. Michelle Grattan (Sydney: New Holland Publishers, 2013), 321.

CHAPTER 10

The Springboks' tour

Of more immediate importance was a question about Prime Minister McMahon's suggestion that an election be held 'on the issue of law and order because of the demonstrations against the South African football team'. The Springboks' tour, dogged throughout by anti-apartheid demonstrators, had started on 26 June in Perth. While the survey was being conducted the team played two matches in Sydney, both of which were disrupted.[22] On 24 July they would play in Brisbane.[23] On 14 July, anticipating their arrival in his State, Queensland Premier Jo Bjelke-Petersen declared a month-long state of emergency.[24] Roughly three-quarters of Spectrum's respondents thought the demonstrations not a 'sufficient reason' to hold an election. However, on the basis of focus groups conducted at about the same time (see below) Spectrum advised Whitlam that 'In the minds of the public, the government is seen as against "lawlessness", therefore the A.L.P. is for it!' It then drew an alarming conclusion. With the government 'unlikely to pass up the opportunity of holding an election on law and order when the South African cricket team arrives [the tour, scheduled for later in the year, was cancelled following the demonstrations over the rugby tour] ... On the basis of our findings there is good reason to believe the Government would receive enough support to remain in power'.[25] Spectrum provided almost no evidence for its conclusion. A year later, its marginal seats survey in

---

22 See Stewart Harris, *Political Football: The Springbok Tour of Australia, 1971* (Melbourne: Gold Star Publications, 1972), 95–103.
23 For the team's itinerary, see https://en.wikipedia.org/wiki/1971_South_Africa_rugby_union_tour_of_Australia.
24 Evan Whitton, *The Hillbilly Dictator: Australia's Police State*, revised edition (Sydney: ABC Books, 1993), 22.
25 Spectrum, 'Political Parties, Leaders & Issues', 60, 71.

New South Wales would show that 'law and order/demonstrations, which is supposed to be the domain of the Liberal Party, comes out in favour of Labor'.[26]

The Party name and the ALP's slogan

The 'It's Time' slogan had been devised before the year was out.[27] The idea was that people would complete it by adding whatever it was they thought 'it was time for'.[28] The slogan drew on 'It's time for a change', used by the New South Wales Division of the Liberal Party for its 1949 campaign theme, though it had used it only 'sporadically'.[29] It also harked back to 'Time for action', the slogan used by Labor in 1963.[30] Freudenberg, thought the 'campaign theme was always going to be along the lines of the well-tried "Time for a change"'.[31] Now the research set out to 'make sure' that the slogan did 'not have any connotations which would harm the Labor Party's image prior to the election'.[32] Election slogans were not new. What was new was the decision to test it.

For this research, conducted in late 1971 or early 1972, Spectrum interviewed 1,177 respondents of voting age in Sydney, Melbourne,

---

26 Spectrum, 'N.S.W. Political Study', Summary, 13.
27 Blewett, 'Labor 1968–72', 9.
28 Spectrum, 'Test of ALP Slogan "It's Time"', 14 February 1972, 1; author's copy.
29 Sally Young, 'Selling Australian Politicians: Political Advertising 1949–2001', Unpublished PhD thesis, (Melbourne: University of Melbourne, 2003), 111, 218. Young collected 79 Liberal Party advertisements from ten daily papers across Australia; the slogan was used only 'in a few'. Robert Crawford, 'Modernising Menzies, Whitlam, and Australian Elections', *The Drawing Board: An Australian Review of Public Affairs* 4, no. 3 (2004): 148, refers to 'It's time for a change' without noting the slogan's restricted circulation at a time when campaigns were State-based.
30 Young, 'Selling Australian Politicians', 219.
31 Graham Freudenberg, *A Figure of Speech: A Political Memoir* (Milton: John Wiley & Sons, 2005), 129.
32 Spectrum, 'Test of ALP Slogan "It's Time"', 12.

CHAPTER 10

Brisbane and Adelaide. Asked to name 'the major political parties' most respondents identified one of them as 'Labor'. Asked 'the best name' for the Party, however, a plurality (48 per cent) nominated the Party's own preferred name: the 'Australian Labor Party'. The name, further questioning revealed, 'ha[d] strong positive appeal'. In second place came 'ALP' (27 per cent). 'Labor', the name most readily used by respondents to identify the party, finished a long way back; only 8% nominated it. Respondents were then shown another card with their preferred name for the Party and the Party's preferred slogan, 'It's Time'. Asked 'Why do you think they [sic] say "it's time"?' the most common responses were: 'Time for a change, a change of government, change in the air, need a new government'; interpretations of this kind were ventured by a third of respondents. Given 'the original intention of the slogan', it seemed to be working 'extremely well', Spectrum reported. 'The general impression is that the slogan will nudge the majority of potential voters to agree that it's time for something or other:- time for a change, time for Labor, time to drop the Liberals.'[33] Neal Blewett notes that there were two ways of interpreting assent to the slogan – one that encouraged an anti-incompetent government campaign, the other that encouraged a pro-Labor's turn in office campaign.[34] This was a distinction to which Spectrum was indifferent.

The South Australian survey

Labor's South Australian branch commissioned its own 'political issues' survey from Spectrum around May 1972. It was conducted not across the State but in selected subdivisions, mostly for reasons

---

33 Ibid.
34 Blewett, 'Labor 1968-72', 12.

that are not clear in seats that were not marginal. It covered national politics and South Australian politics (an election was due in 1973) in equal measure. The questionnaire survives;[35] whether the results survive is unknown. There were also focus groups, apparently. The 'main conclusions' of the survey, as summarised by Laurie Oakes and David Solomon, were:

> the ALP was well ahead of the Liberals in terms of its image; virtually the only image factor favouring the Liberals was that of experience; awareness of Whitlam ... was not as high as the party might like, and Mrs Margaret Whitlam was almost unknown; the ALP was suffering from lack of support among women; most people felt that the ALP had a better approach than its rivals on most major issues; the biggest Federal problems the voters saw were prices, McMahon's leadership, defence and unemployment; and the group discussions revealed the ALP was not acting very positively.[36]

Respondents to the survey were asked to state their positions on just two policy issues. One was on the McMahon Government's 'new education grant' – an announcement made by the government on 11 May that it would provide an extra $215 million over five years to the building funds available to State and independent schools, pay 20 per cent of the running costs of independent schools, or do both.[37] The other issue was immigration; respondents were asked about their attitudes to the number of migrants coming to Australia and the places from where they were coming. At its 1971 Federal conference, Labor had rejected, for the first time, 'discrimination on any grounds

---

35 Spectrum International Marketing Services, 'Proposal: Research on Swinging Seats in N.S.W.', 6 June 1972, 9ff; author's collection.

36 Oakes and Solomon, *The Making of An Australian Prime Minister*, 97. See also Blewett, 'Labor 1968–72', 12–13.

37 Bob Brown, *Governing Australia, Volume 2, 1950–1975* (n.p.: self-published, 2007), 313.

of race or colour of skin or nationality'.[38] Both the funding of private schools and immigration were sensitive issues within the Party. H.R. McCann viewed immigration, as 'a potential disaster area for Labor', electorally.[39]

The New South Wales marginal seat study

While the South Australian study had not focused on marginal seats, the final and most important of the Spectrum surveys did. A study of the New South Wales seats the Party hoped to wrest from the Coalition got underway on 1 July 1972 and was completed on 13 August, two months before the election was called on 10 October.[40] Labor was planning for an election in November or even October, not one in December.

The study focused on eight electorates 'selected by the A.L.P. because of their high potential to swing away from the government' – five in metropolitan Sydney (Cook, in the South; Evans, Mitchell, and Parramatta in the West; and Phillip in the East) and three in rural New South Wales (Gwydir in the North; Hume and Macarthur in the South), the most marginal seats in the State.[41] Eighty respondents were interviewed in each of the metropolitan seats, 100 in each of the rural seats. Samples were drawn 'by a standard random sampling technique' (although the number of males and females that

---

38 Australian Labor Party, *Platform, Constitution and Rules as Approved by the 28th Commonwealth Conference* Launceston 1971, 30.
39 Hansen-Rubensohn-McCann-Erickson, 'Communications Programme', 7 December 1971, 7; Whitlam Institute.
40 Spectrum, 'N.S.W. Political Study', Summary, 3.
41 Ibid., Summary, 6. The seats corresponded to the eight most marginal Coalition seats in New South Wales on the first of the Mackerras pendulums, but they were chosen before the pendulum was published and therefore were not dependent on it; Murray Goot, 'The Transformation of Australian Electoral Analysis: The Two-Party Preferred Vote – Origins, Impacts, and Critics', *Australian Journal of Politics and History* 62, no. 1 (2016): 63–64.

needed to be interviewed was fixed), and the same demographic information recorded as was recorded in South Australia – sex, age, marital status, occupation (reported as 'upper', 'middle' and 'lower'), family income, and education level – although none of these demographic breaks, except sex, figures in the report.[42]

The first interviews were conducted in Phillip from 1 to 9 July. In Phillip researchers wanted to see whether, as well as conducting interviews face-to-face, they could double the number of respondents (from 80 to 160) at no extra cost by mailing the questionnaires and having respondents fill them in. The experiment was abandoned after only 80 questionnaires were completed and mailed back; Spectrum decided to rely on the 80 interviews they had completed by personal interview. Interviews in the other metropolitan seats were conducted between 17 and 31 July, a fortnight that coincided with a petrol strike; as we shall see, this left its mark. Interviewing in rural seats was carried out from 25 July–13 August.[43]

A large number of items covered 'problems' facing the respondents. These questions were open-ended so respondents could raise any problem they wished.[44] About 'the one biggest *local* problem facing this area today which our politicians should be trying to solve', there was no consensus. 'In metropolitan electorates' Spectrum noted, 'pollution and roads' were 'clearly the two local problems which people think politicians should be trying to solve'. Far from being clear, each of these issues was nominated by just 10%. The decision to focus on a 10% cut-off was more or less arbitrary; 'housing' was mentioned by almost as many (7%) as was 'high rise development/home units',

---

42   Spectrum, 'N.S.W. Political Study', Summary, 2, 145–146.
43   Ibid., 3–4, 1, on petrol.
44   Ibid., 64ff, 71ff, 76ff, 88ff.

Table 1. National problems to be solved, marginal metropolitan and rural seats in New South Wales, Spectrum, July–August 1972 (percentages)†

National problems to be solved	Metropolitan seats		Rural seats	
	Biggest	All	Biggest	All
	Total (Women)	Total (Women)	Total (Women)	Total (Women)
Strikes	21 (27)	36 (41)	20 (24)	33 (36)
Prices, inflation, economic planning	18 (16)	36 (32)	19 (19)	40 (38)
Pensions, social welfare	7 (4)	27 (24)	na	na
Pensions	na	na	3 (5)	10 (13)
Social welfare	na	na	2 (2)	4 (5)
Means test	* (*)	* (*)	* (*)	4 (5)
Income taxes	3 (3)	11 (7)	3 (*)	7 (5)
Death duties, probate	* (*)	* (*)	3 (3)	13 (10)
Rural problems and subsidies	* (*)	* (4)	2 (2)	4 (*)
Education	6 (7)	18 (22)	3 (4)	14 (16)
Unemployment	4 (3)	15 (14)	6 (6)	15 (17)
Decentralisation	* (*)	* (*)	5 (3)	15 (12)
Wool problem	* (*)	* (*)	* (*)	5 (5)
Industrial development	* (*)	4 (*)	* (*)	* (*)
Health scheme	* (*)	6 (5)	* (*)	4 (*)
Hospitals	* (*)	4 (5)	* (*)	6 (8)
Pollution	4 (4)	14 (15)	2 (3)	7 (8)
Housing	3 (*)	13 (14)	* (*)	* (*)
Defence, Vietnam, conscription	3 (3)	13 (11)	* (2)	7 (8)
Foreign ownership, investment	3 (*)	10 (8)	3 (*)	8 (5)
Immigration	3 (*)	8 (7)	* (*)	* (*)
Aborigines, land rights	* (*)	10 (11)	2 (3)	10 (13)
Law and order, demonstrations	* (*)	4 (*)	* (*)	4 (5)
Party unity, leadership of both parties	* (*)	* (*)	3 (3)	6 (6)
McMahon's leadership of the government	6 (4)	11 (6)	6 (4)	12 (11)
Poor performance of L.C.P	3 (*)	7 (5)	* (*)	* (*)
Poor performance of A.L.P.	* (*)	* (4)	* (*)	* (*)
Other	* (*)	* (*)	* (*)	* (*)
n	(394) (Women: 196)		(319) (Women: 197)	

†Cook, Evans, Mitchell, Parramatta, Phillip (metropolitan); Gwydir, Hume, Macarthur (rural)

na: not asked

*Issues nominated by fewer than 2% (main problem, rural), 3% (main problem, metro), or 4% (all mentions, rural or metro) were excluded.

Questions:

'Thinking specifically about the national or federal political scene, what do you think is the single biggest problem to be solved there?'

'What other problems are there on the federal scene?'

Source: Spectrum International Marketing Services, 'N.S.W. Political Study', August 1972 for Australian Labor Party, 29 August 1972, 76, 77, 83, 84, 88, 89, 95, 96.

including by 9% of women. Across the rural electorates, local concerns were rather different: 'decentralisation', named by 19% was the issue most frequently mentioned, though only 12% of women mentioned it, followed by 'unemployment' (13%) and roads (9%). A substantial proportion (at least a quarter in the metropolitan seats) failed to name any 'local problem' that needed to be solved.[45]

Asked to name 'the single biggest problem' on 'the *national* or federal political scene', the most frequently mentioned problems in the metropolitan areas were 'strikes' (21% across the whole sample; 27% among women) – though not in Phillip (where 'strikes' were mentioned by only 3%)[46] – and 'prices, inflation, economic planning' (18%); no other issue was mentioned by more than 7%. In rural electorates responses were broadly similar (see Table 1). McMahon's leadership, mentioned by just 6%, ranked equal fourth among problems mentioned in metropolitan seats and equal third in rural seats. Spectrum took its ranking in metropolitan seats (mistakenly described as fifth) to mean that McMahon's leadership 'loom[ed] large in the minds of the electorate as *a national crisis*'.[47] Imagining, perhaps, that it had seen what it hoped to see, Spectrum had let its preconception get the better of its observation.

Adding-in 'other big problems' metropolitan respondents saw 'on the federal political scene' changed the picture somewhat with 'strikes' (36% overall; 41% for women), 'prices/inflation/ economic planning' (36%), 'pensions and social welfare' (27%) still the most frequently mentioned problems, followed (as Table 1 shows) by 'education' (18%), 'unemployment' (15%), 'pollution' (14%), 'defence/Vietnam/

---

45   Ibid., Summary, 8–9, 64, 71.
46   Ibid., 92.
47   Ibid., Summary, 9, 11, emphasis in the original; 76 for the data.

conscription' (13%), 'housing' (13%), 'McMahon's leadership of government' (11%; 6% for women) – in equal ninth place – 'income taxes' (11%), 'Aboriginal rights' (10%), and 'foreign ownership/investment' (10%). Other issues were named by fewer than one-in-ten.[48] Across the three rural electorates what is most striking is the relative infrequency with which some issues were mentioned – 'pensions/social welfare' (14%), 'pollution' (7%), 'defence/Vietnam/conscription' (7%), 'housing' (less than 4%) – and the relative frequency with which others were mentioned: 'decentralisation' (15%), 'death duties/probate' (13%).[49] How prominently state aid figured in 'education' is something either the interviewers didn't probe or Spectrum's coders were not instructed to note. Nor, despite the Party's concerns, did Spectrum attempt to determine what aspect of 'immigration' respondents had in mind.

Respondents were also handed a *list of issues* 'some people have said will be important at the next election' and asked which of them was 'very important or not so important' (Table 2). What mattered to the researchers was not how many thought any of the issues important, or even what they understood the issue to stand for, but how the issues were ranked;[50] the proportion declaring any issue 'very important' had to be discounted, one imagines, not only because of the way it had been framed (respondents were told that others had found the issues 'important') but also because of the tendency of respondents to say any issue is 'important', once they asked. A number of issues retained the top ten ranking they had registered in the open-ended format: 'prices/ inflation/economic planning'; 'strikes'; 'pensions and social

---

48 Ibid., 88–89.
49 Ibid., 95–96.
50 Ibid., 108.

welfare' (metropolitan respondents); 'pensions' (rural respondents); 'education'; 'unemployment'; 'housing'; 'pollution' (metropolitan respondents). However, in the metropolitan seats 'strikes' dropped from the first rank to be equal seventh, 'McMahon's leadership of the government' from ninth to fourteenth ('Whitlam's leadership of the opposition' was not on the list), and 'immigration' from thirteenth to nineteenth; in the rural seats, 'McMahon's leadership' dropped from seventh to eighteenth, 'Aborigines and land rights' from eighth to nineteenth, and 'unemployment' from third to twenty-fourth. Conversely, among respondents in the metropolitan seats 'health' rose from fifteenth to equal seventh, and 'hospitals' from equal seventeenth to tenth; and in rural seats the 'means test' rose from equal nineteenth to eleventh, 'social welfare' rose from equal nineteenth to sixth, and the 'health scheme' from equal nineteenth to fifth.

Responses to the list confirmed Spectrum in the view the 'prices/inflation/economic planning' was 'the main federal issue', although in 'the Sydney metropolitan area pensions and social welfare are equally important'.[51] Had 'prices/inflation/economic planning' been disaggregated into three issues (prices, inflation, economic planning) or even two (prices and inflation, and economic planning) both the first sets of rankings (see Table 1), an artefact of coding, and the second (see Table 2), an artefact of questionnaire design, might have changed. The same is true of 'defence/Vietnam/conscription', 'foreign ownership/investment', 'rural problems and subsidies' and 'law and order/demonstrations'. The effect can be glimpsed by comparing responses to 'pensions and social welfare' in the metropolitan seats with 'pensions' and 'social welfare', addressed separately, in the rural seats (Table 1 and Table 2).

---

51   Ibid., Summary, 11–12.

Table 2. Issues rated 'very important', marginal metropolitan and rural seats in New South Wales, Spectrum, July–August 1972 (percentages) †

Very important issues	Metropolitan Total (Women)	Rural Total (Women)
Prices, inflation, economic planning	93 (93)	91 (94)
Pensions and social welfare	93 (93)	na
Pensions	na	79 (82)
Social welfare	na	70 (72)
Means test	na	64 (66)
Education	86 (88)	85 (90)
Housing	84 (87)	na
Unemployment	83 (83)	40 (36)
Health scheme	79 (80)	76 (80)
Strikes	79 (86)	79 (85)
Pollution	79 (83)	66 (74)
Income taxes	75 (74)	69 (70)
Death duties/probate	na	67 (66)
Hospitals	74 (77)	64 (64)
Defence/Vietnam/Conscription	67 (71)	58 (66)
Foreign ownership/investment	62 (57)	62 (62)
Aborigines and land rights	61 (70)	49 (57)
McMahon's leadership of government	59 (54)	52 (55)
Industrial development	55 (50)	63 (64)
Tariffs	na	37 (31)
Phone costs	na	60 (58)
Law and order/demonstrations	54 (53)	61 (62)
Poor performance of the L.C.P.	48 (44)	na
Immigration	46 (50)	32 (34)
State aid to church schools	41 (43)	na
Poor performance of the A.L.P.	32 (31)	na
Censorship	27 (31)	na
Decentralisation	na	70 (68)
Rates	na	48 (52)
Rural problems and subsidies	50 (53)	na
Rural subsidies	na	44 (45)
Conservation	na	44 (48)
Freight costs	na	43 (45)
Transport costs	na	34 (32)
Wool problem	na	30 (28)
Wheat problem	na	19 (16)
n	(394) (196)	(319) (157)

†Cook, Evans, Mitchell, Parramatta, Phillip (metropolitan); Gwydir, Hume, Macarthur (rural)

na: not asked

Question: 'On the top of the card is a list of things some people have said will be important in the next federal election. How important do you think each of them is, very important or not so important?'

Source: Spectrum International Marketing Services, 'N.S.W. Political Study', August 1972 for Australian Labor Party, 29 August 1972, 100–101, 107–109.

Table 3. Party with best approach on issues, marginal metropolitan and rural seats in New South Wales, by intended vote, Spectrum, July–August 1972 (percentages)†

	Metropolitan seats						Rural seats					
	Labor policies preferred			Coalition policies preferred			Labor policies preferred			Coalition policies preferred		
Policies	Total	ALP	LCP	Total	ALP	LCP	Total	ALP	LCP	Total	ALP	LCP
Pensions & social welfare	66	87	31	19	nr	46	54	82	25	26	nr	53
Means test	na	na	na	na	na	na	47	66	22	26	nr	50
Employment	61	85	22	20	nr	50	44	71	15	28	nr	54
Housing	59	81	26	18	nr	48	na	na	na	na	na	na
Price control	59	78	21	18	nr	51	41	66	16	18	nr	37
Industrial unrest/strikes	56	80	21	23	nr	55	34	64	nr	35	nr	60
Aborigines & land rights	54	75	26	16	nr	43	36	53	nr	24	nr	45
Health scheme	54	78	23	26	nr	nr	42	67	19	40	17	61
Income taxes	52	72	17	24	nr	56	31	nr	15	28	nr	51
Death duties/probate	na	na	na	na	na	na	25	38	nr	22	nr	45
Education‡	51	76	nr	28	nr	73	37	66	nr	44	15	69
Defence/Vietnam/conscription	50	73	nr	38	17	74	32	60	nr	55	25	82
Foreign ownership/investment	49	64	18	26	12	59	37	55	23	25	nr	40
Pollution control, environment	42	62	13	25	nr	nr	20	35	nr	31	15	47
Economic, financial planning	41	65	nr	29	nr	68	25	49	nr	35	nr	59
Law & order/demonstrations	41	61	17	34	15	70	20	42	nr	48	23	69
Immigration	37	56	13	34	17	61	21	43	nr	45	19	64
Decentralisation	na	na	na	na	na	na	22	39	nr	30	15	48
Transport costs	na	na	na	na	na	na	25	41	nr	19	nr	34
Rural problems, rural subsidies	29	46	nr	43	28	72	20	36	nr	42	27	55
Freight costs	na	na	na	na	na	na	22	35	nr	22	nr	34
Censorship	23	37	nr	35	21	61	16	28	nr	45	26	66
n	(394)	(202)	(82)	(394)	(202)	(82)	(319)	(116)	(108)	(319)	(116)	(108)

† Cook, Evans, Mitchell, Parramatta, Phillip (metropolitan); Gwydir, Hume, Macarthur (rural)

na: not asked; nr: not reported

‡ These figures contain an error: metropolitan sample adds to 108%

Question: 'Looking at the next card, which of the two main parties, Labor and the Liberal-Country Party, do you think has the best approach or policy on each issue?'

Source: Spectrum International Marketing Services, 'N.S.W. Political Study', August 1972 for Australian Labor Party, 29 August 1972, 117–177

CHAPTER 10

Issue salience, however measured, is one thing; party advantage, another. Presented with a list of issues and asked 'which of the two[sic] main parties, Labor and the Liberal-Country Party' had 'the *best approach* or policy on each issue', respondents in the metropolitan seats, as Table 3 shows, clearly preferred Labor to the Coalition on 'pensions and social welfare' (by a margin of 47 percentage points), 'employment' (41 points), 'housing' (41 points), 'price control' (41 points), 'industrial unrest/strikes' (33 points), 'Aborigines and land rights' (38 points), the 'health scheme' (28 points), 'income taxes' (28 points), 'education' (23 points), 'defence/Vietnam/conscription' (12 points), 'foreign ownership/investment' (23 points), 'pollution control/ environment' (17 points), and 'economic/financial planning' (12 points)'. On only two issues did the Coalition come out clearly ahead: 'rural problems and subsidies' (14 points), and 'censorship' (12 points). On other issues – law and order/demonstrations' (7 points) and 'immigration' (3 points) – the differences were not statistically significant.[52]

Two things should have been especially heartening for the campaign. First, Labor was preferred to the Coalition on the issues that had registered as being of most concern: 'price control/economic/ financial planning', 'pensions and social welfare', 'industrial unrest/ strikes', 'education' and 'employment' (assuming, bravely, that 'employment' would have rated as highly as 'unemployment'). Second, the issues on which Coalition respondents said they preferred Labor's approach to that of the Coalition's: the 'health scheme' (Labor preferred by 23 percentage points), 'industrial unrest/strikes' (Labor by 21 points), 'law and order/demonstrations' (Labor by 17 points), and 'immigration' (Labor by 13 points), the Party's concerns about its changes on 'White Australia' notwithstanding. Less heartening

---

52 Ibid., 117.

were the issues on which Labor respondents preferred the Liberal-Country Party's approach, including: 'immigration' (the Coalition was preferred by 17 points), 'defence/Vietnam/ conscription' (the Coalition by 17 points), and 'law and order/demonstrations' (the Coalition by 15 points). These, however, were issues that had registered in both the open-ended and closed questions as being of relatively little concern.

In the rural seats the pattern was different. While Labor was preferred on six issues ('pensions and social welfare', the 'means test', 'employment', 'price control', 'Aborigines and land rights', and 'foreign ownership/investment'), the Coalition was preferred on five ('defence/Vietnam/conscription', 'law and order/demonstrations', 'immigration', 'rural subsidies', 'censorship'), opinion on the other ten being fairly evenly divided. None of the issues on which Labor was behind the Coalition showed up as a matter of great moment on either measure of salience.

Not only was Labor ahead of the Coalition as the party with the best approach to most policy areas; it appeared to outscore the Coalition in terms of *party image*. More respondents thought Labor rather than the Coalition: 'concerned about people' (Labor's margin on this measure was 39 percentage points), 'energetic' (30 points), 'progressive' (23 points), 'forward looking' (23 points), 'in touch with the times' (20 points). Respondents put the Coalition well ahead on only two measures: 'experienced' (by 39 points), and 'respected outside Australia' (18 points). On several other measures – 'capable', 'united', 'stable' and 'trustworthy' – there was little if any difference.[53] Spectrum viewed all these factors as important. But which of them really was important it could only guess.

---

53   Ibid., 113.

CHAPTER 10

By contrast with the attention given to policy areas and party images, the attention given to the *political leaders* and the performance of the parties was small. It was also uneven. Forty-six per cent of respondents thought that McMahon's performance as prime minister had been 'only fair' and 37% considered it 'poor'; few rated it 'good' (15%) let alone 'very good' (2%). These figures were not very different from those elicited by the question about the 'sort of job the Liberal-Country Party [had] done in, say, the last year': 48% rated this 'only fair' and 33% 'poor compared with 16% 'good' and 2% 'very good'.[54] Of those who rated the government's performance 'very good' or 'good' nearly half (48%) rated McMahon's performance 'only fair' or 'poor'. On this evidence McMahon seemed more of a drag on the government's standing than a dynamo that might lift it.

The questions respondents were asked about the Leader of the Opposition started with whether respondents knew his name (90% did), whether they had 'seen or heard of his wife' (67% had) and whether they knew 'her first name' (40% of the women but only about 16% of the men did). Asked about the 'sort of job' Mr Whitlam would do 'if he were elected Prime Minister this year', respondents were 'not overwhelmingly convinced that Whitlam would do a good job'. Nearly half thought Whitlam would do either a 'very good' job as Prime Minister (11%) or a 'good' job (38%), while 28% thought the job he would do would be 'only fair' and 12% thought it would be a 'poor'.

Whitlam's relatively high standing compared to McMahon's was underlined by the marked differences in their scores on a series of personal attributes. The proportion that thought Whitlam 'a good speaker' exceeded the proportion that thought McMahon 'a good

---

54   Ibid., 129. Respondents were also asked the 'main reasons' for their answers.

speaker' by 46 percentage points. On the measure of 'attractive personality' the difference was 45 points; 'in touch with the people', 42 points; 'a good leader', 39 points; 'dynamic and forward looking', 35 points; 'has Australia's interests at heart', 12 points; 'intelligent', 10 points; 'honest and sincere', 9 points. On only one positive attribute did McMahon (by 12 points) come out ahead: 'respected outside Australia'. Conversely, McMahon scored higher then Whitlam on a number of negatives: 'a poor leader' (by 46 percentage points); lacking 'appeal to women' (31 points); 'evasive' (30 points); 'insincere' (14 points); 'a puppet for his party' (14 points); 'arrogant' (14 points); 'egotistical' (14 points); 'effeminate' (14 points); and 'immature' (14 points). On only one negative did Whitlam (by 13 points) come out on the wrong side: 'a mudslinger'.[55]

Asked how they had voted at the last federal election (the actual vote across the eight electorates is in brackets), 36% (44.4%) said Labor, 44% (47.3%) Liberal-Country, 2% (2.3%) Democratic Labor Party (DLP), 2% (3%) Australia Party, 4% did not know or would not say, and 12% said they had not voted. Spectrum's comparison between the votes cast in 1969 and the votes respondents recalled casting was 'close enough', it argued, 'to be regarded as statistically reliable'.[56] Hardly. The Coalition vote was underreported in the metropolitan seats – massively in Cook (by 14 percentage points) and Phillip (by 20 points). The Labor vote, underreported in four of the five metropolitan seats (it was over-reported in Mitchell) was underreported in each of the rural seats – massively. The vote for the DLP and the Australia Party was underreported in almost every seat as

---

55   Ibid., 135–137.
56   Ibid., Summary, 7.

CHAPTER 10

well.[57] Asked how they would vote at the next federal election, 45% said Labor, 27% Liberal-Country, 3% DLP, 2% Australia Party, and 1% Other. The remaining 22% either would not or could not say,[58] a figure best explained by the absence of any attempt by interviewers to push or probe; the Gallup Poll's practice had long been to push respondents on this.[59] Based on how respondents said they had voted in 1969, there had been a swing of 17 percentage points away from the Coalition 'across all sub-groups, i.e. males, females and all age groups'; but a swing of only 9 points to Labor.[60] 'Even by allocating most of the 22% who are undecided to the L.C.P.', the report noted, 'Labor appears to be in an extremely strong position in New South Wales'.[61] The overall vote in these seats on 2 December would be: Labor, 47.5%; Liberal-Country, 42.3%; DLP, 3%; Australia Party, 2.9%; Other, 4.2%.[62] Spectrum would have had to allocate almost all the 'undecided' to the Coalition to have come close.

Focus groups

Much of Spectrum's research was not quantitative but qualitative. It wasn't polling that distinguished the research behind 'It's Time'; it was the use of focus groups. Although 'merely a free-wheeling discussion', so far as respondents are concerned, focus groups, Spectrum argued, were where respondents 'inevitably revealed their real attitudes to the topics under discussion'.[63] That this

---

57 Ibid., 55–62; Colin A. Hughes, *Voting for the Australian House of Representatives 1965–1984* (Department of Government, University of Queensland, 1995), 32–37.
58 Spectrum, 'N.S.W. Political Study', 53.
59 See Goot, 'Labor's 1943 Landslide', 161.
60 Spectrum, 'N.S.W. Political Study', Summary, 7, 53.
61 Ibid., Summary, 7.
62 Derived from Hughes, *Voting for the Australian House of Representatives 1965–1984*, 67–71.
63 Spectrum, 'Political Parties, Leaders & Issues', 3–4.

might raise questions about the validity of the survey data passed without notice.

The 'pilot study'

In August 1971, Spectrum assembled seven different groups: 'young A.L.P. confirmed voters'; 'young A.L.P. swinging voters'; 'Liberal confirmed and swinging voters'; 'Australia Party voters'; 'undecided swinging voters'; 'middle-aged female voters' and 'young first-time voters'.[64] These were rather different from those Spectrum had originally proposed – 'journalists', 'sub-editors' and 'ALP members' among them.[65] What parts of Australia the groups came from was not disclosed. However, internal evidence – notably, respondents' apparent familiarity with the leaders' wives – suggests that most if not all of the groups were convened in Sydney; both McMahon and Whitlam lived there and Spectrum had its office there.

The study was designed to help produce 'a marketing plan to sell the A.L.P. to the electorate' by 'provid[ing] a new way of looking at familiar and often frustrating problems'.[66] The key was to document 'the electorate's images' of the alternative prime ministers (Whitlam, in particular), their wives, and their parties.[67] The reasons for prioritising the image of the leaders were 'because a) people most readily identify with *people*, not parties or objects b) few people have the slightest idea about any other members of the parties, c) as must be obvious, the leader represents the focal point of his party and is essentially the "personification" of that party in people's minds'.[68]

---

64 Ibid., 4.
65 W L Young to M Young, 28 May 1971, 2.
66 Spectrum, 'Political Parties, Leaders & Issues', 1.
67 Ibid., 10.
68 Ibid., 11; emphasis in the original.

CHAPTER 10

The feed-back on Whitlam made depressing reading; from Spectrum's four-page summary of 'the Image of Whitlam', Whitlam ordered that the last three be removed.[69] 'The overwhelming majority of respondents' had 'an image of Whitlam that was at best neutral and at worst, extremely negative,' this section of the report started. Instead of being seen as 'direct', subsequent sections noted, Whitlam was seen as 'evasive'. Characterising his 'leadership' respondents used words like 'negative' and 'timid'. In terms of 'loyalty' he was judged 'not a Labor man'. He scored high on 'negativism', 'always opposing the government' and 'not constructive'. His arguments were 'often only partially comprehended'. Far from being 'persuasive', he justified his statements at such length 'that people [began] to doubt him'; ditto for 'sincerity'. He lacked 'warmth'; he was 'cold'. He lacked 'naturalness', respondents describing him as 'unctuous' and 'oily'. Far from being recognised for his 'strength', he seemed weak – certainly when compared to Bob Hawke, President of the Australian Council of Trade Unions (ACTU). He didn't score well on 'openness', respondents complaining that they had 'never seen the real Whitlam' only the 'mask'. As for 'sex appeal', Whitlam had these pages removed as well. Only on 'seriousness', it appears, did Whitlam score well; but even here, 'not many *positive feelings* came out'.[70]

If McMahon had 'image problems' they were not as pervasive. Though there was a 'consensus' that he was not a 'good P.M.', he 'enjoy[ed] some distinct image advantages over Whitlam'. He may have been 'pompous', 'boring', 'a better Minister than a P.M.' and the sort of man who 'would kiss you on the cheek and stab you in the back';

---

69 Ibid., 14–16. Oakes and Solomon report concerns in the 'Labor camp' and the 'high content of comment' in Spectrum's reports; *The Making of an Australian Prime Minister*, 97.
70 Spectrum, 'Political Parties, Leaders & Issues', 16–36; emphasis in the original.

but he was also 'forceful, shrewd and direct'. Above all, he appeared 'a little more human than Whitlam'. There was a 'certain physical "cuteness"' about McMahon, 'which seem[ed] to appeal to some women and which to some degree mitigate[ed] against his cold calculating ruthlessness'; there was 'his wife, who obviously enhance[d] his "appeal"'; and there was 'the rub-off from the general Liberal Party image which in total [was] warmer, more personal than the A.L.P.'.[71] Of these attributes '[t]he first and probably most important electorally [was his wife] Sonia', who amongst other things 'imbue[d] him with sex appeal'. Margaret Whitlam was not as well known; but she, too, was 'potentially a vote getter', although not perhaps among 'blue-collar women'. 'Among the swinging Liberals, the A.P. [Australia Party] voters and the swinging A.L.P. voters, Margaret Whitlam is good news'.[72] The contrast with the South Australian study, which ten months later found that 'only 40%' of respondents were 'aware Whitlam [was] married and only 6% [knew] Margaret's name',[73] is striking. Spectrum recommended that Margaret Whitlam 'take a more active role'. She did. It also recommended that she 'be seen and photographed more often with Whitlam'. She was.[74]

McMahon's advantages over Whitlam were reinforced by the Coalition's advantages over Labor. While Labor lacked 'credibility ... as an alternative because of overwhelming negatives', there was a 'widespread acceptance of the government as "probably knowing more about things" and therefore [sic] general willingness not to question

---

71 Ibid., 39–41.
72 Ibid., 42–43.
73 Spectrum, 'N.S.W. Political Study', Summary, 17.
74 See, for example, Oakes and Solomon, *The Making of an Australian Prime Minister*, 107; Jenny Hocking, *Gough Whitlam: The Biography A Moment in History, Volume 1* (Carlton: Miegunyah Press, 2008), 391; Susan Mitchell, *Margaret and Gough* (Sydney: Hachette, 2014), 165.

CHAPTER 10

their actions'. Not only was Labor not 'seen as offering any real alternative in many cases'; there was 'no one', it seemed, who was 'really incensed at the Government's apparent ineptitude'. Underlying the Liberals' advantage was a sense that 'just by being there' they would 'bring about "natural progression and advancement"', the bonus that accrued to 'the winning team'.[75]

Labor, by contrast, was still seen as 'pretty old-fashioned', however 'progressive' its policies; it was 'not even a "fun" institution'. Respondents were concerned about its being under 'communist influence' and hostage to 'union militancy'. Labor was 'disunited'. Labor was 'a closed club' that didn't 'really represent the people'. Where were 'the women'? The "faceless men" controlled the parliamentary party; Whitlam was just "a mouthpiece". And whereas the Liberal Party seemed 'open to individuals who want[ed] to "have a go"' – respondents thought of themselves, as of most Australians (other than unionists), as "little capitalists" – Labor seemed almost 'designed to avoid attracting popular support'.[76]

When it came to policies, the 'only things' that were 'clear' about Labor were its 'basic stances on Vietnam and conscription', although the latter was 'clouded' by Whitlam's failure to say whether he wanted Labor to 'introduce a civilian alternative'. Whitlam came across 'as trying hard not to offend anyone by actually committing himself to A.L.P. policy' that 'might appear contentious e.g. Vietnam'. 'This', the report continued, did 'two things: (1) it reinforce[d] Whitlam's own negative image (2) it detract[ed] from the policy's credibility'. In the absence of any knowledge of the party's positions there was 'a general feeling' that Labor would 'cut defence, up education, pensions, health

---

75 Spectrum, 'Political Parties, Leaders & Issues', 44.
76 Ibid., 45–49; emphasis in the original.

benefits and taxation'. In each of the groups, there were '[s]ome' who 'expressed a vague idea that the A.L.P's health plan was good but this didn't get widespread confirmation [sic]'. Again, there was 'some awareness that the A.L.P. was concerned about education but no one knew if the party had any specific answer to what were perceived to be the major problems'. On foreign policy, Labor was seen to be moving to friendlier relations with our northern neighbours', but 'at the expense of our allies'. On this '[o]pinion was mixed'.[77]

What placed Labor at a disadvantage was not that respondents knew more about the government's plans; it was that the government did not need plans. Policies, in the sense of plans for the future, were considered 'to be things that only Opposition parties have' – or need. For governments 'policy is historical fact'. Whereas there seemed ready acceptance of government "policy"', Labor's efforts were characterised as 'opinion, untried, guesswork, head in the clouds, idealistic, unreal'. The contrast was 'expressed again and again by "better the devil you know, then [sic] the devil you don't"'.[78]

The New South Wales political study

In mid-1972, Spectrum undertook another focus group study designed to provide 'lists of the issues and problems the electorate had on its mind for inclusion in the subsequent door-to-door survey' and 'to reveal some of the reasoning and feelings behind the attitudes expressed by voters, in a situation which allowed those attitudes to be discussed in depth'. Respondents, it appears, were drawn from the New South Wales marginal seats Spectrum would later survey. However, the impact of the study on the Summary document at the

---

77   Ibid., 53–54.
78   Ibid., 54.

CHAPTER 10

beginning of the report on the marginal seats appears to have been limited; the document concentrates on the survey results. Since focus groups were promoted to the Party as the way to access voters' 'real attitudes', the decision to down-play them seems curious.

In an echo of its findings a year earlier the document reported that 'virtually no one [knew] what the A.L.P. would do about specific issues'. This was not because of inadequate media reporting of Labor's policies or the inattentiveness of the respondents to such reports, it implied. Rather, '[t]here [was] an awareness creeping into voters' minds that the A.L.P. [was] deliberately lying low and not taking positive stands on issues'. Respondents didn't see this as a 'bad strategy' by Labor. 'Most people', the authors continued, '"feel" that the A.L.P. would do something about the issues that concern them'.[79] Another observation was not about hopes but about fears. 'From the groups', the report said, 'it appears there are some areas of fear still associated with the A.L.P., particularly for women: strikes, union domination, nationalisation, black migrants, increased taxes'.[80] A third observation was about Whitlam's image, which 'still [had] many worrying negatives'. In particular, he was 'still seen as untrustworthy and not in control of the party'.[81] Nothing, apparently, emerged from the focus groups about Margaret Whitlam. Perhaps the moderator hadn't asked.

Impact

'[M]arket research', Mick Young wrote after the 'It's Time' campaign, 'was an integral part of all our decision-making at the campaign

---

79 Spectrum, 'N.S.W. Political Study', Summary, 11.
80 Ibid., Summary, 15.
81 Ibid., Summary, 18.

level'.⁸² However 'integral', it is not clear which parts were integrated – or integrated into which of the multi-level campaigns.

Some of the advice Spectrum offered the Party was ignored because it was beyond the bounds of what the Party could do; the injunction, for example, that Labor should 'guard against the Libs' actions, which could be mostly positive from here on in'.⁸³ Some advice had to be ignored for other reasons. 'It is imperative', the report said, 'that advertising commence as soon as possible'.⁸⁴ It was 'imperative' because Labor needed both to 'consolidate' the 'advantage' it was enjoying as a result of 'the government's mistakes' and 'to combat the weaknesses which the research [had] turned up'.⁸⁵ But no election had been called. And even if it had been called sooner rather later, as Labor expected, the Party didn't have the funds to sustain a campaign of months rather than weeks.⁸⁶ Some advice had to be ignored lest Party members thought the Party was running dead; the suggestion, for example, that party do away with pamphlets.⁸⁷

Other advice may have been treated with caution because the campaign committee was not entirely convinced. Spectrum had advised the Party to avoid 'negative ads'. Attacks on the Liberals 'only resurrect the old A.L.P. image of "negativeness", "carping" etc.', the Party was told.⁸⁸ However, about 30% of the Party's ads in the metropolitan dailies (excluding those for particular candidates or

---

82   Young, 'The Build up to 1972', 98.
83   Spectrum, 'N.S.W. Political Study', Summary, 22.
84   Ibid.
85   Ibid.
86   But see Blewett, 'Labor 1968–72', 13–14.
87   Spectrum, 'N.S.W. Political Study', Summary, 22; Vicki Braund, 'Timely Vibrations: Labor's Marketing Campaign', in *Labor to Power*, 21.
88   Spectrum, 'N.S.W. Political Study', Summary, 21. See also Maxwell, 'The Anatomy of an Undertaker', 32.

CHAPTER 10

notices of broadcasts of meetings) were 'negative' ads – a much lower proportion than in 1969, certainly, but on a par with the proportion in 1966.[89] 'Negative' ads signalled to Party members that the party was campaigning – and in the style that senior members of the Party wanted.[90] Without Spectrum's advice would the proportion of 'negative' ads have been more like the proportion in 1969 or more like the proportion in 1966? No one can say.

A good deal of advice designed to introduce 'modern marketing methods'[91] – including the slogan, the 'It's Time' song (though not who would sing it), and the use of Margaret Whitlam – was taken on board, including the need to appeal to women.[92] One of the more remarkable pieces of advice that was accepted had to do not with national but with local campaigning. Spectrum advised candidates that its research had shown that 'the people in your electorate are not interested in [your] making phoney promises', since these have been 'shown to be unbelievable and not credible [sic]', Spectrum told the candidates in the seats in which it had polled. The research also 'reveals that if you show genuine concern on[sic] subjects and issues which the electors are also concerned about, this will reveal you as a credible politian [sic] with whom they can identify'.[93] So, instead of sending out 'old style' pamphlets that sought to persuade voters by stating the Party's policies on issues that were – or ought to be – of local or national concern, candidates were advised to send out new style

---

89 Young, 'Selling Australian Politicians', 110–111, 300, 648–649.
90 Maxwell, 'The Anatomy of an Undertaker', 31–32.
91 W L Young to M Young, 28 May 1971, 1.
92 Blewett, 'Labor 1968–72', 8–9; Braund, 'Timely Vibrations', 21; Oakes and Solomon, *The Making of an Australian Prime Minister*, 103–104, for the words of the song.
93 Spectrum, 'N.S.W. Political Study', Summary, 21.

'brochures' that *sought* constituents' views on issues of local or national concern. H.R. McCann prepared a marketing 'kit' for candidates in the form of three brochures. Each had 'been designed to incorporate about six questions' though '[t]he grouping of the questions is best left to your discretion', candidates were told, with 'substituting' according to 'your own personal specifications' allowed 'where desirable'; 19 questions from which the 'groupings' were to be arranged were attached. The first brochure was to be mailed to constituents 'as soon as possible'. A second, 'say three weeks later, and the third about two to three weeks before the election'. These were 'intended to replace normal campaign literature'.[94] When the questionnaires were returned, all the candidates did 'was put them straight in the rubbish bin'.[95] The point was not to know their electorate; it was for candidates to show their 'concern'.

Conclusion

Mick Young has long been credited with running Labor's first 'modern' campaign.[96] Among the features that were distinctive and would 'continue in all subsequent elections', Colin Hughes has argued, was the 'substantial use of polling to test the acceptability of policies, identify issues [and] monitor performance through the campaign'.[97]

---

94 Hansen-Rubensohn-McCann-Erickson, 'Directions for Use', n.d., Labor Party, SLNSW 5095 Box 856, Item 2577, House of Reps 2/12/1972. Whether the questionnaires were distributed to candidates other than those in the New South Wales seats in which Spectrum had polled is unclear. The author has a copy of the first questionnaire sent out on behalf of Allan Mulde (Evans).

95 Paul Jones, author interview, 21 August 1980.

96 Kim E Beazley, *Father of the House: The Memoirs of Kim E. Beazley* (Fremantle: Fremantle Press, 2009), 175.

97 Colin A Hughes, 'Australia and New Zealand', in *Electioneering: A Comparative Study of Continuity and Change*, eds. David Butler and Austin Ranney (Oxford: Clarendon Press, 1992), 102–103. See also Terence W Beed, 'Opinion Polling and the Elections', in *Australia at the Polls: The National Elections of 1975*,

CHAPTER 10

This is misleading. It is true that Labor used polling to 'identify issues'. However, its use of 'polling to test the acceptability of policies' was minimal. Beyond education, in a narrow way, and immigration, in a broader way, the market research was not used to test policies; a number of Wayne Young's proposals, most notably his proposal to test Labor's 'policy planks', were not encouraged. Nor was polling used to 'monitor performance through the campaign'. There was no polling during the campaign. Labor's research came to an end nearly two months before the election was called. To boast that 'nothing was left to chance'[98] is to exaggerate the influence that any team can have on the course of a campaign. To do so on this occasion was to suggest a range of things that never happened and were barely contemplated.

If polling is a marker of modernity, then Labor had begun to modernise nationally and in some of the States long before 'It's Time'. From the early 1960s it had not only commissioned polling through Marplan; it had done so in marginal seats, an approach the Liberals would take a long time to adopt. Nor was the use of 'image politics' entirely new. In her study of newspaper ads in federal elections from 1949 to 2001, Sally Young shows that from 1954 to 1966, Menzies appeared in over 60 per cent of Liberal ads; that from 1954 to 1961, Evatt and then Calwell appeared in at least 60 per cent of Labor ads; and that while Whitlam appeared in 60 per cent of Labor's ads in 1972, in 1969 he appeared in every Labor ad.[99]

---

ed. Howard H Penniman (Washington, D.C.: American Enterprise Institute for Public Policy Research, 1977), 227. Elsewhere Hughes argued that what was distinctive about 1972 was that 'television took over' as the 'principal' campaign techniques, polling not making an impact until much later; Colin A. Hughes, 'Prime Ministers and the Electorate', in *Menzies to Keating: The Development of the Australian Prime Ministership*, ed. Patrick Weller (Carlton: Melbourne University Press, 1992), 154–155.

98 Braund, 'Timely Vibrations', 28; also Hocking, *Gough Whitlam*, 384.
99 Young, 'Selling Australian Politicians', 231, 621.

Much has been made of the fact that the campaign was 'centralised'. The market research, however, was not. Spectrum's surveys were organised through Mick Young in South Australia and Peter Westerway the New South Wales State Secretary; their respective State branches were responsible for raising the finance – $6,500 in South Australia, $15,000 in New South Wales. Far from being part of a 'national' effort, Mick Young thought Spectrum's South Australian survey would be 'of no assistance to other States'. He undertook to provide the NCC with a copy simply to provide 'an insight as to the part to be played in campaigning by privately employed market research teams'.[100] Indeed, not until July 1972 did the NCC formally agree that the campaign would be centralised.[101] Even then, other research was organised by Labor's Victorian branch through P.A. Consulting.

How important was the campaign? Stephen Mills insists that '"It's Time" was a powerful slogan'.[102] Patricia Amphlett ('Little Pattie') assures us that the "It's Time" commercial was more effective than anyone could have imagined'.[103] Tom Uren thought 'the slogan ... and the euphoria behind it put us over the line'.[104] Paul Jones, who helped devise the campaign, thought he had been 'the difference between

---

100 M J Young, 'Report to National Campaign Committee to serve as an agenda for their meeting N.S.W. Party offices, Sydney, Thursday 10th July [1972] 9.30 a.m.', 4; ALP–Federal 72 Election RH9/Z/F12, Bob Hawke Collection, University of South Australia.

101 Ibid., 2–6.

102 Stephen Mills, *The Professionals: Strategy, Money and the Rise of the Professional Campaigner in Australia* (Collingwood: Black Inc., 2014), 84; but cf. *The New Machine Men: Polls and Persuasion in Australian Politics* (Ringwood: Penguin Books, 1986), 153, where Mills poses the power of the campaign as an unanswered question.

103 Patricia Amphlett, 'It's Time, the Arts and Cultural Policy', in *The Whitlam Legacy*, ed. Troy Bramston (Sydney: The Federation Press, 2013), 266.

104 Tom Uren, *Straight Left* (Sydney: Random House Australian, 1994), 220.

CHAPTER 10

life and death'.[105] However, arguments for the power of the campaign fail to account for the fact that, in the end, Labor won quite narrowly. They fail to account for the net loss of two Labor seats in Western Australia and one in South Australia. In Mills' telling the losses in Western Australia are blamed on its State campaign director, dismissed as a troglodyte who resisted the professionalisation of the party, while the loss in South Australia (Mick Young's home State that ran 'an almost pure national campaign') is passed over in silence.[106] Above all, they fail to consider alternative explanations of Labor's victory.

Rubensohn was a great believer in the old saying that Oppositions didn't win elections, governments lost them. Early in 1972, an analysis of the patterns of support in the public opinion polls for the parties and for the party leaders had concluded that it was 'going to be very hard for Whitlam to win the next election; but quite easy for McMahon to lose it'.[107] Commenting in August 1972 on their marginal seat research, Spectrum noted that the swing towards Labor was 'mainly due to the feeling that the current government has had its day and it's time to give the opposition a go'. After the election there were those close to the campaign – the Labor member for Hindmarsh, Clyde Cameron, among them – inclined to agree that Whitlam had won the election largely because McMahon had lost it, notwithstanding the importance of party reform in Victoria and New South Wales and Labor's policy changes.[108] Or as David

---

105   Maxwell, 'The Anatomy of an Undertaker', 29.
106   Mills, *The Professionals*, 84–85. Chamberlain, in 1969, had presided over an extraordinarily good West Australian result.
107   Murray Goot and R W Connell, 'Presidential Politics in Australia?' *Australian Quarterly* 44, no. 2 (1972): 33.
108   Clyde Cameron, *The Cameron Diaries, 1976–1977* (North Sydney: Allen & Unwin Australia, 1990), 155. In *The Confessions of Clyde Cameron 1913–1990 as told to Daniel*

Butler put it, 'if over the previous few years the Liberal leadership had shown even moderate skills in politics and public relations, it is hard to believe they could not have saved the day'.[109] On this view the swing was not, as Oakes argues, a product of Whitlam's 'drive, his energy, his determination, his ideas'.[110] It was not a 'Whitlam swing', as Malcolm Mackerras has dubbed it.[111] It was mostly an anti-Liberal (McMahon), and to a lesser extent, an anti-Country Party (Anthony) swing.[112]

How important was 'the program'? For Mills, 'It's Time' was a slogan that 'encapsulated both Labor's electoral strategy and Whitlam's policy program'; this despite the fact that even in the 'It's Time' ad 'not a single policy is hinted at'.[113] For Nick Cater, 'It's Time' was 'a tacit admission that much of middle Australia had yet to be convinced that the country needed change'.[114] Donald Horne averred that 'throughout' Whitlam's campaign, 'audiences became bored with long parts of his programme'.[115] Jones, the advertising man at the centre of Labor's campaign, insisted that even voters who knew about the policies would still have been swayed by their 'emotional response'.[116]

    Connell (Crows Nest: ABC Books, 1990), 199–200, Cameron insists that with Gorton as Prime Minister the Liberals would have won.

109 David Butler, 'Thoughts on the 1972 Election', in *Labor to Power*, 5.

110 Oakes, *Whitlam PM*, 228.

111 Malcolm Mackerras, 'The Swing: Variability and Uniformity', in *Labor to Power*, 235

112 Malcolm Mackerras, 'Victories, Defeats and Electoral Politics', in *The Whitlam Legacy*, 69.

113 Mills, *The Professionals*, 76, for the first quote; *The New Machine Men*, 97, for the second.

114 Nick Cater, 'Hearts and Minds: The Meaning of "It's Time"', in *The Whitlam Legacy*, 53.

115 Donald Horne, *Time of Hope: Australia 1966–72* (Sydney: Angus & Robertson, 1980), 8.

116 Maxwell, 'Anatomy of an Undertaker', 33; see also Braund, 'Timely Vibrations', 25–26, 28.

CHAPTER 10

Evidence from Spectrum's *surveys* suggests that across most policy domains respondents preferred Labor's positions to those of the Coalition's. Evidence from its *focus groups* showed that on most issues respondents did not know what Labor's position was.[117] These findings were never reconciled. What is clear, on the evidence of Spectrum's research, is that Whitlam's program was not widely understood. If that's the case, one can hardly say that the slogan encapsulated the program or that the electorate endorsed it. Whitlam may have believed that his first government 'had been given a specific mandate to implement each part of the program set out in the 1972 policy speech'.[118] The Party's research, however, suggested otherwise.

117　Spectrum, 'N.S.W. Political Study', Summary, 13.
118　Gough Whitlam, *The Whitlam Government 1972–1975* (Ringwood: Viking, 1985), 26. See also Jenny Hocking, *Gough Whitlam: His Time, Volume 2*, Revised edition (Carlton: Miegunyah Press, 2013), 60–62. For an extended discussion of how the emergence of survey research undermined some claims to a 'specific mandate' while strengthening others, see Murray Goot, 'Whose Mandate? Policy Promises, Strong Bicameralism and Polled Opinion', *Australian Journal of Political Science* 34, no. 3 (1999): 327–352.

Chapter 11

E G WHITLAM

Reclaiming the initiative in Australian history

Greg Melleuish

How are we to understand the place of the Whitlam government in Australian history?

My starting point is an observation that history is not only contingent but our understanding of it is nominalist. That is to say that it does not have a necessary, or natural, structure. We make, and re-make, narratives according to the way in which we arrange and re-arrange what we know about what has happened in the past. Human beings crave a satisfactory narrative to explain the past as a means of understanding the present but, in so doing, they usually have to make use of the imagination which can be a misleading, indeed treacherous, friend.

We are all prone to impose templates on history as a means of making sense of what has happened. Such templates make it easier to grasp complexity and to reduce it to something which can be more easily grasped. In so doing we run the risk of not only becoming blinkered hedgehogs but also of being captured by powerful myths which, for a whole range of reasons, we want to believe, even if they fly in the face of the available evidence.

CHAPTER 11

Clive James made the following comment in his *Times Literary Supplement* review of John Howard's biography of Sir Robert Menzies:

> Perhaps the most resonant fact was that the Prime Minister who abolished the last vestiges of the White Australia policy was not Whitlam but Harold Holt. Whitlam gets the credit because of the power of myth, which plays a worryingly large part in Australia's politics and in its writing of history. In my view – admittedly only the view of a cultural critic, and an expatriate as well – the intellectual life of Australia since the Whitlam years has been increasingly weakened by the reluctance of almost the entire educated population to deal with past events whose implications might undermine their heartfelt views.[1]

James may have got some of the details wrong, Whitlam drove the last nail into the coffin of White Australia, but the general point, regarding the tendency to view the recent past in partisan terms, is well made. Such partisanship marks both those who have a positive and a negative view of Whitlam. The 'Whitlam years' play an important role in a particular narrative of Australian history which gives a unique place to those years as a time of rapid and beneficial social, political and cultural progress. Of course, such a narrative only makes sense if one accepts that there is a meaningful idea of progress, or perhaps in the current climate, the endless need for this thing called 'reform'. Progress, and its wayward child reform, has been perhaps the most important myth underlying Australian politics, especially for what Jill Roe once termed the 'thinking classes'.[2]

---

1 Clive James, 'Australia Fair,' *Times Literary Supplement*, 15 April, 2015, www.the-tls.co.uk/tls/public/article 1543967.ece.
2 Jill Roe, *Beyond Belief: Theosophy in Australia 1879–1939*, (Sydney: UNSW Press, 1986), xvi.

One could say: how could it have been otherwise in a settler society born in an age in which the West had its moment of glory, perhaps its one efflorescence, in world history? The odd thing is that there has been virtually no scholarly interest in tracking the idea of progress in Australia, although one can discern a number of different varieties, including a Scottish Enlightenment stadial model in the mid-nineteenth century and an Idealist vision of spiritual and moral growth in the first half of the twentieth century.[3]

Of course, where there are narratives there are also counter-narratives, all competing for our attention. The most famous was the vision of history presented by C H Pearson in the early 1890s of a world in which the dynamic of liberal individualism had been exhausted and all that remained was to live from day to day in a socialist state.[4] Sixty years later philosopher John Anderson defined progress as the 'going on of what goes on', and championed the intellectual superiority of an approach based on pessimism and decline to one founded on optimism and progress.[5]

But despite the extraordinary events of the twentieth century, which the West inflicted on itself and the world, a mood of pessimism, and surrender to inevitable decline, were very much minority tastes in Australia. Even where critics were scathing in their criticism the failings of the country, they seemed to remain positive that the future would be a better place. This was a pattern which can be traced back to the 1850s in New South Wales when the failings of the present were contrasted with the glorious possibilities of a democratic

---

3   Gregory Melleuish, *Cultural Liberalism in Australia*, (Cambridge: Cambridge University Press, 1995).
4   C H Pearson, *National Life and Character: a Forecast*, (London: MacMillan, 1894).
5   John Anderson, *Education and Inquiry*, ed. D Z Phillips, (Oxford: Blackwell, 1980), 55.

future.⁶ It has been this dynamic of an acute awareness of the failings of the present and a hope that the future will see those failings overcome which has often fuelled the way in which political narratives have been constructed in Australia.

The hope has been one of social progress, democracy and the creation of a more equal society. At a popular level this is probably summed up by the notion of rough justice embodied in the term 'fair go'. This term, however, says little about what a 'fair go' means in terms of policy. Equally, it cannot form the basis of a narrative of progress without much ideological elaboration. The most popular of these narratives in the context of Australian history is that of party of initiative and party of resistance. It can be traced back to W K Hancock and beyond to Clarence Northcott.⁷ As Henry Mayer put it in his classic critique of the thesis in 1956:

> The Australian Labor Party is presented as the party which, whether in or out of power, has been the "magnetic pole by which all political ships must set their courses". Labor, pretty generally, has been awarded the prize for "positive initiative". Deakin's "necklace of negatives", originally intended for Reid, has been mass-produced and hung around the neck of the Nationalists and the United Australia Party by almost everyone. The Country and Liberal Parties have also been adorned, but with rather more hesitation.⁸

Mayer was in turn criticised for his critique, but the point remains that it nevertheless remained as a powerful narrative for understanding

---

6   Greg Melleuish, 'Utopians and Sceptics: Competing Images of Democracy in Australia', in *Australian Political Ideas*, ed. Geoff Stokes, (Sydney: New South Wales University Press, 1994), 114–133.

7   W K Hancock, *Australia*, (London: Benn, 1930), Clarence H Northcott, *Australian Social Development*, (New York: Longmans, Green & Co., 1918).

8   Henry Mayer, 'Some Conceptions of the Australian Party System 1910–1950,' *Historical Studies: Australia and New Zealand* 7: 27, 254.

the course of Australian political history, a template which could be used to make sense of that history. In part, the narrative comes out of the peculiar turn of events of the first decade in Australia, including what most fascinated observers, both local and foreign, of the rise of the Labor Party and its assumption of office. Deakin, the initiator of liberal progress, was forced to 'fuse' with those around whom he had hung the "necklace of negatives"; his last major political act was to lead the campaign against the attempts by the Labor Party to extend Commonwealth power in the 1911 referendum.

How then did the Whitlam government come to be seen as embodying 'progress'? It all goes back to its foundation myth, the jingle 'It's Time'.

It's Time

It's time for freedom,
It's time for moving, It's time to begin,
Yes It's time

It's time Australia,
It's time for moving, It's time for proving,
Yes It's time

It's time for all folk,
It's time for moving, It's time to give,
Yes It's time

It's time for children,
It's time to show them, Time to look ahead,
Yes It's time

Time for freedom,
Time for moving, Time to be clear,
Yes It's time

CHAPTER 11

Time Australia,
Time for moving, It's time for proving,
Yes It's time

Time for better,
Come together, It's time to move,
Yes It's time

Time to stand up,
Time to shout it, Time, Time, Time,
Yes It's time

Time to move on,
Time to stand up, time to say 'yes',
Yes It's time[9]

The implication of the jingle would seem to be that Australia at that time under a Coalition government was stationary and lacking in freedom, history had become stalled and the country turned into a stagnant pool where little of note happened. This contrast between stagnation and activity is very reminiscent of the way in which orientalism operated in which a dynamic West was pitted against a stagnant and decaying East. It has strong overtones of J S Mill who placed a great emphasis on movement and intellectual activity. Consider the following quotes from Mill's 'Considerations on Representative Government':

> This question really depends upon a still more fundamental one, viz., which of two common types of character, for the general good of humanity, it is most desirable should predominate – the active, or the passive type; that which struggles against evils, or that which endures them; that which bends to circumstances, or that which endeavours to make circumstances bend to itself.
>
> All intellectual superiority is the fruit of active effort.

---

9   'It's time', www.whitlamdismissal.com/government/its-time.

> In proportion as success in life is seen or believed to be the fruit of fatality or accident, and not of exertion, in that same ratio does envy develop itself as a point of national character. The most envious of all mankind are the Orientals.[10]

Whitlam was presenting himself as the active type who struggles against evils and his opponents as passive types who merely bend to circumstances. Now there would be action after a period of stagnation. There is an emphasis on rupture, not continuity, it was time to move, time to begin.

This emphasis on movement, change and rupture is confirmed by some of the key sentences and phrases of Whitlam's policy speech:

> The decision we will make for our country on 2 December is a choice between the past and the future, between the habits and fears of the past, and the demands and opportunities of the future. There are moments in history when the whole fate and future of nations can be decided by a single decision.
>
> We have a new chance for our nation. We can recreate this nation. We have a new chance for our region. We can help recreate this region.
>
> We want to give a new life and a new meaning in this new nation to the touchstone of modern democracy – to liberty, equality, fraternity.[11]

The rhetoric has a 1789 feel to it.[12] It is marked less by socialist zeal, in fact there is very little socialism in it, than by a repudiation

---

10   J S Mill, 'Considerations on Representative Government' in *Three Essays*, (London: Oxford University Press, 1971), 190, 191, 192.

11   It's Time: Whitlam's 1972 Election Policy Speech, http://whitlamdismissal.com/1972/11/13/whitlam-1972-election-policy-speech.html

12   The *Sydney Morning Herald* editorial the following day certainly saw it as such, depicting Whitlam and Bob Hawke as 'irresponsible revolutionaries' and the Labor party's policies as 'directed, openly or covertly, to the destruction of the existing order'. in 'Gough Whitlam, the Father of Modern Australia' *Sydney Morning Herald* editorial, 22 October 2014.

CHAPTER 11

of what could be described as the Burkean liberalism of the Menzies' era. François Furet has argued that there was a crucial point in 1789 when the leaders of the French Revolution ceased thinking in terms of reform within the existing order and began to look to constructing a new order.[13] Whitlam, of course, like Deakin before him, remained staunchly Burkean on constitutional matters (in particular the supremacy of parliament). Also like Deakin, he was radical on issues of public policy. Radicalism implies the repudiation of the past, of tradition, and in that sense Whitlam can be viewed as a radical liberal, as an heir of John Stuart Mill.

The only problem with a radicalism which seeks to 'recreate the nation', as the National Assembly discovered after 1789, is that it also generates opposition from those who feel threatened by radical change. As change pertains to the 'glory' of a government rather than its power, and hence has a strong symbolic dimension, the focus and emphasis on change is potentially divisive. Whitlam wanted to be seen as an agent of change; whether that was the best approach to take to achieve actual change is a different matter. Menzies's approach was fundamentally Burkean; change there would be but it would be gradual and built on what had been inherited from the past. But they were both at heart liberals; one the heir of Edmund Burke, the other of John Stuart Mill. Deakin was the heir of both.

The idea that a rupture with the past was required implied that the faults of Australia were manifold and the country in need of a complete regeneration if it was to achieve its destiny of being dynamic, democratic and devoted to achievement. Intellectuals in Australia

---

13   François Furet, *Interpreting the French Revolution*, Trans. Elborg Forster, (Cambridge: Cambridge university Press, 1981).

have long mocked its ordinariness, its devotion to 'middling standards' and 'the spreading rash of nineteenth century suburbanism'.[14]

D H Lawrence also characterised Australians as apathetic and passive. Consider the following passages:

> And in this state, this very Australian state, you could hardly get a word out of him ... The indifference, the marvellous bedrock indifference. Not the static indifference of the east. But an indifference based on real recklessness, an indifference with a deep flow of loose energy beneath it, ready to break out like a geyser.

> The aboriginal *sympathetic* apathy was upon him, he was like some creature that has lost his soul, and simply stares.

> The indifference – the fern-dark indifference of this remote golden Australia. Not to care – from the bottom of one's soul, not to care. Overpowered in the twilight of fern-odour. Just to keep enough grip to run the machinery of the day; and beyond that to let yourself drift, not to think or strain or make any effort to consciousness whatsoever.[15]

Just as D H Lawrence had felt a kind of revulsion for Australian life in *Kangaroo* in the 1920s so Brian Penton, writing in the early 1940s, expressed a disquiet with the way in which Australia had developed. Penton believed that the promise which Australia had demonstrated in the 1890s, an age of vitality and activity, had been dissipated and Australians had lost the plot. As with Hancock, he believed that something had gone wrong in twentieth century Australia:

> Once in the nineties, it looked as though Australia was going to have a national credo. That was in the days when the *Bulletin* talked about a republic for Australia and scorned imported

---

14   W K Hancock, *Australia*, (London: Benn, 1930), 273, 285.
15   D H Lawrence, *Kangaroo*, (Harmondsworth: Penguin, 1986), 200, 202, 203.

CHAPTER 11

hokum. A promising time. It looked as though the Labour Party was going to get itself a national philosophy – but what came of it? A muddle-headed outfit consisting of a few militant realists, a lot of sectional trades unionists, and some scared, respectable politicians who compromised the half-expressed aims of the party's founders out of existence till, in the last election, you could not really tell Labour from the U.A.P.[16]

Moreover, argued Penton, the blame for this failure lay with the Australian Labor Party:

> The failure of Australians to get a national consciousness, a national credo, a sense of their own identity … may be laid entirely at the door of the Australian Labour Party. Looking back over the past troubled ten years you will find the Labour Party initiating not a single great liberal campaign … On all big issues and in all crises the Labour Party is timid or downright reactionary.[17]

Not that the other side of politics was much better. The sickness was at the heart of the Australian body politic: 'I admit that at the end of this inquiry you will find yourself disenfranchised – between a hesitant, gutless, confused, and complacent Labour Party at one end of your voting ticket and an unctuous money-grubbing conservative party at the other'.[18]

In this regard it is worth remembering that Lloyd Ross depicted the 1890s as a new Elizabethan Age, an age of intellectual vitality.[19] The whole myth of the 1890s was founded on a distinction between ages of energy and vitality and ages of stagnation and passivity in

---

16 Brian Penton, *Think – Or Be Damned*, (Sydney: Angus & Robertson, 1941), 61–62.
17 Ibid., 64
18 Ibid., 72
19 Lloyd Ross, *William Lane and the Australian Labor Movement*, (Sydney: Hale & Iremonger), 3.

the history of Australia, with passivity being linked to so-called bourgeois values and being obsequious to the empire. From this perspective, the 1890s were the touchstone of what could be described as an Australia which possessed and exhibited Millian vitality. The hope was that post-1972 would be such an age.

The passivity of Australians is also linked to a tendency by the educated classes to look down on the ordinary Australian with contempt, even loathing. This is not a new phenomenon. Witness the following passage by A J Marshall in *Australian Limited* in 1943:

> You can spot an Australian in London or on the Continent at thirty yards, because he usually wears a kangaroo, a boomerang or map of Australia in some conspicuous position. (In many ways this is a very good thing as it enables civilized people to avoid him.)[20]

Marshall continues with such statements as 'Most Australians don't think at all' and then presents the case for 'trained scientists' to solve the problems of the country.[21] (This reminds one of the BAAS Victorian Handbook of 1914 which has, as its first chapter, 'The problems in the State of Victoria which await scientific solution'[22]). These sorts of attitudes are not dissimilar to those described by Fred Siegel in his work *The Revolt against the Masses* which tracks similar disdain for ordinary people amongst American intellectuals in the twentieth century.[23] For intellectuals like Marshall, education becomes

---

20 A J Marshall, *Australia Limited*, (Sydney: Angus & Robertson, 1943), 7.
21 Ibid., 11, 21
22 J W Barrett, 'The Problems in the State of Victoria which await Scientific Solution,' in *British Association for the Advancement of Science Australian Meeting 1914: Handbook to Victoria*, eds A M Laughton & T S Hall, (Melbourne: Government printer, 1914), 29–69.
23 Fred Siegel, *The Revolt against the Masses: How Liberalism has Undermined the Middle Class*, (New York: Encounter, 2013).

the great panacea for all which is wrong with Australia. Of course, in 1943 this is not a very large group in Australia; by 1963 it has increased in size considerably.

English expatriate J D Pringle, who came to Australia to be editor of the *Sydney Morning Herald*, found a similar emptiness of the spirit in Australia in the 1950s. He claimed that 'If then, culture is to be judged by the general standard of education and the arts among the population, once again it must be said that Australia has little or none'.[24] This was a not uncommon view of the intelligentsia of the time; although it was generally not restricted to any particular political party. Anti-intellectualism was seen to be a central feature of Australian life across the political spectrum. This view found full expression in one of the most influential books ever written about Australia, Donald Horne's *The Lucky Country*, Horne claimed that 'in a sense – Australia does not have a mind'.[25] He went on to characterise Australian public life, like Lawrence, in terms of its emptiness and vacuity. He asserted that 'the public emptiness of Australian politics comes from its lack of intellectual strength'.[26] Horne linked the supposed deficiencies of Australian public life with the long years of Liberal/Country Party government under Sir Robert Menzies:

> an archaic flavour in political affairs, a sense that much of this might have been happening at some earlier period in history. Even for Australia the deadness was remarkable. Politicians seemed pompous and out of touch. They seemed to be conducting a political debate that they had read about in an old book. Politicians did not project the symbols of modern life ... men of

---

24 J D Pringle, *Australian Accent*, (London: Chatto and Windus, 1958), 116.
25 Donald Horne, *The Lucky Country*, (Melbourne: Penguin, 2005), 10–11.
26 Ibid., 192.

the Menzies-Calwell generation became virtually exiles in their own century.[27]

The sin of Menzies, and it should be noted of then Labor Party leader Arthur Calwell, was that they were yesterday's men. Horne's comments are somewhat extraordinary in that they provide no evidence and are simply a rhetorical denunciation. Hence the emphasis on deadness and a 'political debate that they had read in an old book' and 'virtually exiles in their own country'. This was rhetorically impressive but essentially meaningless. Of course the 1950s and early 1960s was a time of old rulers, from Eisenhower to Churchill to Adenauer. If one looks closely at Menzies one can see that he did have a sort of a 'steady as it goes' approach but that attitude was informed by the terrible events he had lived through during the first half of the twentieth century.

In a slightly different vein Manning Clark wrote regarding Menzies as 'a man who had not understood the forces of the age; or, if he understood them, seemed to resist humanity's march from the darkness into the light, and paid a terrible price for so doing'.[28] Again, this owes more to rhetoric than to reality. Clark claimed to have looked into Menzies's soul at the funeral of H V Evatt, but Clark had a clear capacity to see what he wanted to see.

From another perspective, F W Eggleston wrote a decade earlier that 'Australians once prided themselves on being in the vanguard of social progress, but they have now allowed themselves to lag far behind'.[29] But as a Liberal who believed in social cooperation and

---

27 Ibid., 193.
28 Manning Clark, *Speaking Out of Turn: Lectures and Speeches 1940–1991*, (Melbourne: Melbourne University Press, 1997), 11.
29 F W Eggleston, *Reflections of an Australian Liberal*, (Melbourne: Cheshire, 1953), 153.

CHAPTER 11

the need for individuals to make the public interest paramount, he did not look to Labor, which he saw as a party which worked for the interest of the trade unions as the means of achieving that goal. Labor was the party of initiative insofar as it took initiatives which favoured its own sectional interest. Eggleston saw the Liberal Party as representing 'a policy which is a truer expression of the Australian pattern of culture than any other' because it was not bound to a sectional interest, even if its weakness was its lack of willingness to change that pattern'.[30] This was not an unfair statement, and reflected the Burkean nature of liberalism under Menzies. But then, in his debt to philosophical idealism and his belief in social cooperation, Menzies had much in common with Eggleston. Eggleston also bemoaned the lack of 'the publicist, the man detached from politics but able and well-informed' in Australia.[31]

There were others who shared Eggleston's less than positive estimation of the Labor Party. Consider J D Pringle's description of a typical Labor politician, 'not usually a man who cares much about ideas ... a tough, shrewd opportunist, a master of the more disreputable political arts, but utterly ignorant and contemptuous of wider horizons ... a good mixer, genial, often with a racy, down to earth turn of speech. You see him at the races or drinking in a hotel bar surrounded by his cronies, red-faced, big-bellied, hard-eyed, the image of Tammany all the world over'.[32] Craig McGregor, writing in the mid-sixties, described the Labor Party as 'fundamentally conservative, meliorist, non-Socialist ... in many ways, rather old-fashioned ... It is suspicious of intellectuals and has again and again

---
30   Ibid.
31   Ibid., 255.
32   Pringle, *Australian Accent*, 52.

turned down the help of the academics and thinkers'.[33] This description is not all that dissimilar to that made by Brian Penton some twenty years earlier. Writing in 1958, Colin Clark who had worked for the Queensland Labor government before becoming a professor at Oxford, bemoaned the small number of Labor members of parliament with university degrees. Clark observed that 'on the whole, it remains a very badly-educated party'.[34] Admittedly a jaundiced observer, he also described unscrupulous practices by Queensland Labor Party, including forged ballot papers, which he claimed were 'perhaps unique in the history of the British Commonwealth'.[35]

McGregor also commented on the party of progress/party of resistance model and its inapplicability to contemporary Australian politics. In fact he remarks favourably on the capacity of Liberal governments to adapt to changing circumstances:

> What the Liberal Government has shown itself to be, however, is fairly flexible and responsive to community pressures, readier than the ALP to depart from political theory for the sake of practical solutions ... it is susceptible to the political currents (including reform movements) around it.[36]

Equally, not every commentator saw Australia as a cultural and intellectual wasteland. Colin Clark, wrote that 'the scholastic standards attained by Australian school-children are generally comparable with those of English school-children of the same age and type of school'[37] Clark thought that the source of Australia's problems was its attempt to use excessive tariffs to protect Australian manufacturing

---

33 Craig McGregor, *Profile of Australia*, (Ringwood: Penguin, 1966), 202.
34 Colin Clark, *Australian Hopes and Fears*, (London: Hollis & Carter), 190.
35 Ibid., 244.
36 McGregor, *Profile of Australia*, 188.
37 Clark, *Australian Hopes and Fears*, 295

industries, a problem exacerbated by what he saw as the outdated ideas produced by its academic social scientists.[38]

This survey of ideas indicates that the situation was much more complex, and interesting, than Horne and Manning Clark would have us believe. Of course, in all of this we are dealing with the way commentators saw Australia rather than with the reality of Australian social, cultural and political life. Nevertheless, what is apparent is that the political situation in the early 1960s was not clear cut. Standing in 1960 it would have been difficult to predict how Australian politics and political culture would develop. Both of the major political parties could be, and were, accused by intellectuals of belonging to an outmoded world. Both were led by men who had grown to manhood in the shadow of 1914. Coming back to my original point about contingency, one wonders what might have eventuated if the Labor Party had won the 1961 election. Or going back even further, Australia would be a rather different place if the 1954 Labor split had never occurred. Certainly 'It's Time' as a rhetorical strategy would not have been possible if there had been a memory of a Calwell led government fresh in the public mind.

In this regard I think that Nick Cater's recent analysis in *The Lucky Culture* is very plausible; the rise of the newly minted educated class is crucial. Responding to John Douglass Pringle's claims of 1958, Cater states bluntly that 'more than fifty years later Australia has its educated class'.[39] It was members of this class, which had barely existed during Eggleston's lifetime, who were to create what can be described as the new party of initiative – party of resistance paradigm

---

38   Ibid., Chapter XI.
39   Nick Cater, *The Lucky Culture and the Rise of an Australian Ruling Class*, (Sydney: HarperCollins, 2013), 28.

in Australia. Donald Horne argued that the 1950s had seen the end of a chapter in Australian history but the new Australia was struggling to be born; the real problem, according to Horne, was that there was at that time no place for 'the kind of extraordinary man who can see the new shapes of the future – or present – and enjoy challenge, living life at a fuller pitch'.[40] 'Material prosperity in the future,' he claimed, 'is likely to lie, for the first time in history, with clever, educated people. He also identified Whitlam as someone who seemed to recognise this need for a 'new tone and style'.[41]

It was, of course, Menzies who was responsible for extending Commonwealth funding to universities, allowing for considerable university expansion, much to the applause of someone such as Hugh Stretton, in the hope, which was soon dashed, that it would produce people like himself and Eggleston, devoted to the advancement of the liberal ideal of the public good. Building on the foundations laid by Chifley in enabling returned servicemen to attend university after World War II[42], Menzies clearly believed in the role which clever people would play in Australia's future. It was the massive expansion of the universities, and the newly created Colleges of Advanced education in the 1960s, which created the audience for Horne's ideas.[43] Don's Party would be unthinkable without Menzies's reforms. They were Menzies's children.

What way would this new knowledge class jump? It was most certainly not a foregone conclusion that they would jump to the left. It was by no means certain that the Liberal Party would move towards

---

40   Horne, *The Lucky Country*, 13.
41   Ibid., 11.
42   Stuart Macintyre, *Australia's Boldest Experiment: War and Reconstruction in the 1940s*, (Sydney: NewSouth, 2015), 328–9.
43   See Greg Melleuish, 'Sir Robert Menzies and Australian Education,' in *Menzies*, ed. John Nethercote, (Ballarat: Connor Court, 2016), 257–78.

CHAPTER 11

a greater appreciation of conservatism. Even as late as the 1980s B A Santamaria was predicting a split on the Right in Australia between conservative and liberal groups.[44] Perhaps it was the influx of Catholics into the Liberal Party which was crucial in the re-making of the Liberal Party. This is a poorly understood process much in need of systematic investigation. Again it was, I think, contingency, not necessity, which provides the best explanation. In this regard Whitlam may have been crucial in creating the image of a Labor Party which was the friend of the educated class, something which Pringle and Colin Clark would have found extraordinary.

If Cater is correct then what matters is not so much what the Whitlam government was actually like, but the image which Whitlam managed to project, very successfully, into the wider community, and how that government has come to be portrayed in Australian history. In this sense, Manning Clark was very prescient; history, or perhaps historians, have been much kinder to the Whitlam government than the voters who, quite sensibly in 1975, decided that they had had enough of a dysfunctional government.[45]

In this way, the whole notion of party of initiative/party of reaction could be resurrected in a new guise, one which emphasised the Labor Party as the party of ideas and the natural representative of the new knowledge class. The party of anti-intellectualism in Australia had become the party of the intellectuals. It could be represented as the party of modernisation and progress, of energy and ideas; it could claim the Millian heritage which is very important in Australian political culture. When *On Liberty* was published in 1859 it received

---

44 B A Santamaria, *Australia at the Crossroads: Reflections of an Outsider*, (Melbourne: Melbourne University Press, 1987), 79.
45 Manning Clark, 'History will be Kinder to Labor than the People,' in his *Occasional Writings and Speeches*, (Sydney: Fontana, 1980), 203–208.

major attention in newspapers in both Sydney and Melbourne.[46] This is not to say that under Whitlam, and even today, the Labor Party continues to contain elements which are decidedly unreconstructed. Of course, here I am talking in terms of image, or to be more fashionable, discourse or narrative. The reality, as can be seen in the recent documentary on Rudd and Gillard, is often quite different; Tammany Hall has not yet been laid to rest.

The great achievement of Whitlam, and I say Whitlam because there were many in his government who were very traditional and old-fashioned, was to create this image, and to convince many others in the knowledge class, especially intellectuals such as Horne and Manning Clark, that he was the transformative hero for whom they had been waiting. He was their John Galt, their social democratic equivalent of a Randian hero.[47] And, it can be argued, Randian heroes have an impeccable ancestry stretching back to Ralph Waldo Emerson. I say this advisedly because Rand became the hero of the educated classes in America who established Silicon Valley.[48] She is the philosopher of self-esteem and feeling good about oneself. For a variety of reasons, she has only ever been a minority taste in Australia. Nevertheless, educated Australians wanted to be individualistic and creative, but in a way somewhat different from their American cousins. At heart, and this is what the 'It's Time' jingle captured, they were the heirs of J S Mill, not of Karl Marx. Whitlam appealed to them for exactly this reason; it was energy and vibrancy which they craved, not the dullness of an 'end of history' socialist paradise.

---

46   Greg Melleuish, 'Introduction: Liberalism and Conservatism,' in Greg Melleuish, *Liberalism and Conservatism*, (Ballarat: Connor Court, 2015), 6–12.
47   John Galt is the hero of Ayn Rand's novel *Atlas Shrugged*.
48   See the documentary 'All Watched over by Machines of Loving Grace,' Part 1, 'Love and Power' made by Adam Curtis.

CHAPTER 11

One can see from the following quote the sort of emphasis which Manning Clark placed on the role of individuals who he saw as creative thinkers as agents of positive social change: 'So the men and women with the creative gifts were the true psychedelic agents of their age; they expanded our minds and helped us to see ourselves as we really are.'[49] Despite the shades of Timothy Leary, Clark, like Horne, believed that bold creative thinkers were the true transformative agents of positive political and social change. Whitlam was such a figure for him, although Clark's notion of hero, like his prose style, owed more to Thomas Carlyle than Ayn Rand. Whitlam was the prophet who should have transformed Australia:

> It seemed then that the years of unleavened bread were over. At long last we had a teacher who had the chance to lead us out of the darkness into the light, always provided THEY did not cut him down, that THEY spared him a little before he went from hence and was no more seen.[50]

What does Clark mean by the years of unleavened bread? If he is referring to Corinthians 1.5 then this seems to mean the need for Australians to be re-made with new leavening, with perhaps Whitlam as a Christ figure. Of course, this is very much in line with the way in which Whitlam's coming to power had been portrayed in both the 'It's Time' theme song and Whitlam's policy speech. There will be a rupture with the bad old days; a great man would liberate the creative, dynamic and progressive values of the Australian people, or at least, its creative elite. The self-actualisers will finally be rewarded and those whose needs are merely the 'lower needs' of

---

49   Manning Clark, *Occasional Writings and Speeches*, (Melbourne: Fontana, 1980), 201–202.
50   Ibid., 202.

social approval and safety will be put in their place. Of course, this vision of human nature may be ascribed to Maslow in the 1940s[51] but its true roots lie in liberalism:

> This individual vigour, then, and manifold diversity, combine themselves in originality; and hence, that on which the whole greatness of mankind depends – towards which every human being must ceasely direct his efforts, and of which especially those who wish to influence their fellow-man must never lose sight: individuality of energy and self-development.[52]
>
> All intellectual superiority is the fruit of active effort. Enterprise, the desire to keep moving, to be trying and accomplishing new things for our own benefit or that of others, is the parent even of speculative, and much more of practical, talent.[53]

The years of Whitlam were a time of true transformation, and this was because he had appreciated what the creative Randian and Millian heroes of Australia had to offer: 'So in those three halcyon, golden years, in contrast to the pro-British archaic, philistinism of their predecessors, Whitlam gave the men and women with creative gifts a place of honour and respect in Australian society'. But, alas, Whitlam had been cut down by the philistines. Writing of 11 November 1975 Clark stated that 'It may be the day which proved once and for all just how hopelessly wedded we, as Australians, are to the petty-bourgeois values, to that very sickness which the progressive part of the world is shedding and destroying'.[54] It is very likely that Clark saw himself when he looked at Whitlam. Just

---

51   A H Maslow, 'A Theory of Human Motivation', 1943, psychclassicsyorku.ca/Maslow/motivation.htm.
52   Wilhelm von Humboldt, *The Limits of State Action*, ed. J W Burrow, (Indianapolis: Liberty Fund, 1993), 12.
53   Mill, 'Considerations on Representative Government', 190–191.
54   Clark, *Occasional Writings and Speeches*, 208.

CHAPTER 11

as C H Pearson's depiction of a world entering old age reflected his own aging, it can be argued, Clark's empathy with Whitlam came out of his own suffering at the hands of the 'philistine' critics of his *History of Australia*. Australians just could not recognise, nor understand, their creative heroes.

This led to Clark viewing Whitlam as a tragic figure, a prophet of progress and 'the light' who had been betrayed and destroyed by those who could not appreciate his true worth; but the image is Christian, with Whitlam as Christ, not Platonic as is described in the allegory of the cave in the *Republic*. Mark McKenna suggests that Clark was sculpted by Whitlam in the image of Thucydides.[55] To see Whitlam in terms of Thucydides is a little misleading. Thucydides' *History* can be read as a tragedy culminating in the devastation of the Sicilian campaign and the work is meant, as is that of Herodotus, as a warning against hubris and the dangers of imperial ambition. But none of the major figures from Pericles to Cleon to Alcibiades are in any sense Christ like and are invariably inflicted with the failing of hubris. Clark manifestly failed to see Whitlam's hubris, as McKenna admits 'he could only see his idealism'[56]; Whitlam lacked the humility required to be a Christ figure. The tragedy, for Clark, comes from Australians failing to recognise who Whitlam is and how he has come to save them from themselves. The tragic narrative follows on from a view of history which emphasises a corrupt present and the hope of a glorious future. That future will invariably not be realised and the disappointment created by that failure will need to be explained.

---

55 Mark McKenna, *An Eye for Eternity: The Life of Manning Clark*, (Melbourne: The Miegunyah Press, 2011), 582.
56 Ibid., 580.

A good comparison is with W K Hancock's *Australia* written in 1930. For Hancock the chief character is the Australian people. They did not require a prophet or Randian hero to goad them down the road of justice. One can read in Hancock's account of the Australian people a 'tragedy' but it is one caused by their virtues, or rather the excesses which those virtues generate. Australian are a kind open hearted people who fail to understand their own moral failings and so end up creating something quite different to what they set out to achieve. Seeking justice, they create injustice. Hancock's solution to the problem is to wait for a time when Australians are more mature, as is expressed in his parable of the dog.[57]

In another way Clark's depiction of Whitlam also resonates with the Gallipoli narrative. It may have been a massive defeat but it was a glorious defeat, one well worth celebrating. Whitlam should be celebrated as a Sisyphean hero struggling to achieve the light but constantly thwarted; Australian history then becomes the tale of a series of such heroes. A careful reading of Clark's monumental *History of Australia* indicates that this was indeed Clark's historical vision. In this regard, the idea of a hero leader, as espoused by Manning Clark and Donald Horne, with an emphasis placed on their capacity to stimulate intellectual capacity and creativity is something new in Australian culture, but something in line with the way in which Australian democracy has moved over the past 50 years.

If we attempt to look behind the sort of mythology which came to be associated with Whitlam what can be discerned as going on?

Whitlam was attempting to 'modernise' the ALP and to portray that modernisation as also extending to Australia as a whole. He was taking a Tammany Hall Trade Union Party, which was in many ways

---

57   Hancock, *Australia*, 288–289.

CHAPTER 11

decidedly traditionalist, and turning it into a vehicle for progress. He was making the party much more Millian. This should be seen in the context of a Labor Party which has a long tradition of controlling its politicians and being opposed to individuals who demonstrated initiative.[58] Modernisation meant making the Labor Party the party of individual emancipation as opposed to a party which sought to control individuals. It also meant making the Labor Part shed much of its Tammany Hall image and seem to be a party of honesty.

That modernisation was very much linked with the coming to age of the new knowledge class which was the product of the extension of secondary education in the 1950s and tertiary education in the 1960s. This was a massive change in a country which had never been renowned for an excessive interest in education. It was linked to the development of manufacturing industry. If Australia was to remain in the forefront of progress it needed to have modern industries and a modern education system. It was effectively a new vision for Australia based on an updated notion of what constituted progress and national development in which education was central.

That process was inaugurated by Menzies through both his schools and universities policies, including Commonwealth funding of universities and Commonwealth involvement in the funding of schools.[59] But as with most things, Menzies did not rush these changes, but he was a convinced advocate of the importance of education, not just in terms of technological progress but also because he believed that education would create engaged citizens who would seek the public good.

---

58 V G Childe, *How Labour Governs: A Study of Workers' Representation in Australia*, ed. F B Smith, (Melbourne: Melbourne University Press, 1964).
59 Melleuish, 'Sir Robert Menzies and Australian Education'.

With regard to education there is no substantive difference between Menzies and Whitlam. Both believed in the ideal of an educated Australia. The major difference between them was the rate of change; Whitlam took what Menzies had begun and took the educational ideal to its logical conclusion by making university education free. The alternative vision to such policies were figures such as B A Santamaria and Colin Clark who retained a sort of rural sentimentality founded on Chesterton and Belloc. Santamaria would come to see the universities as a major corrupting force in Australian culture.

Whitlam can be seen as a new version of Menzies. Most certainly Craig McGregor considered him as such in the mid-1960s.[60] Like Kevin Rudd 40 years later Whitlam was not traditional Labor, but a 'clean skin' outsider in the sense that he could not be identified by the likes of John Douglas Pringle as belonging to Tammany Hall.

For a variety of reasons Whitlam sought to adopt a view of Australian history not all that dissimilar from Horne and Clark. Australia had been asleep since the 1940s and in need of a new 'leavening' to make it once again dynamic and progressive. This was a clever strategy for Whitlam for both reasons internal to the Labor Party and as a means of selling himself to the Australian public. It was an intelligent strategy for an outsider who was not carrying too much in the way of traditional Labor baggage and wished to transform both Labor and the country.

The subsequent failings of the Labor government from 1972 to 1975, many of which were a consequence of its unreconstructed nature, were mythologised from within this renewed narrative of progress and modernisation. Hence we arrive at a sort of tragic narrative.

---

60   McGregor, *Profile of Australia*, 204.

CHAPTER 11

The key outcome was that Labor was successful in winning the ideological battle, even as it lost the battle for power, at least in the short term. After a somewhat confused situation in the 1960s Labor came to be seen as the natural political expression of the new knowledge classes. This enabled it to be re-anointed as the 'party of initiative'. The Whitlam government may have been a miserable failure in many ways but it was a great success in winning the battle of ideas. Its self-image came to dominate the historical record; Manning Clark was right.

It is worth reflecting on the fact that there has never been a Conservative Party in Australian politics. Menzies was very careful to re-launch a Liberal Party in 1944 after nearly 30 years. I think that there were reasons for the need to 'own' the word liberal, much of which has to do with the dominance of a discourse of progress in Australian political culture. Liberalism in Australia was founded on a doctrine of progress, even if, as Stephen Chavura and I recently argued in relation to the Federation debates, it could contain powerful Burkean elements.[61] Menzies clearly believed that he, and the Liberal Party which he led, were agents of progress, both in a national and international sense. As was discussed earlier, Frederic Eggleston, saw liberalism, and especially its capacity to create enhanced social cooperation, as crucial to possible future progress in Australia.

It can be argued that Whitlam, with the sort of Millian principles proclaimed in 1972, enabled the Labor Party to lay very strong claim to the heritage of liberal progress in its new form with a powerful

---

61   Stephen A Chavura and Greg Melleuish, 'Conservative Instinct in Australian Political Thought: The Federation Debates, 1890–1898,' *Australian Journal of Political Science* 50, no. 3 (2015): 513–528.

emphasis on the transforming power of education. The two most important sources of a more pessimistic approach to politics in Australia, the secular Calvinism of John Anderson and the conservative political Catholicism of B A Santamaria, were to find a home in the Liberal Party. Together, they formed the intellectual underpinning of the major Australian conservative intellectual journal of the second half of the twentieth century *Quadrant*. Anderson did not believe in progress; he did not support the expansion of the universities in the 1950s. Santamaria believed that the expansion of the universities was one of the biggest mistakes which Menzies ever made and he was a significant critic of the new educated classes. He was, in many ways, the father of the 'culture wars' of the early twenty first century. Menzies was said to be close to Santamaria in retirement; both John Howard and Tony Abbott had connections with Santamaria. With Whitlam's second election victory at the 1974 double dissolution, the DLP went out of business and the Liberal Party became the natural home of conservative Catholics. This transformed the Liberal Party.

On the surface the re-birth of the party of initiative-party of resistance model with the Whitlam government appears to be a natural flow-on from earlier developments in Australian history. But such a model works best when it does not touch the real world of politics. By the 1960s the model no longer seemed to be relevant for an understanding of Australian politics. It was difficult to present the Labor Party as a party of change and social progress. Whitlam's great achievement was to claim the heritage of Millian liberalism for the Labor Party, to present it as the party of change and dynamism, just at the time when a new educated group emerged in Australian

CHAPTER 11

society seeking the freedom and individual autonomy which Mill espoused. It need not have happened that way; there is a certain irony in the fact that Whitlam turned out to be the beneficiary of an act of which Sir Robert Menzies was rightly proud: the reform of Australian higher education.